When a city's major industry is illegal drugs, horrible things happen to its government and its people. El Cajon, California had earned its title, "Crystal Meth Capital of the World." George Wills called it "The Medallion (*a city in Columbia famous for its production of Cocaine*) of Crystal Meth."

To build a great church is not easy. To build one in El Cajon is harder. To turn El Cajon around is harder still. David and Mark Hoffman, brothers, have let God show them how.

Even more exciting, El Cajon's miracle can be duplicated wherever sin has taken over. In *On Earth as It Is in Heaven*, Mark tells us how. If you face impossible odds, the book you hold in your hand is must reading. Warning, wait until your day off... once you start, you won't be able to put it down.

For anyone who wants to see God lift not only his church but his city, Mark Hoffman's *On Earth as It Is in Heaven* is an essential handbook. I've known and loved Mark for more than 10 years; they don't come any better.

Harald Bredesen
International Christian Statesman
Founder, Prince of Peace

On Earth as It Is in Heaven is a great book because it's a Kingdom book. It's a Kingdom book because Mark Hoffman truly understands the Biblical priorities of God and of His church. This is not a book to be taken lightly. If you want to carry on in an average ministry with average results for years to come, then this book isn't meant for you. In fact, you only need to read the section on creating a "Kingdom-driven Church," to change your ministry forever. But, read the whole thing. Why? Because it will take you one step closer to building your church on earth as it is in heaven.

Bill Wilson
President and Founder,
Metro Ministries New York

If truth is like a nail, Mark Hoffman's book is a hammer. Page after page drives home the message of the Kingdom of God.

This book is not abstract or vague, but a very practical application of eternal truth. The message is timeless, but also very timely for our generation.

Mark has been given a gift from God to all of us who care about the Kingdom of God, and how the Church should function within it. He also addresses how we should be, and can be affecting the culture around us.

Charles Simpson
Author, Conference Speaker
Chairman of the Board, CSM Publishing

Don't read this book if you are complacent and want to remain that way. Do read this book if you are willing to rethink the nature and purpose of the church. Mark is not a "lightweight." He is a "heavy hitter."

I have the privilege of pastoring a church near Mark's church. Mark lives Kingdom principles. I see it in him. I hear it when he talks and shares. Simply put, he's serious about it – and acts like it. That's one of the reasons I love to call him "my friend." I love what happens to me when I am around him. He ignites my heart. Beware, his book may have the same impact on you!

Dr. Jim Garlow
Author, Radio Commentator
Senior Pastor, Skyline Wesleyan Church

In *On Earth as It Is in Heaven*, Southern California Pastor Mark Hoffman challenges today's Church to return to the Gospel of the Kingdom, to forsake her current fascination with end-time evacuation in favor of a mindset of occupation. Astonishingly, he has managed to present a broad survey in very readable fashion. In an era of demographic studies and church growth statistics, he has given us a picture book of the Kingdom of God.

Jim Gilbert
Missionary, Author
Founder, Nehemiah Project

On Earth as It Is in Heaven is a must read for most western world Christians. It is a prophetic and Biblically-based call back to the fundamental message of seeking first the Kingdom of God. I have been both a friend and an associate of Mark Hoffman for almost 20 years. And during that time, he has not only preached the Kingdom of God without compromise, but more importantly, he has lived a Kingdom lifestyle. For those called to leadership in the Body of Christ, the final two chapters alone are worth the price of the book!

I can give a wholehearted endorsement. I am looking forward to this being released with excitement.

Marc Dupont
Author, Conference Speaker
Founder, Mantle of Praise Ministries

I have known Mark Hoffman for 18 years. I have seen the increase of God's Kingdom through Mark's ministry. It is with great excitement that I recommend to you *On Earth as It Is in Heaven* a must read for the serious-minded believer wanting a clear and well-illustrated understanding of God's Kingdom purposes.

George Runyan
Founder and Director, City Church Ministries

The message of the Kingdom was the message of Christ, the mystery revealed to the Apostle Paul and his passion, and it is the message most needed today in the Body of Christ.

Pastor Mark Hoffman does not just teach principles of the Kingdom of God, but has lived this message. His book is filled with fresh revelation on the Kingdom of God, the purposes of our King, and the call of the church to be the church, taking the Kingdom to the world. Very few books written today are truly life changing...but *On Earth as It Is in Heaven* is one.

Stan DeKoven, Ph.D.
President, Vision International College and University

ON EARTH AS IT IS

IN HEAVEN

THE POWER OF GOD'S KINGDOM

AT WORK

MARK HOFFMAN

ON EARTH AS IT IS IN HEAVEN

THE POWER OF GOD'S KINGDOM AT WORK

ISBN: 1-59352-009-3

CREATIVE SERVICES AND PRINTING THROUGH:

CSN BOOKS
833 Broadway, Suite #201
EL CAJON, CA 92021
TOLL FREE: 1-866-484-6184
www.CSNbooks.com

PRINTED IN THE UNITED STATES OF AMERICA

DEDICATION

To my beautiful and beloved wife and life partner, Linda; my three sons, Neil, Brice, and Will, who fill my heart with joy and pride; my brothers David and John who are my partners in ministry at FCF; and to all the many people who have over the years opened up the Kingdom of God to me, I gratefully dedicate this book.

TABLE OF CONTENTS

SECTION THREE
LAYING HOLD OF THE KINGDOM

SECTION FOUR
FOR PASTORS AND CHURCH LEADERS

INTRODUCTION

This book was not planned. It was begun, unknowingly, as a short sermon series in response to the tragic events of September 11, 2001. It further developed and began to take shape in response to a request by my friend George Runyan to teach a seminar on the Kingdom of God at a local Bible college. But it was only after teaching this material at a pastors' conference in Seoul, South Korea, at the invitation of my friend Marc Dupont that the concept for a book came into being.

As I sat in my Jacuzzi, trying to recover from the effects of that long flight home from Korea, I had one of those Divine Moments. I felt the wonderful presence of God encompass me, and I instantly knew that God was directing me to write this book. So clear was His direction that I have never doubted it to this moment. This conviction has sustained me over the long 15 months it took me to complete this project.

Having stated my conviction that God directed me to write this book does not imply that I blame Him for everything in it. It reflects my sincere study of the subject of the Kingdom of God as revealed in the Bible and informed by my own experiences of watching God work in my own community. (Many of these accounts are recorded in this book, especially in the third section.) I would welcome comments and corrections that might help me to have a more accurate understanding of this most important subject, the Kingdom of God.

This book serves as a companion to my first book, Breakthrough Kingdom Living, written some years ago. This present book serves as more of a macro-view of the Kingdom, and the former serves as a more micro-view of how the Kingdom of God intersects with an individual's life. I would suggest reading them in the reverse order in which they were written, if that is convenient (though it is certainly not necessary).

Finally, this book is written with a conviction that much of the American church has lapsed into a defeatist and defensive (almost passive) mindset toward our present opportunity and has therefore been enticed to settle for aiming at individual ministry success rather than true cultural transformation.

It is my conviction that neither the church at large nor most individual Christians truly understand the level of responsibility (and therefore real opportunity) that we have been given to determine the future of our world. God has not predetermined a dark future for our world (as many Christians apparently believe). Quite the contrary, He has restored to us the opportunity to successfully fulfill our original mission. He has done this by establishing a new humanity under a new Head, Jesus Christ. His Body lives under His invincible Kingdom and has been given the irresistible powers of that Kingdom. Under Jesus, the future is ours to determine.

The highest heavens belong to the Lord, but the earth He has given to Man.

Psalm 115:16 (NIV)

Section One

Seeing the Kingdom

Truly, truly, I say to you, unless one is born again he cannot see the Kingdom of God.

John 3:3

CHAPTER 1

TURBULENT TIMES AND
UNSHAKABLE PEOPLE

The late nineteenth and early twentieth centuries were the golden age for England. The British Empire was at its height. Everywhere, her power and influence reigned supreme. This island nation's navy was so vast that it was said: "Britain rules the waves." Her economy was the dominant economy of the world and her colonial empire stretched around the world. It was said: "The sun never sets on the British Empire."

At home, English society was in full bloom during the glorious "Victorian age" of Queen Victoria. Patriotism and public morals were at an all-time high along with the economy. The British felt that they would continue to reign unchallenged and that nothing could sink their economy or expanding World Empire. As a symbol of her invincibility, England built the largest and most lavish passenger ship ever made. They named it *The Titanic*. The ship was a marvel, and with its 16 separate watertight compartments, it was considered unsinkable. *The London Times* quoted one of her builders as saying: "This is a ship that not even God could sink."

The world's wealthiest and most powerful people vied for the tickets for her maiden voyage in April of 1912. She steamed out of the harbor bound for New York while brass bands played and huge crowds cheered. Aboard her were nobility, politicians, industrialists and business tycoons such as John Astor, Benjamin Guggenheim and Isidor Straus.

So confident were they in the ship's invincibility that *The Titanic* carried only half of the needed lifeboats. They brashly sailed into dangerous waters at top speed through the darkness of night. Just before midnight on April 14, 1912, ninety-five miles south of the Grand Banks of Newfoundland, she struck an iceberg. Although to the passengers dining and dancing the night away it seemed to be just a minor jolt, the iceberg did its damage and ripped a tear in the side of the ship, puncturing 5 of the watertight compartments, which quickly filled with water. Within 3 hours *The Titanic* would be at the bottom of the sea. Of the 2,220 people on board, 1,513 would die, including some of the world's most powerful people. Two years later, Britain would be thrust into World War I, her economy ruined, and her colonial empire beginning to unwind.

The above serves as an important reminder that the kingdoms of men are fragile, as are their plans. Those who fail to understand this face severe disillusionment or worse.

WORLD TRADE CENTER

On September 11, 2001, our nation was jolted by a series of events that took away our breath and left us dazed and confused. The symbols of our military power, our economy and our democratic institutions were targeted. The twin towers of the World Trade Center, the mega-center of our economic markets, came tumbling down with the loss of over 3,000 lives. The Pentagon, the symbol of our military might, was partially destroyed with the loss of additional lives. Only the courageous actions of several passengers on a fourth plane averted disaster at either the White House or Capitol Hill (the symbols of our Democracy) by causing the plane to crash in the hills of Pennsylvania, short of its intended target. Our national political leaders were forced into hiding in undisclosed locations. To make matters worse, the terrorists, armed only with boxcutters, turned our vaunted technology into weapons against us by using our own jet airliners as powerful bombs.

Part of the great shock we felt as a nation can be understood by realizing that our national idols were toppled. That is to say, the things that we put our confidence in, instead of God, failed us. Neither our government (through its intelligence agencies), nor our technology, nor our economy, nor our military were able to protect us. As it turned out, many of the terrorists were students at our colleges and universities and so our great trust in the ability of education to change people and solve problems proved empty.

The effect on our national life was profound. Jaded newscasters wept on national T.V. People sat at work and stared at computer screens unable to work for days. Whole industries were brought to the brink of bankruptcy. Psychiatrists reported a surge in people complaining of depression and anxiety attacks, and pharmaceutical companies did a record business. Likewise, church attendance swelled in the weeks following the attacks. People began to speak of how everything had changed after 9/11.

STANDING WHILE OTHERS FALL

The truth is that people were shaken because their confidence had rested in things that could be shaken and toppled. The Bible points out the difference between things that can be shaken and those that cannot. It counsels us to know the difference, and to live accordingly.

> *And His voice shook the earth then, but now He has promised, saying, "Yet once more I will shake not only the earth, but also the heaven." And this expression, "Yet once more," denotes THE REMOVING OF THOSE THINGS WHICH CAN BE SHAKEN, AS OF CREATED THINGS, IN ORDER THAT THOSE THINGS WHICH CANNOT BE SHAKEN MAY REMAIN. Therefore, since we receive a Kingdom which cannot be shaken, let us show gratitude, by which we may offer to God an acceptable service with reverence and awe.*
>
> Hebrews 12:26-28

The above passage makes several clear points.

1. In life, shaking happens. Events will transpire in the lives of individuals and nations that shake them to their roots.

2. This shaking is included as a part of God's plan to show the difference between the temporary which can be shaken and the eternal which can never be shaken.

Times of stress, transition, and loss are usually the times in which we reevaluate our lives, priorities and values. This is true for nations and societies as it is for individuals. In these times, we see more clearly the difference between truth and error. These times allow us to see the difference between God's higher wisdom and our limited thoughts, and between His works and ours. They help us to gain His perspective.

God sees everything from an "eternal perspective." He always sees the big picture. This means that He views your life, circumstances and choices from a perspective that may be very different from the one you now have. Things that we may consider very important, He may know to be relatively unimportant in the long run. On the other hand, we often let people, tasks and values get crowded out of our lives that God knows should be our priorities.

It's critical to realize that God's perspective is the right one, and that God's priorities for our lives and society are the ones that lead to blessedness and success.

SEEING THE UNSEEN

In 2 Corinthians 4:17-18, the Bible gives us an important understanding of God's perspective. It gives us a glance at ultimate reality.

For momentary light affliction is producing for us an eternal weight of glory far beyond all comparison, while we look not at the things which are seen, but at the things which are not seen, for the things which are seen are temporary, but the things which are not seen are eternal.
                                                            2 Corinthians 4:17-18

As these verses point out, life is made up of things both visible and invisible, both physical and spiritual. God sees the eternal and invisible just as clearly as the physical and visible. He knows that the spiritual, eternal and unseen are just as real as the physical, temporary and visible. Arriving at this perspective demonstrates spiritual maturity. A spiritually mature person knows that the security of God's promises is more real than the security of a seven-figure bank account. They know that the power of faith is more than the power of money or position, and that the power of love is greater than the power of a gun. This is the reality that Jesus lived and that He taught His disciples to live as well.

Our problem stems from the sin nature that is in each of our hearts, along with the busyness of life, and the influences of our culture and humanistic education. Unbelief comes very naturally to us. The visible and temporary seems very pressing and real, while the unseen and eternal seems far away and unreal. The things of God are easily forgotten amidst the allurements and pressures of this life.

In allowing shaking to occur, God seeks to redirect us to that which is eternal and true. These are times when it becomes clear which things are temporal and can be shaken, and which are lasting and of Him. In these times, we must trust God and come to learn both the reality and power of faith. This is certainly true in our personal life. Health problems, financial reversals and loss of loved ones can often refocus us on God, and such things as our character or our family. All of a sudden we see things more clearly and know what is truly important.

My close friend Kevin had an experience like this. Although He had given his life to Christ when he was younger, he was now drifting through life without any clear purpose. One night he was robbed at gunpoint. A gun was pointed right in his face and he was told to lie face down in the road. As he lay there, he realized that these might be his last moments of life. He looked at the pavement beneath him and realized that it might be the last thing he ever saw. He quickly thought about the life he was living. He realized that his priorities were all wrong and that the excuses he had been giving himself for living that way were not true. He resolved in his heart to live differently from that day if he survived. The robbers took what they wanted and left (the next day he read in the newspaper that those same robbers killed someone several miles up the road in a second robbery). This "shaking" had a profound effect on Kevin's life. He immediately began to give priority to those things "which cannot be shaken" in his life. He began to seek God in earnest, become more involved in church, and serve in a ministry. His whole character and lifestyle changed.

Times of shaking are often times of growth. Often at these times we have our "moments of truth" where we grow up and learn wisdom. Just as it is true of individuals, it can also be true of societies and cultures. The Old Testament is full of times in Israel's history where, because of their folly in turning from God, they encountered a national tragedy and would begin to "cry out to God in heaven" once again (passages such as Judges 4:1-3 and 6:1-6 illustrate this). Even in our day, events such as those that occurred on September 11, 2001 with the destruction of the World Trade Center, or the stock market crash of 1929, or the bombing of Pearl Harbor cause many people to re-evaluate their lives and priorities.

Unfortunately, it seems to be true that when everything is going smooth and easy, people and nations have a tendency to move away from truth and dependence on God. It appears that difficulty and tragedy are necessary to help us face reality. The Prophet Isaiah said it this way:

> *For when the earth experiences Thy judgments, the inhabitants of the world learn righteousness. Though the wicked is shown favor, he does not learn righteousness.*
>
> Isaiah 26:9-10

DISCOVERING HIS KINGDOM

God's ultimate purpose in allowing "shaking experiences," however, goes far beyond our simply gaining wisdom. God's purpose is to reveal to us a Kingdom that cannot be shaken. Remember the passage we looked at earlier from Hebrews 12:26-27?

> *This expression, "Yet once more," denotes the removing of those things which can be shaken, as of created things, so that those things that cannot be shaken remain. THERE-FORE, SINCE WE RECEIVE A KINGDOM WHICH CAN-NOT BE SHAKEN, let us show gratitude, by which we may offer to God an acceptable service with reverence and awe.*
>
> Hebrews 12:27-28

God's ultimate purpose in allowing shaking is to reveal to us, and to establish us in, His Kingdom that can never be shaken. All around us men and women are building their kingdoms. The plans, purposes and works of men are meant to establish their wills, desires, and dreams, what we might call their kingdoms. However, all of these can teeter and fall when shaking comes. All of these fade and pass away with the passage of time and are replaced by others. Only one Kingdom cannot be shaken or pass away or be replaced by any other kingdom. This is the Kingdom of God, the realm where God works to establish His plans and purposes. When shaking comes, then the things that can be shaken are removed and in their place the Kingdom of God, and the people of that Kingdom, are established.

When God's people understand this, then they no longer need fear any calamity when it comes. When God allows shaking to come, it is to elevate and empower His people. To the extent that believers are shaken by predictions of coming troubles, to that extent their hearts are not established in God's unshakeable Kingdom. Christians who are fearful about the future do not understand the teaching of God's Word regarding this.

> *I have set the Lord continually before me; because He is at my right hand, I will not be shaken.*
>
> Psalm 16:8

> *Cast your burden upon the Lord and He will sustain you; He will never allow the righteous to be shaken.*
>
> Psalm 55:22

> *He only is my rock and my salvation, my stronghold; I shall not be shaken.*
>
> Psalm 62:6

> *It is well with the man who is gracious and lends; He will maintain his cause in judgment. For he will never be shak-*

en; the righteous will be remembered forever. He will not fear evil tiding; his heart is steadfast, trusting in the Lord.

Psalm 112:5-7

The righteous will never be shaken, but the wicked will not dwell in the land.

Proverbs 10:30

He who dwells in the shelter of the Most High will abide in the shadow of the Almighty…You will not be afraid of the terror by night, or of the arrow that flies by day; of the pestilence that stalks in the darkness, or of the destruction that lays waste at noon. A thousand may fall at your side and ten thousand at your right hand, but it shall not approach you. You will only look on with your eyes and see the recompense of the wicked.

Psalm 91:1, 5-8

Many Christians face the future with fear and trepidation. They expect the worst to happen and for circumstances to cause the wicked to rule over the righteous. But God purposes that the events and circumstances of life would dispossess and displace the unrighteous and elevate and empower His people to take their place. This is everywhere taught in scripture. Psalm 37 is a wonderful psalm for every believer to study and meditate on. Consider just these few verses from it:

For evildoers will be cut off, but those who wait for the Lord, they will inherit the land. Yet a little while and the wicked man will be no more; and you will look carefully for his place and he will not be there. But the humble will inherit the land and will delight themselves in abundant prosperity. The Lord knows the days of the blameless, and their inheritance will be forever. They will not be ashamed in the time of evil, and in the days of famine they will have abundance. I have been young and now I am old, yet I have not seen the righteous forsaken nor his descendants begging bread.

Psalm 37:9-11, 18-19, 25

Jesus promised His followers that if they would just be careful to follow His words and teachings, that in a time of great storms and problems when others' houses and works are destroyed, theirs would still stand.

Everyone who comes to Me and hears My words and acts on them, I will show you whom he is like; he is like a man building a house, who dug deep and laid a foundation on the rock;

and when a flood occurred, the torrent burst against that
house and could not shake it, because it had been well built.
Luke 6:47-48

STANDING TALL

Shaking presents the church with her greatest opportunity.
When all around us everything is shaking and on shifting ground, then
the people of God who have faith and stand up, confident in their God's
supply, will rise to the top and lead. It was the great earthquake in
Philippi, when Paul was in prison, that opened the prison doors and
broke off his shackles. As a response, the Philippian jailer came to Paul
and, falling on his knees, asked him how he might be saved (Acts 16).

It was the terrible storm and shipwreck, when Paul was being
taken to Rome as a prisoner, that caused him to become, in effect, the
leader of the expedition. When the twenty-seventh chapter of Acts
begins, Paul is a prisoner in chains in the hold of a ship bound for
Rome. By the time the story ends in Chapter 28, Paul is an honored
guest in the home of the leading citizen of the island, and all the people of the island are coming to him for help and honoring him. What
caused the reversal? Why, it was the terrible storm and shipwreck, as
even a casual reading will reveal.

Difficult times are the best times for Christians to arise. When such
times come, they serve as a test of what is in the heart of a Christian.
If a believer becomes shaken and worried, then it means that the world
has a grip on his heart. If the Kingdom is established in his heart, then
he remains unshaken. When the Church truly is established in God's
unshakeable Kingdom, then it will make great advances during difficult and turbulent times. In the coming chapters, we will explore this
unshakeable Kingdom.

YOU ARE INVITED TO A

Before and After Party

Before New Years and After Christmas

<u>Date:</u>   December 29, 2012 (Saturday)

<u>Time:</u>   2pm till whenever

<u>Location:</u>   Scott and Ronda's House (call for directions)
        29420 Lilac Drive, Campo, CA 91906   619-478-2582

<u>What to Bring:</u>   YOU – and oh yeah – a side dish

We will have karaoke & A Gift Exchange Game for the Adults!
"each adult that wants to play bring a wrapped gift of $10 or !
Game time around 6pm.

CHAPTER 2

THE UNSHAKABLE KINGDOM

In 1923, a very important meeting was held at the Edgewater Beach Hotel in Chicago. In attendance were nine of the world's most successful financiers. These men had come together to help direct the economy of this country for their mutual benefit. Present at the meeting were: Charles Schwab, the largest producer of steel; Samuel Insull, president of the largest utility company; Howard Hopson, president of the largest gas company; Arthur Cotton, the greatest wheat speculator; Richard Whitney, president of the New York Stock Exchange; Albert Fall, a member of President Harding's cabinet; Leon Fraser, president of the Bank of International Settlements; Jesse Livermore, the great "bear" investor on Wall Street; and Ivar Krueger, head of the nation's most powerful monopoly.

Certainly, this was a gathering of some of the most powerful people in the world. These were people who sat as "kings" above their "kingdoms." These were people who saw themselves as "movers and shakers." But let's see where these "kings and their kingdoms" were just 25 years later.

Charles Schwab had died in bankruptcy, living the last 5 years of his life on borrowed money. Samuel Insull had died penniless, a fugitive from justice in a foreign land. Howard Hopson had gone insane and had to be institutionalized. Arthur Cotton had died bankrupt in a foreign land. Richard Whitney had spent time in Sing Sing prison. Albert Fall had been pardoned from a prison sentence so that he could die at home. Jesse Livermore, Ivar Krueger and Leon Fraser had all died by suicide.

ASHES, ASHES, WE ALL FALL DOWN...

The sad truth is that the kingdoms of men are shaken and they fall. Only that which is of God remains unshakable. Over the years, many men have stood up to try to destroy the Kingdom of God. The caesars of Ancient Rome persecuted the early church, killing and imprisoning thousands of Christians, yet the church grew until it became the official religion of Imperial Rome.

Lenin and Stalin arrested and executed tens of thousands of Christians and church leaders, and yet they could not extinguish the faith in the Soviet Union and their empire collapsed. Chairman Mao of China deported all of the Christian missionaries from China and outlawed the church. The result? China underwent the fastest growth of the Church in history.

Others, such as the French thinker Voltaire, have declared that Christianity was outdated and would pass from the stage of history. Instead, many years later, Voltaire is a footnote in history, the Kingdom of God is greatly enlarged over the face of the earth, and the Bible Society is printing Bibles in the former home of Voltaire.

Certainly it is the height of folly for mere humans to plot against God and His Kingdom. Psalm 2 gives us God's perspective on the unfolding of human history. Every Christian should be thoroughly familiar with it, perhaps even memorize it, before listening to the ever-changing opinions of so called "experts" and commentators. Consider just these portions of that Psalm:

> *Why are the nations in an uproar and the peoples devising a vain thing? The kings of the earth take their stand, and the rulers take counsel together against the Lord and against His Anointed One...He who sits in the heavens laughs; the Lord scoffs at them...Ask of Me and I will surely give the nations as Your inheritance, and the very ends of the earth as Your possession...Now therefore, O kings, show discernment; take warning O judges of the earth. Worship the Lord with reverence and rejoice with trembling. Do homage to the Son that He not become angry, and you perish in the way...*
> Psalm 2:1, 2, 4, 8, 10-12

Men and nations come and go. They make their plans, and declare their pronouncements. In the end, God's purposes go on unchanged. His will and His Word will come to pass. God is absolutely committed to His Word and His Kingdom.

> *All flesh is grass, and all its loveliness is like the flower of the field. The grass withers, the flower fades, when the breath of the Lord blows upon it; surely the people are grass. The grass withers, the flower fades, but the Word of our God stands forever.*
> Isaiah 40:6-7

God's Unchanging Purpose

God's purpose has always been to establish His Kingdom, unshakeable and chief among all other kingdoms. Throughout the Old Testament, God spoke concerning the establishment of His Kingdom upon the earth. A proper understanding of the flow of history and the future of our planet is not possible without a study of the prophets of the Bible. These inspired prophets reveal that the driving force in history is the Kingdom of God. What these prophets of long ago saw and prophesied has great relevance to you today.

In the Book of Daniel, in the second chapter, Nebuchadnezzar, the king of Babylon, the mightiest nation on the earth at that time, was given a dream. In the dream, the king saw a great image or statue of a man. The head of the statue was made of gold, its breast and arms of silver, its belly and its thighs of bronze, its legs of iron, and its feet a mixture of iron and clay. As the king continued to watch in the dream, a great stone was cut out of a rock without the use of hands. This great rock flew through the air and hit the statue in the feet and crushed it. The entire statue collapsed and turned to dust that was blown away by the wind. But then something even stranger happened. The stone that had crushed the statue grew into a great mountain that continued to grow until it filled the whole earth.

The king was greatly troubled by the dream. He called in the magicians of his kingdom. He required that they tell him what he dreamed as well as its interpretation. None could do it. Finally the Jewish prophet and leader Daniel was called in.

Daniel was shown the dream and its interpretation by God. He related the dream to the king and then told him its interpretation. Because he was the king of the first great world empire, God had shown him the five dominant world empires that would follow his. Even a cursory study of history reveals the identity of these coming kingdoms as they appeared on the stage of history. The head of gold was Nebuchadnezzar's own kingdom of Babylon. Next would come the Medo-Persian Empire, then the empire of the Greeks, and finally the legs of iron and feet of iron and clay referred to the Roman Empire, which split into the Western Empire (centered in Rome) and the Eastern Empire (centered in Constantinople). Notice I said five great kingdoms were pictured in the dream. Yet the statue only pictures four. The last and final dominant Kingdom, Daniel tells us, is pictured by the stone which destroyed the great statue. Then he gives us the key to understand our times.

> *In the days of those kings* (i.e., the Roman caesars – which is Latin for king) *the God of Heaven will set up a Kingdom which will never be destroyed, and that Kingdom will not be left for another people (i.e., no other kingdom will arise after it to supersede it); it will crush and put an end to all these kingdoms, but it will itself endure forever.*
>
> Daniel 2:44

Daniel prophesied that during the last of these great Gentile kingdoms, the Roman Empire, God would establish a Kingdom among men that would grow and increase until it came to fill the whole earth. It would never be defeated. It would grow and grow and never recede or suffer defeat (as Isaiah the prophet had made clear many years earlier in Isaiah 9:6-7). Many Jewish scholars, after the time of Daniel, must have wondered what this future Kingdom would look like.

THE MYSTERY REVEALED

Remember that for four centuries, prior to Daniel, Israel had been a sovereign kingdom. From its first king, Saul, to its last king, Zedekiah, the nation had known both glory and shame. Under its second and third kings, David and Solomon, Israel had become the greatest kingdom in the Middle East, if not the entire world. But by the time of the third king, Rehoboam, Israel began to go into decline. Under Solomon's son, Rehoboam, the kingdom split into the northern kingdom, which would retain the name Israel, and the southern kingdom, which would become known as Judah. Though there would be some periods of national revival and national glory, the next three centuries would be marked by idolatry, unrighteousness and, finally, rejection by God.

The northern kingdom, Israel, would be destroyed in 722 B.C. by Assyria. The Babylonians would destroy the southern kingdom of Judah in 586 B.C., Jerusalem would be completely demolished and burned with fire. The survivors would be carried off to Babylon as slaves. The Jews would not have a sovereign nation again for more than 2,500 years, except for a brief period under the Hasmoneans. Although many Jews would return to their homeland, they would be ruled by foreign nations. *The kingdom of Israel had failed and passed away. Whatever Kingdom God was promising would be something different.*

Daniel was given a further revelation of this coming Kingdom. It would be associated with a King who would be a mysterious heavenly figure, somehow different from the kings of the failed kingdom of Israel.

> *I kept looking in the night visions, and behold, with the clouds of heaven One like a Son of Man was coming, and He came up to the Ancient of Days and was presented before Him. AND TO HIM WAS GIVEN DOMINION, GLORY AND A KINGDOM, THAT ALL THE PEOPLES, NATIONS, AND MEN OF EVERY LANGUAGE MIGHT SERVE HIM. His dominion is an everlasting dominion which will not pass away; and His Kingdom is one which will not be destroyed.*
>
> Daniel 7:13-14

This coming King came to be known to the Jews as the long-awaited Messiah (which translated means "Anointed One"). Isaiah prophesied that His victory would be a spiritual and not a military victory, and that He would defeat enemies far worse than Israel's kings had ever faced.

> *Surely our griefs He Himself bore, and our sorrows He carried; yet we ourselves esteemed Him stricken, smitten of God, and afflicted. But He was pierced through for our transgressions, He was crushed for our iniquities; the chastening for our well-being fell upon Him, and by His scourging we are healed. All of us like sheep have gone astray, each of us has turned to his own way; but the Lord has caused the iniquity of us all to fall on Him.*
>
> Isaiah 53:4-6

So there it was. A mysterious King would come and establish a triumphant Kingdom unlike any kingdom they had ever known. And it would arise during the time of the Roman Empire more than 5 centuries later.

Chapter 3

The Forgotten Gospel

If someone asked you to sum up the message that Jesus came to preach in one sentence, how would you do it? Some might suggest, "God loves you and will forgive your sins," others might suggest, "Receive Me and you can be born again," or someone might suggest, "Love one another as I have loved you." These are all good and true statements, however they fall far short of the essence of Jesus' message.

The simple answer would be to say that Jesus came to announce or preach the gospel. But what is the gospel? Many would say that the gospel could be summed up in this way: "Jesus was sent down from Heaven to die on a cross in our place and thereby win for us forgiveness and entrance to heaven by paying our debt." Would you agree that this sums up the heart of the gospel? I think that most people would. They would point to John 3:16 as being perhaps the best verse to summarize the gospel.

For God so loved the world that He gave His only begotten Son, that whoever believes in Him shall not perish but have everlasting life.

John 3:16

If that is true, however, how do you explain such verses as Mark 1:14?

And after John (the Baptist) had been taken into custody, Jesus came to Galilee, preaching the gospel of God...

Mark 1:14

How could Jesus have preached the gospel before He was crucified? If the essence of the gospel is that we can be forgiven because Jesus died on the cross for our sins, then how could He have preached the gospel more than two years before He was crucified?

Even more puzzling, how could the twelve disciples have been sent out to preach the gospel while Jesus was still with them? Certainly the Bible makes clear that they did not foresee the crucifixion of Jesus and the plan of God.

And He called the twelve together, and gave them power and authority over all the demons and to heal diseases...And departing, they began going about among all the villages preaching the gospel and healing everywhere.

Luke 9:1, 6

The Bible says that even John the Baptist preached the gospel:

So with many other exhortations also, he (John) *preached the gospel to the people.*

Luke 3:18

If you check the context of the above verse, you will see that this was even before God revealed to John the identity of Jesus as the Messiah (compare Luke 3:21-23 with John 1:29-34). Now, give this some thought. How could John the Baptist have preached the gospel before Jesus was crucified for our sins, and in fact, even before it was revealed to John that Jesus was "the Lamb of God who takes away the sin of the world" (John 1:29)?

The answer is that he could not have, nor could the disciples. Not, that is, if what is meant by the term "the gospel" is what so many Christians think that it means.

The answer to this dilemma is to realize that most Christians today misunderstand the gospel. They have reduced the gospel (literally the "good news") to a gospel of forgiveness or to a gospel of John 3:16 instead of what it really is.

THE GOSPEL JESUS PREACHED

What is the gospel? It is simple. The Bible tells us very clearly in several places. Look again at Mark 1:14-15. Here, the gospel is defined.

Now, after John (the Baptist) had been taken into custody, Jesus came into Galilee, preaching the gospel of God and saying, "The time is fulfilled, and the Kingdom of God is at hand; repent and believe in the gospel."

Mark 1:14-15

The gospel that John the Baptist, Jesus, and the disciples preached was this; "The time is fulfilled, and the Kingdom of God is at hand." In other words, that which was promised from of old throughout the Old Testament is about to happen. God is about to break into history and establish His Kingdom among men.

Remember at the beginning of this chapter, I asked you to try and reduce Jesus' message to one sentence? Well the Bible does summarize

Jesus' message to one 9-word sentence.

> *From that time Jesus began to preach and say, "Repent, for the Kingdom of Heaven is at hand."*
>
> Matthew 4:17

Here the substance of Jesus' message is reduced to one sentence. "Repent, for the Kingdom of heaven is at hand." In fact, the gospels of Mark and Luke summarize it in the same way. We have already looked at Mark's summary in Mark 1:14-15 above. Now consider Luke's summary of Jesus' preaching mission.

> *I must preach the Kingdom of God to the other cities also, for I was sent for this purpose.*
>
> Luke 4:43

SHRINKING DOWN THE GOSPEL

Most of the church is guilty of practicing "gospel shrinking," that is, they have shrunk down the gospel to a mere message about personal forgiveness of sins. But Jesus' gospel of the Kingdom was a much larger message. In essence, Jesus said, "Wake up, a new Kingdom is being brought in and nothing will ever be the same. There is a new power and a new level of Divine blessing available to you. From now on, all the rules change."

What Jesus meant by the gospel, the message He came to proclaim, is made clear by His declaration at the beginning of His ministry. After He returned from the desert, where He was tempted by the devil, He returned to Nazareth to inaugurate His public ministry. He entered the synagogue on the Sabbath day, and opening the scroll of Isaiah, He quoted from Isaiah 61:1 to declare His mission and define His "gospel."

> *The Spirit of the Lord is upon Me, because He has anointed Me to preach the gospel to the poor. He has sent Me to proclaim release to the captives, and recovery of sight to the blind, to set free those who are downtrodden, to proclaim the favorable year* (i.e., the Old Testament "Year of Jubilee") *of the Lord.*
>
> Luke 4:18, quoting Isaiah 61:1

Jesus obviously meant more by the term "gospel" than forgiveness and eternal life. He meant it to include healing, deliverance from the oppression brought about by both men and demons, freedom from addictions and anxieties, the lifting up of the downtrodden, and justice for all people. All this and more is included in His above declaration.

Even a brief overview of Jesus' preaching mission reveals how consistently the healing of the sick, casting out of demons and feeding of the hungry accompanied His preaching of the gospel. Note also how often Jesus, in the midst of His gospel-preaching mission, challenged and rebuked the Jewish leaders present who were oppressing the people.

Jesus announced the "good news" that a new Kingdom had arrived to displace the kingdom of Satan and destroy all the works of Satan's kingdom. In fact, the Apostle John said this was a central reason for Jesus' coming.

The Son of God appeared for this purpose, that He might destroy the works of the devil.

1 John 3:8

We must preach healing, deliverance, and blessing just as boldly as we preach the forgiveness of sins. If we do not boldly announce these things and practice these things, then we have shrunk down the gospel and are no longer preaching the same gospel that Jesus and His followers did. If we are not trusting God to empower us to destroy every manifestation of Satan's kingdom, just how "Christian" can our preaching be?

The gospel of the Kingdom is the gospel Jesus preached. It is the gospel He sent the twelve disciples out to preach.

Jesus summoned His twelve disciples and gave them authority over unclean spirits, to cast them out, and to heal every kind of disease and every kind of sickness...These twelve... Jesus sent out after instructing them: ..."And as you go, preach, saying, 'The Kingdom of heaven is at hand.'"

Matthew 10:1, 5, 7

It is the gospel that He later sent the 70 out to preach.

Now after this the Lord appointed seventy others, and sent them in pairs ahead of Him to every city and place where He Himself was going to come... "Whatever city you enter and they receive you, eat what is set before you; and heal those in it who are sick, and say to them, 'The Kingdom of God has come near to you.'"

Luke 10:1; 8-9

Jesus has instructed us that this is to be our message as well.

This gospel of the Kingdom shall be preached in the whole

world for a witness to all the nations, and then the end will come.

Matthew 24:14

FOLLOWING JESUS

The gospel that we must preach is, and always has been, "The Kingdom of God is at hand," that is, it is present and available to you now. The reason that so many churches are allowed to go on year after year in their community without controversy or coming under attack is because they have surrendered the full gospel of Jesus. That is the price for the peace and respectability they "enjoy." Jesus said:

If they persecuted Me, they will also persecute you.

John 15:20

Why are so few churches facing persecution like Jesus did? Is it because we are wiser and more loving than Jesus? Of course not. The answer is that, "persecution arises because of the word" (Matthew 13:21). Once we surrender the word of the Kingdom, we will no longer be a threat to destroy the "works of the devil," and therefore no longer be a threat to him or his kingdom. But just begin to pray for the sick, cast out demons, home school your kids, or start a Christian school, and you will face increasing criticism and persecution. Just try to organize and pull down the strongholds of injustice and deception in your community and you will know real persecution.

Much of the Church today is laughed at and ignored, rather than opposed, because it is just a shell of what it should be. *The Church is brought about by the preaching of the gospel, and it will conform to the size of the gospel it preaches.* If it preaches a "shrunk down" gospel it will be a "shrunk down" Church.

Since most of the Church is not preaching the same gospel (that is the gospel of the Kingdom) that Jesus and the apostles preached, they are not getting the same results nor facing the same opposition.

The great need of the Church today is to rediscover the message of the Kingdom and get back to its mission of preaching the gospel of the Kingdom.

CHAPTER 4

THE MISSION OF JESUS

A family had a hobby of putting together jigsaw puzzles. The father regularly brought home puzzles of greater and greater difficulty. One night he presented his family with a puzzle of over one thousand pieces. Immediately they tackled it. After an hour, however, the family was frustrated. No matter how hard they tried, they couldn't get the puzzle started. The father then discovered that he had accidentally switched the box top with the top from another puzzle. The picture they were looking at wasn't the puzzle they were working on.

One major reason that the church in America has not been more effective is because many Christians have the wrong box top in front of them. They do not have a correct view of what Jesus is attempting to bring about. Since they do not fully grasp the mission of Jesus, they are confused in their efforts to serve Him. What was the center of Jesus' mission and plan?

In studying the gospels, one thing becomes apparent. The Kingdom of God was the central core of Jesus' message. He taught on this subject more than on any other subject. The subject of the Kingdom of God appears over a hundred times in the four gospels. It is the main subject in the parables that Jesus taught. In fact, seventeen of the thirty parables told by Jesus specifically mention that their intent is to explain the Kingdom of God or the Kingdom of Heaven.

Teaching about the Kingdom of God was crucial to Jesus' plan. If you were to ask most people why Jesus came to earth, no doubt most Christians would answer in somewhat the following way. They would say that He came to earth to die on the cross to pay the penalty for our sins, and rise from the dead for our justification (Romans 4:25). This is true as far as it goes, however it is an incomplete answer. Think about it. It only took Jesus three days to be crucified and rise from the dead. And yet His ministry was for over three years. What was His purpose for the rest of the time? Remember His words that we read in the gospel of Luke?

I must preach the Kingdom of God to the other cities also,
FOR I WAS SENT FOR THIS PURPOSE.
Luke 4:43

One reason for the three year ministry was that it took three years to adequately proclaim the Kingdom message in all the cites and villages of Israel. A second and more important reason is that it took this long to adequately instruct a group of men in the truths of the Kingdom of God.

JESUS' PRIVATE LESSONS

Jesus chose twelve men to teach them the secrets of the Kingdom of God. His purpose was that they would teach these to the church that He would form after His ascension. This fuller understanding concerning the Kingdom would not be made known to the masses until after His crucifixion, resurrection, and the coming of the Holy Spirit on the day of Pentecost. Jesus' method of instruction was often to teach the masses in parables and then to fully explain these parables to His disciples later.

With many such parables He was speaking the word to them, so far as they were able to hear it; and He did not speak to them without a parable; but He was explaining everything privately to His disciples.
Mark 4:33-34

One day the disciples approached Jesus and asked Him, "Why do you speak to them in parables?" Jesus answered them in this way.

To you it has been granted to know the mysteries of the Kingdom of Heaven, but to them it has not been granted.
Matthew 13:11

The disciples had been chosen as those who would teach these principles and secrets to those would receive Jesus as Savior and Lord after He finished His earthly mission. He spent most of His earthly ministry instructing His disciples (both the twelve but also His wider circle of disciples) in the truths of this Kingdom He had come to inaugurate. This is what prepared them for their later ministry. But even the twelve were not ready for all the mysteries about this Kingdom until Jesus had risen from the dead. This explains a puzzling fact in the Book of Acts.

In Acts chapter one, we read in the first three verses that Jesus presented Himself alive to the disciples over a period of forty days.

Now the obvious question is this: If Jesus' work was finished with His crucifixion and resurrection, and perhaps several post resurrection appearances, what was the purpose of the extra forty days? Well, the Bible gives us the answer.

> *To these also He presented Himself alive after His suffering, by many convincing proofs, appearing to them over a period of forty days and speaking of the things concerning the Kingdom of God.*

Acts 1:3

Jesus spent these forty days doing the same thing that He had done for the past three years. He taught His disciples about how to operate and live in this Kingdom He had come to establish. He was now able to teach them things that they would have not been able to accept just one month earlier.

RECOGNIZING THE KINGDOM

Teaching the mysteries and truths about the Kingdom of God was central to Jesus' mission. Just how faithful are our churches to Jesus if we hardly ever mention or study this Kingdom that was the central concern of His teaching and ministry? Think about it, when was the last time you heard a message on the Kingdom of God? How well do you understand it? How can we recognize the Kingdom of God?

A kingdom exists wherever a king's will and authority are in effect. God's Kingdom exists wherever God's will is being accomplished through God's love, power and provision. We may think of God's Kingdom as being present wherever:

- God's will is being done on earth as it is in heaven (Matt. 6:10).

- The works of God are accomplished through faith and dependence on God.

- God is truly glorified and people are reconciled to God and each other.

- People are restored, the sick are healed, and demons are cast out.

- The King (Jesus) is manifestly present.

- The culture of heaven is being lived out rather than the culture of the sinful world.

- God's love, truth, blessing and increase are found.

God's Kingdom is the realm of God's presence, peace, power and supply that we are invited to live in. God's Kingdom is comprehensive; that is, it reaches into every area of life and society. There is no area of life which the King Jesus does not claim as His own and over which He does not have a plan and a will. He brings salvation, deliverance and righteousness into every arena of life.

The Kingdom of God is the reign of God and the government of God. It is established on earth by our repentance, faith and obedience. Every time the gospel is believed and obeyed by a sinner, the Kingdom of God is expanded. Each time God's love and power sets a soul free from alcoholism, addiction, bitterness or fear, the Kingdom of God grows on earth. Whenever a couple in a troubled marriage humbles themselves before God, forgives one another and reconstructs their marriage on God's principles, there also God's Kingdom is established. If, as you read this, you are captured and held by sin and destruction, the good news is; "The Kingdom of God is at hand (i.e., 'within your reach'). Repent and believe the good news."

Jesus came to establish this Kingdom on earth. *Now all the love and power of heaven are available on earth to meet every human need.* This is the reality that Jesus and the early church lived out. They overcame class divisions and racial enmity, healed the sick, multiplied resources to feed the poor, cast out demons, reconciled people through the love of God, and eventually changed their culture. They destroyed the kingdom and works of Satan. Jesus came and declared cosmic war on Satan. This is the Kingdom of which you are now a citizen.

The Kingdom of God is more than the church. The church is brought about through the Kingdom and is to be the instrument of the Kingdom. The church exists to serve the Kingdom. When we make serving the church the ends rather than the means of building up the Kingdom, we fall prey to a subtle form of idolatry. The purpose of the church is more than to just "have church." That is, its purpose is more than to just have services and run programs. Its purpose is to see the advancement of God's Kingdom among men. God's Kingdom is the power and love of God let loose among people to set them free and bring them into the loving purposes of God. But just how does God's wisdom, power, and protection reach us? How can we receive what He has promised to give us so freely? This will become clearer to you as you study this book. *God's answers and blessing are awaiting you in His Kingdom.*

CHAPTER 5

CROWN HIM KING OVER ALL

Whenever a president is elected or whenever a king ascends to his throne, they must formally receive authority and power to rule. This principle was also true of Jesus Christ. After His resurrection, He ascended to heaven to receive his Kingdom. This is similar to the coronation of a king or the inauguration of the President. It is at this time that they receive their authority and power to rule.

With this in mind, let's read together the incredible Scripture passage in the first chapter of Ephesians.

I pray that the eyes of your heart may be enlightened, so that you may know what is the hope of His calling, what are the riches of the glory of His inheritance in the saints, and what is the surpassing greatness of His power toward us who believe. These are in accordance with the working of the strength of His might which He brought about in Christ, WHEN HE RAISED HIM FROM THE DEAD, AND SEATED HIM AT HIS RIGHT HAND IN THE HEAVENLY PLACES, FAR ABOVE ALL RULE AND AUTHORITY AND POWER AND DOMINION, and every name that is named, not only in this age, but also in the one to come. And He put all things in subjection under His feet, and gave Him as head over all things to the church, which is His body, the fullness of Him who fills all in all.

Ephesians 1:18-23

This verse tells us that God established "the surpassing greatness of His power" and "the strength of His might" in Christ when He raised Him from the dead and seated Him at His right hand in Heaven. From this position, He rules over "all rule and authority and power and dominion." Here His name is chief above every other name.

Centuries earlier, Daniel the prophet was given a glimpse of this still far-off day of coronation. Daniel has a vision of heaven.

I kept looking until thrones were set up and the Ancient of Days took His seat; His vesture was like white snow and the hair of His head was like pure wool. His throne was ablaze with flames, its wheels were a burning fire. A river of fire was flowing and coming out from before Him; thousands upon thousands were attending Him, and myriads upon myriads were standing before Him; the court sat, and the books were opened.

Daniel 7:9-10

A comparison with visions by prophets such as Ezekiel and John in the Book of Revelation demonstrate without question that the setting here is the throne of God (Revelation 5:11; 20:4; Ezekiel 10:2, 6; etc.). As Daniel continues to gaze into this heavenly vision, something quite shocking takes place. A human appears on the scene.

*I kept looking in the night visions, and behold with the clouds of heaven **One like a Son of Man was coming, and He came up to the Ancient of Days and was presented before Him. And to Him was given dominion, glory and a Kingdom,** that all the peoples, nations and men of every language might serve Him. His dominion is an everlasting dominion which will not pass away; and His Kingdom is one which will not be destroyed.*

Daniel 7:13-14

This is a clear picture of Christ's ascension and coronation. In Acts we have another picture of the ascension of Christ.

And after He (Jesus) *said these things, He was lifted up while they were looking on, and a cloud received Him out of their sight.*

Acts 1:9

This "cloud" that "received Him" probably should not be thought of as a water vapor cloud. It was likely the glory cloud, which appears throughout Scripture. It is the cloud that veils God's glory from our eyes. It was the pillar of cloud that led the Israelites in the desert wanderings (Exodus 13:21-22). It was the cloud out of which God spoke on the Mount of Transfiguration (Matthew 17:5). It appears throughout Scripture and is what is in view in our passage in Daniel 7 where it is referred to as the "clouds of heaven."

In other words, Jesus at His ascension was received into the clouds of heaven. Upon passing through those same clouds, He then appeared before the throne of His Father to receive His Kingdom. Upon finishing His work on earth, He reported to His Father, "Mission accomplished," and then received, as His due, all power and authority.

Remember what Jesus said to His disciples when He gave them the great commission?

All authority has been given to Me in heaven and on earth.
Go therefore and make disciples of all nations...

Matthew 28:18-19

When Jesus said this, He was referring to His coronation pictured in Daniel 7 where He received all power and authority and took possession of His Kingdom.

Daniel's vision was of Jesus "coming on the clouds of heaven" to receive all power and authority and a Kingdom. What a difference it would make if the church would focus on and teach about this "coming" to Heaven to receive authority and a Kingdom which He now offers to us. Instead, the church is obsessed with the "second coming" to earth at the end of the world. The church's neglect of this "heavenly coming" in place of wild, misguided speculation about world conditions and the time of the "second coming" has led the church to surrender the authority and dominion that Jesus has won for it and instead become defeatist and escapist in our thinking.

JESUS AND THE PROPHECY "EXPERTS"

When Jesus' disciples were starting to fall into this trap of "end time" speculation, Jesus rebuked them and refocused them on their assignment.

So when they had come together, they were asking Him, say-
ing, "Lord, is it at this time You are restoring the kingdom to
Israel?" He said to them "It is not for you to know the
times or epochs which the Father has fixed by His own
authority; but you will receive power when the Holy Spirit
has come upon you; and you shall be My witnesses both in
Jerusalem, and in all Judea and Samaria, and even to the
remotest part of the earth."

Acts 2:6-8

What a tragedy that we have rejected Jesus' clear injunction here and have instead confused and wounded ourselves with our end-time speculations. Jesus says in effect, "That is not your concern, you concentrate on the assignment I have given you and the surpassing power I am sending you."

Jesus said, "It's not for you to know." He said, "Of that day and hour no one knows" and that included the angels and Jesus Himself

(Matthew 24:36). It has not been given that we can know either the timing or details of the end. And yet in our arrogance we try to know what we are not to know. As a result, Scriptures meant for former times are misapplied to our time and misinterpreted.

As one who has listened to the so called "Bible prophecy experts" for nearly 30 years, I can tell you they have been wrong in every one of their predictions. Not a single thing they have ever predicted has come to pass. Every date they have set has been wrong. I can not think of a single thing they have ever warned us of that has ever come about. The Y2K scare was just one of many false predictions. The occult clairvoyants that make predictions in the National Enquirer have a better track record than many of our most famous "Bible prophecy experts." If ever anyone deserved the title of "false prophets," these so-called Bible prophecy experts do. Multiplied millions of dollars have been lost and thousands of opportunities missed while evangelical Christians have run around like Chicken Little waiting for the sky to fall in. Never once have I heard these "experts" apologize to the many Christians whose lives have been disrupted by their predictions.

Instead of being rebuked and disciplined by the church, they continue to amass great wealth by writing new books with new "predictions."

The result is a diabolical mythical scenario that has robbed Christians of a sense of victory. It has caused us to question our power and authority and to be distracted from our assignment. The truth is that many Christians in America have adopted an End-Times scenario which has been popularized in novels and movies. If you think about it, however, the particular "eschatology" is in complete contradiction to the parables and teaching of Jesus and the messages of the Bible as a whole. It has the effect of producing a "self-fulfilling prophecy" for the church. The church expects things to get worse and guess what, as a result, they often do. In other words, it matters what box top you are looking at when you put the puzzle together.

A Parable for Today's Church

There was a farmer who lived in the middle of Kansas, and he raised two sons. Both of his sons joined the Navy. The farmer's brother was a psychologist, and he came to visit. At dinner, the farmer said, "You're a psychologist. I want you to tell me how a farmer living in the middle of Kansas, where there's almost no water, can raise two sons who join the Navy and love it."

The psychologist said, "That's a good question. Let me think about it."

That night, he spent the night in those boys' room. The next morning when he got up, he came downstairs and told his brother, "I think I've got an answer for you. Come up to this room with me."

They walked into the boys' room, and the first thing they saw was a picture on the wall. It was a beautiful picture of the sea, and in the middle of the sea was a ship. The psychologist told his brother, "I want you to lay down on the bed and tell me what you see when you get up from the bed." The psychologist said, "The first thing you see when you walk into this room is this picture. The last thing you see at night is the picture. And the first thing you see in the morning when you get up is the picture of this ship on the sea. Did the boys have this picture for a long time?"

The farmer said, "Yes, since they were about 3 years old." The brother said, "If you think about a picture like that long enough, you might become a sailor yourself." It matters what you put before your imagination. We will tend to get what we expect, believe, and preach. If we place before our imagination the coronation of Jesus and the glory of his unstoppable, ever-advancing Kingdom, we will become different people indeed. And, as surely as night follows day, we will change our world.

CHAPTER 6

THE PLAN REVEALED

Every four years, a great contest takes place in America. Tens of millions of dollars are spent. Banners, signs and bumper stickers appear in every corner of America and literally thousands of people walk neighborhoods, make phone calls, and engage in various other related activities. The contest is, of course, the presidential election. The great question being decided is "Whose administration will rule over America?"

In America, a president is elected on the basis of his campaign promises, what we might call his political agenda. People vote for the candidate because of what he promises to accomplish. The very first act of the winning candidate, even before he assumes office, is to set up his administration. He begins by appointing his Cabinet members. These are people like the Secretary of State, the Secretary of Defense, the Secretary of Transportation, among others. These are the executives that will manage his administration under him. Before he takes office, his administration must be in place. This is because there is no way for him to deliver on his campaign promises except through his administration. Without this administration in place, he could never put his political agenda into action.

If he made promises regarding education, he will try to deliver on those promises through the Department of Education. If he made promises to veterans, those promises can only be fulfilled through the Department of Veteran Affairs. If a veteran wants to receive the promised benefits, he must apply through the Department of Veteran Affairs. If he does not apply through this Department, he cannot receive the benefits. If he tries to apply for them through any other institution or organization he will not receive them.

These benefits are only available through the properly appointed channel. This system of administration is how a President brings the proper government aid or service to the individual citizen. *It is the connection between each individual citizen and the President.*

Not only do presidents have administrations, so do governors and mayors. There is no other way for them to serve us. A mayor offers pro-

tection for your life and property through the police and fire depart-
ments. If you feel menaced and put in danger and want protection, you
must call the police department. Don't like the police? Don't want to
call them? Then the Mayor cannot offer you any protection. Don't want
to call the fire department because you are mad at the Fire Chief? In
that case your house will burn.

THE KING'S ADMINISTRATION

*What does all of this have to do with the Kingdom of God? The
answer to that question could totally change your life and your experience of God.* You see, Jesus also has an administration through which
He works to bless His people and fulfill His promises. Let's look at the
first chapter of Ephesians.

> *He made known to us the mystery of His will, according to
> His kind intention which He purposed in Him **with a view
> to an administration suitable to the fullness of the
> times**, that is, the summing up of all things in Christ, things
> in the heavens and things on the earth...*
>
> Ephesians 1:9-10

The first sentence of this passage tells us that God made known to
us the mystery of His will. The Greek word "musterion" which appears
here, and from which we get our English word "mystery," refers to
something which is hidden and unknowable until it is revealed to us.
In other words, God's will and plan was known only to Himself. No
human could fathom it. The plan of God was a mystery to all of the
world until He revealed it to us. For long ages, people would look at the
state of the world and wonder, "What is God up to?" They would ask,
"How is God going to straighten out this mess and keep the promises
He made to us?"

Then, at just the right time, God revealed His plan and put it into
action. His plan would center in a man (i.e.,"which He purposed in
Him," v.9). He would send His Son as a man to become Savior and King
of all people. Then He would set up under Him an "administration"
through which He would rule.

The phrase "the fullness of the times" refers to the period of the
final covenant, or "new covenant," under Jesus within which God
would finish His plan and restore all things. This is the period we now
live in, the period between the resurrection of Jesus and His second

coming. This "administration" would be "suitable" to these times, that is, it would be perfectly fitted to accomplish God's purposes for this final period. That purpose is to "sum up" all things in Christ. To "sum up" means to bring everything under Christ's rule and thereby reconcile it to God the Father.

Here in these two verses, the Bible puts the plan of God into a nutshell. Phase one would involve Jesus in an earthly ministry of removing the sin and guilt of the world. This would remove the barrier between God and us. The second phase would be to set up an "administration" through which He would heal and restore people to live as the sons and daughters of God. Through this administration, He would supply grace and mercy to transform whole societies.

The Greek word translated "administration" here is the word "oikonomia" which itself is made up of two other Greek words. Those words are "oikos," which means "house," and "nomos," which means "law" or "rule." Literally, the word means "house rules." This word came about in relation to the large farms and estates of noblemen of the ancient world. Like the plantation system that existed in our own south years ago, many of these estates were very large with many workers and slaves. Feeding and caring for the basic needs of the estate population was a big task that would fall to the steward. The steward would supply the needs of the residents by following the rules and system that the owner would establish. This system of managers and rules became known as the "oikonomia" of the estate.

As Roman society developed and the power of the caesar (Latin for "King") increased, this word was used to refer to his system of ruling over and supplying his empire. This was the understanding of the term when Paul wrote the letter to the Ephesians.

Paul means us to understand that Jesus has set up, and rules through, an administration. This is how *The New American Standard* translated the word. *The King James* translation uses the word "dispensation," which is also good because a "dispensation" is a system of dispensing, distributing or administrating something. *The New International Version* here ignores the word all together for some inexplicable reason.

Think about it. Jesus rules through an administration. Jesus fulfills His promises and brings His supply through an administration. Consider what this means for your life. Think how much a person will miss out on by not understanding this and by not working through the administration.

Jesus' administration includes, of course, the church and its ministries, the Bible, the Holy Spirit, the family and civil government, as well as several other channels. We will study these in Chapter 13. In understanding the Kingdom of God, we must remember that it is only through relating to Jesus' administration that we can enter it and receive of its power and riches.

CHAPTER 7

HOW HE WINS

What happened next after Jesus received all power and authority and His Kingdom? What was the next step in God's plan?

Following Jesus' ascension and coronation, which we looked at in Chapter 5, we see a clear order take place. First, as we have already read, Jesus took His seat at the right hand of the Father (Ephesians 1:20-21). This is the place of ultimate authority. From this position, He fulfilled His promise to His followers by sending forth the Holy Spirit. This is made clear in Peter's sermon on the day of Pentecost to the crowds who gathered because of the signs and wonders which accompanied the coming of the Holy Spirit.

> *This Jesus God raised up again, to which we are all witnesses. Therefore, having been exalted to the right hand of God, and having received from the Father the promise of the Holy Spirit, He has poured forth this which you both see and hear.*
>
> Acts 2:32-33

Now Jesus' plan to build His church could begin. The very power that Jesus had in His earthly ministry was given to His followers to continue His work of destroying the devil's kingdom and extending Jesus'.

But one thing was still lacking. As we saw in the last chapter, every king must reign and rule through an administration. This would be His next order of business.

Several chapters later in Ephesians, Paul makes this clear. He begins by quoting from Psalms 68:18:

> *Therefore it says, "WHEN HE ASCENDED ON HIGH, HE LED CAPTIVE A HOST OF CAPTIVES, AND HE GAVE GIFTS AMONG MEN..." And He gave some as apostles, and some as prophets, and some as evangelists, and some as pastors and teachers, for the equipping of the saints for the work of service, to the building up of the body of Christ;*
>
> Ephesians 4:8,11-12

Here we see Jesus, upon His ascension, beginning to set up His administration through which He would rule. An important part of this administration would be known as His church. Over this church Jesus appointed officers or administrators. These officers, or fivefold ministers (apostles, prophets, evangelists, pastors and teachers), are called and specially gifted to evangelize, gather, build up, and equip the church, which is Christ's administration. It is they who dispense His grace and riches and help the whole church to mature to its full potential and achieve its destiny.

THE DESTINY OF THE CHURCH

And just what is the potential and destiny of the church? Before we answer this question, please make sure that you are sitting down. If you truly grasp it, your head will spin and you may never be the same again. This is because the destiny of the church is beyond what any of us are experiencing and beyond what any one of us truly understand.

Remember the passage we were studying earlier that spoke of Jesus taking His place seated at the right hand of the throne of God the Father (Ephesians 1:18-22)? Now the time has come to study the last half of that passage. Paul had been speaking of the "greatness of His (God's) mighty power"...

...which He brought about in Christ, when He raised Him from the dead, and seated Him at His right hand in the heavenly places, far above all rule and authority and power and dominion, and every name that is named, not only in this age, but also in the one to come. And He put all things in subjection under His feet, and GAVE HIM AS HEAD OVER ALL THINGS TO THE CHURCH, WHICH IS HIS BODY, THE FULNESS OF HIM WHO FILLS ALL IN ALL.

Ephesians 1:20-23

Christ is seated at the right hand of the Father, where all things have been placed under His authority. There is nothing in heaven or earth, physical or spiritual, that is not under His authority. The church is His body (I Corinthians 12:27). He is the head and we are the body. All things have been placed under His feet. The feet are part of the body. Think of what this means. All things have been placed under the authority of His administration, which is the church.

The head is in heaven, His feet are on the earth. It is the Body of Christ which connects His authority in heaven to His rule on earth. In other words, CHRIST'S PLAN IS TO RULE EARTH FROM HEAVEN THROUGH HIS CHURCH. Think what this means, WHEN THE BODY IS PROPERLY CONNECTED TO THE HEAD (TAKING ITS DIRECTION FROM THE HEAD), AND FILLED WITH HIS SPIRIT, THEN THERE IS NO GREATER AUTHORITY, POWER OR FORCE ON THE FACE OF THE EARTH.

How is this possible? It is possible because of what Christ has given and invested in the church. In verses 22-23, we read that the church is His body "the fullness of Him who fills all in all." Think what this means, the church is the fullness of Christ.

Imagine that I had two glasses, one empty and one full. If I poured the contents of the full glass into the empty glass, then I would have poured its fullness into the empty glass. Everything that had been in the formerly full glass would now be in the formerly empty glass. In the same way, everything that Jesus had in His earthly ministry has now been emptied into the church through the Holy Spirit. All the miraculous, healing power that flowed through Jesus has now been poured into the church. The knowledge and wisdom of Jesus is likewise now in the church. All the resources that were available to Jesus are now available to us. We have the power, love, wisdom, knowledge and miraculous supply available to us to see Jesus' rule accomplished on earth through His administration, the church.

THE EXAMPLE OF THE EARLY CHURCH

The early church understood and experienced this power, authority and supply, and transformed the Roman Empire. Although the church began as just a handful of men and women without power or money who lived in an obscure corner of the Roman Empire, they transformed the greatest empire in world history. Despite gross misrepresentation and savage persecution, the church marched on victorious. Temples were abandoned, idols toppled, laws were changed, family life restructured, and customs changed. Society was transformed from pagan to Christian. Official persecution ended with the edict of Milan in 313 and Christianity continued to expand until it became the official state religion of the Empire.

The difficulties and odds facing the early church were so much greater than those facing us today and yet she triumphed over them. The resources that those first Christians possessed were so much less than what the church today possesses. And still she triumphed. So too can we triumph. Only one thing is lacking. We must recover the power, authority and supply that are in the Kingdom of God.

In speaking of Christ's rule on earth, we must make an important point. Failure to understand this point would result in terrible mistakes being made. While the church is the primary component of Christ's administration, it is not the only component. Nor is its rule to be political or military.

Rather, the rule through the church is spiritual. It is exercised by changing people's hearts and lives and transforming them through the forgiving and regenerating power of the gospel. It is furthered by establishing people in the teaching of Jesus and establishing them in a transformed community. In a future chapter, we will look at the other spheres of Christ's authority and administration.

CHAPTER 8

THE UNSTOPPABLE ADVANCE

What is the destiny of the Kingdom of God on earth and what are its prospects for the future?

One of the great problems today is that so many American Christians have lost sight of the intent of Christ to make His Kingdom grow until it ruled the earth. They do not expect Christ to gain dominion of this world despite clear statements of Scripture. Remember the famous prophecy of the coming Messiah that is found on so many Christmas cards from Isaiah 9:6-7?

> *For a child will be born to us, a son will be given to us; and the government will rest on His shoulders; and His name will be called Wonderful Counselor, Mighty God, Eternal Father, Prince of Peace. THERE WILL BE NO END TO THE INCREASE OF HIS GOVERNMENT OR OF PEACE... from then on and forevermore. THE ZEAL OF THE LORD OF HOSTS WILL ACCOMPLISH THIS.*
>
> Isaiah 9:6-7

The above quote is clear and unambiguous. The coming Messiah (King) would establish a government that would NEVER STOP INCREASING AND GROWING as would the peace that it would bring with it. Furthermore, this promise comes with the assurance that it would not be left up to the flagging efforts of men to accomplish this, but that GOD HIMSELF WOULD BRING IT TO PASS OUT OF HIS OWN ZEAL AND POWER. God has actually tied His reputation to His ability to accomplish this task. There is hardly any room here for the defeatist attitude of so many Christians.

The above prophecy has certainly been the story of history since then. For 2,000 years His Kingdom has continually advanced. From a small, powerless group in Palestine, His followers have become the dominant force in the world.

On the day that Jesus died on a cross as a rebel outside the city of Jerusalem, the world was held in the grip of gross darkness. Idolatry, demon worship, warfare, witchcraft and cruelty were the norms of the day. A great percentage of the world's population was slaves. Women and children were without rights or protection. True freedom and democracy did not exist anywhere in the world. Besides Israel, no nation worshipped the One True God. Every other nation worshipped nature or a pantheon of idols and "gods" who were in fact demons (1 Corinthians 10:19-20). Jesus' few followers were hiding in an upstairs room behind locked doors (John 20:19). They were seemingly powerless and inconsequential in the greatest empire that has ever existed. An empire unified by its worship of the Emperor as god and held together by the greatest army in history.

But this Kingdom of Jesus grew until it overfilled Palestine and spilled out throughout the entire empire, and despite savage persecution multiplied until the great pagan Roman Empire was converted to Christianity. Across England, Ireland, Russia and North Africa, the Kingdom grew as idols were destroyed and pagan temples abandoned. Then across North and South America, through Africa; and now into China and Korea and many other lands, the Kingdom continues to grow at a rate unprecedented in history.

Today, more people identify with Jesus as their King than with any other religion, philosophy or movement. Already, about one third or more of the earth's total population claims Jesus as their Savior and Lord. The Bible has become the most published, translated, and loved book on the planet. Even our calendars trace themselves to Jesus. Year one was calculated to be the year they believed to be that of our Lord's birth. Years followed by the letters BC refer to "before Christ" and AD for "Ano Domini," or "the year of our Lord." And evangelical Christianity is spreading faster than at any other time in world History.

The growth of Christ's Kingdom is impressive and what's more, it's accelerating. The percentage of the world's population that would describe itself as Christian is generally estimated to be between 32-39 percent, making it by far, the largest religion or movement on the face of the earth. However, when stricter definitions are used to identify true believers, the numbers are smaller. However, you figure it, the growth of Christianity is impressive and it is accelerating!

Mission Frontiers using a definition attempting to identify true believers shows the following growth of believers by a ratio of total world population.

RATIOS REGARDING THE GROWTH
OF CHRISTIANITY:

In 100, there were 360 non-Christians for every Christian.
In 1000, there were 220 non-Christians for every Christian.
In 1500, there were 69 non-Christians for every Christian.
In 1900, there were 29 non-Christians for every Christian.
In 1950, there were 21 non-Christians for every Christian.
In 1980, there were 11 non-Christians for every Christian.

In 1989, there were 7 non-Christians for every Christian (Mission Frontiers, November 1990, quoted in "Global Glimpses," *Quarterly Missions News*, ed. Helen Temple, no. 3, January 1991, n.p.)

The highly respected U.S. Center for World Missions, identifies what it calls "Great Commission Christians." Those who are born-again and are working to fulfill the Great Commission Jesus gave us in Matthew 24. This stricter definition yields somewhat smaller number but no less sensational acceleration in growth.

PER "GREAT COMMISSION BELIEVERS"

Year (A.D.)	World Population per believer
100	360 to 1
1000	270 to 1
1500	85 to 1
1900	21 to 1
1970	13 to 1
2000	9.3 to 1

But the Kingdom of God's influence has not been limited to those who have officially become Christians. All people have benefited from the peace that His Kingdom has brought. As His followers and teachings have spread throughout the earth, so has justice and righteousness. It is a plain fact that it was the followers of Jesus who stopped the barbaric practices of Ancient Rome like the murderous gladiator games at the Coliseum and the widely practiced infanticide of female or handicapped babies. Likewise, it was through the efforts of Christians that slavery was abolished throughout the earth, women and children were accorded basic human rights, and democracy was established. Almost all positive social and political reforms have been introduced in countries with a Christian base and then spread throughout the world. This is a fact beyond dispute. The teachings of Jesus historically lead to freedom, democracy and justice.

Freedom House, the independent and well-respected monitor of political and civil rights, publishes a survey every year showing how nations around the world are faring in terms of basic human rights. It stated recently that never before in all of human history have so many people lived in freedom, testifying to the spread of Christ's peace.

In its most recent publication, "Freedom in the World 20012002," they listed the nations of the world in terms of freedom. Of the ten least-free nations, seven are Islamic (Afghanistan, Iraq, Libya, Saudi Arabia, Sudan, Syria, and Turkmenistan), two are atheistic (Cuba and North Korea) and one is Hindu (Burma). Notice that none are Christian-based. In fact, of the 48 nations listed as "not free," not a single one was Christian. Rather, nearly all of the nations with a Christian background received a perfect or near-perfect score. In fact, there were only two nations that were not of a Christian background that consistently scored perfect or near-perfect over the past decade. They were Israel (which is based on Old Testament values) and Japan (survey available at their website, www.freedomhouse.org). As Christianity has circled the globe, so has freedom and democracy.

In addition, much human suffering has been alleviated through Jesus' followers. Around the world hospitals, schools, orphanages and leper colonies have been built by Christians and by governments of Christian nations. The increasing rule of Christ in the hearts of people has bettered the lot of people all over the globe.

NEBUCHADNEZZAR'S DREAM

But this is what we should expect to find if the prophecies of Daniel are to be believed. In Chapter 2 we briefly looked at an incredible prophecy by Daniel which gave a panoramic view of the future of world history. In about 600 B.C., Nebuchadnezzar, King of Babylon, the first of the great world empires, had a dream. This dream was meant to reveal all the great world empires that would follow his. Each of these kingdoms would rise to dominate the world of their time. In this dream, he was shown a giant statue of a human figure that was crushed by a huge stone cut from a mountain.

Although Nebuchadnezzar knew that this dream had tremendous significance, he could not interpret its meaning. He was greatly disturbed and asked his wise men and advisors to interpret his dream for them. Because he was desperate to be sure that he had the true interpretation, he made an impossible requirement. He required that they not only interpret the dream, but that they relate the dream to him without his having revealed it to them. None could do it until the Jewish prophet Daniel was summoned. He was able to relate the dream and its interpretation.

> *You, O king, were looking and behold, there was a single great statue; that statue, which was large and of extraordinary splendor, was standing in front of you, and its appearance was awesome. The head of that statue was made of fine gold, its breasts and its arms of silver, its belly and its thighs of bronze, its legs of iron, its feet partly of iron and partly of clay. You continued looking until a stone was cut out without hands, and it struck the statue on its feet of iron and clay and crushed them. Then the iron, the clay, the bronze, the silver and the gold were crushed all at the same time and became like chaff from the summer threshing floors; and the wind carried them away so that not a trace of them was found. BUT THE STONE THAT STRUCK THE STATUE BECAME A GREAT MOUNTAIN AND FILLED THE WHOLE EARTH.*
>
> Daniel 2:31-35

As we pointed out in Chapter two, the statue represented Babylon, Persia, Greece, and Rome. The stone which was cut out without human hands and which crushed all the other empires and replaced them is the Kingdom of God, which Jesus, the Messiah, came to establish. This stone then grew until it became a GREAT MOUNTAIN WHICH FILLED THE WHOLE EARTH.

YEAST AND MUSTARD SEEDS

This concept that His Kingdom would continue to grow until it had filled the whole earth and become preeminent over all other kingdoms is exactly what Jesus taught. Jesus' favorite way of teaching was through parables. Many of His parables illustrated His clear conviction that His Kingdom would do just this; that it would be forever advancing, enlarging, and victorious.

In the Parable of the Leaven (or yeast), Jesus makes the point that His Kingdom and movement would penetrate every part of the world and transform it all just as the yeast transformed the whole loaf of bread.

He spoke another parable to them, "The Kingdom of Heaven is like leaven, which a woman took and hid in three pecks of flour UNTIL IT WAS ALL LEAVENED."

Matthew 13:33

In the parable of the mustard seed, Jesus states that His Kingdom would start out small and insignificant like the mustard seed. But just as the mustard plant grows until it becomes larger than any other plant in the garden, so His Kingdom would grow to be larger than all, providing protection and shelter to any who would come to it.

And He said, "How shall we picture the Kingdom of God or by what parable shall we present it? It is like a mustard seed, which, when sown upon the soil, THOUGH IT IS SMALLER THAN ALL THE SEEDS that are upon the soil, yet when it is sown, IT GROWS UP AND BECOMES LARGER THAN ALL THE (other) GARDEN PLANTS and forms large branches; so that the birds of the air can nest under its shade."

Mark 4:30-32

In the Parable of the Sower, Jesus tells us that the seed the farmer sows is "the word of the Kingdom" (Matthew 13:19), or the gospel of the Kingdom. Jesus emphasizes the incredible growth potential of His Kingdom. Every seed has life within it, and when it falls in good soil it brings a multiplied harvest.

And the one on whom seed was sown on the good soil, this is the man who hears the word and understands it; who indeed bears fruit and brings forth, SOME A HUNDRED FOLD, SOME SIXTY, AND SOME THIRTY.

Matthew 13:23

Wow, every seed brings forth an increase of 100 times (10,000% return), 60 times or 30 times. This incredible power to multiply is in the very DNA of Jesus' Kingdom. His Kingdom bursts forth with the power and life of God.

There is not a hint anywhere in Jesus' teachings that He expected His Kingdom to stop growing or to fade away or to fail. He expected it to continually triumph and grow. He knew the power that was in His Kingdom. He knew that it had authority over all other kingdoms.

A GUARANTEED PROFIT

Only when you understand this can you make sense of some of His other parables, like the Parable of the Talents (Matthew 25:14-30) or the Parable of the Minas (Luke 19:12-27). In these parables, the master of the estate (who represents Jesus) divides up his resources among his servants to be responsible for until he returns. When he returns, he calls his servants to come and report before him. Those who brought forth increase are rewarded with more; however, any servant that has not brought forth increase is cast out as unworthy and excluded from the master's house.

> *And the one also who had received the one talent (a measure of money – about 75 lbs of silver) came up and said, 'Master, I knew you to be a hard man, reaping where you did not sow and gathering where you scattered no seed. And I was afraid, and went away and hid your talent in the ground. See, you have back what it yours.'*
>
> Matthew 25:24-25

To most of us, the man's attitude seems completely reasonable and understandable. It would be a terrible thing to lose your master's investment. He might hold you responsible. Perhaps the man lacked confidence in his business ability. Perhaps he was inexperienced in handling money. Yes, the safest course would be to hide the money and return it safe and sound rather than risk losing it. It seems reasonable and even prudent.

That is why for many of us the master's response seems harsh and unfair. After all, the marketplace can be risky and investments can be lost. How can we explain the reaction of the master?

> *But his master answered and said to him, 'YOU WICKED, LAZY SLAVE, you knew that I REAP WHERE I DID NOT SOW AND GATHER WHERE I SCATTERED NO SEED. Then you ought to have put my money in the bank, and on my arrival I would have received my money back with interest. Therefore take away the talent from him and give it to the one who has ten talents.'*
>
> Matthew 25:26-28

The master's response only becomes understandable when you remember that this is a parable about the Kingdom of God, not a story about the risks of the marketplace. While it is true that the marketplace is liable to unforeseen events and anything invested in it is at some risk, this is not true of the Kingdom of God.

The Kingdom of God cannot fail. The Kingdom of God is absolutely certain of growth and victory. It is backed by the reputation of God. It is filled with the power and life of God. It is built by the zeal of the Lord of Hosts. Its King always reaps a harvest. He reaps where he planted no seeds. Even where His enemies planted seeds, He is the one who goes in and reaps the harvest. God uses even the plans and actions of His enemies to advance His purposes and Kingdom. Just ask the Pharaoh of Moses' time. Just ask Pontius Pilate, Caiaphas the High Priest, or even Judas Iscariot. In fact, even Satan, who inspired Judas to betray Jesus (John 13:27) found that his action only brought about his defeat and Christ's victory.

To invest time, energy, abilities or money in the Kingdom of God, this parable tells us, is as certain of growth as money in the bank with guaranteed interest. *Therefore, there is no other reason possible for failing to advance and grow than unbelief, laziness or wickedness.*

What other excuse can we offer our Lord for the state of the church in our nation today than human wickedness, unbelief and laziness? The truth is, we often use wicked defeatist doctrines that are absolutely unworthy of the followers of the King of Kings and Lord of Lords. I hear Christians throw up their hands at the condition of the world and say; "Well, what can you do? We know things are going to get worse and worse."What a wicked and demonic doctrine this is! How we use it to excuse our unbelief and lust to pursue the things of this world!

Because of some highly questionable interpretations of mysterious and difficult apocalyptic passages, we ignore the clear commandments of the Lord. Where did Jesus tell us to become irrelevant and preoccupied in our own pursuits because, "it's just going to get worse and worse anyhow and there is ultimately nothing you can do about it"?

THE "IMPOSSIBLE" ASSIGNMENT

Jesus certainly did not expect that the forces of the devil would overcome His Church. He certainly did not mean anyone to derive from any of His teachings that "things would just get worse at the end and then He would come to rescue us." Jesus taught that He was bringing in an indestructible, invincible Kingdom that could not be overcome and could not fail. This explains why Jesus could give such an incredible commission to a small band of seemingly powerless followers.

ALL AUTHORITY HAS BEEN GIVEN TO ME IN HEAVEN AND EARTH. GO THEREFORE AND MAKE DISCIPLES OF ALL THE NATIONS, baptizing them in the name of the Father and the Son and the Holy Spirit, teaching them to observe all that I have commanded you; and lo, I AM WITH YOU ALWAYS, even to the end of the age.

Matthew 28:18-20

It is only because of the invincible nature of His Kingdom that Jesus could give them this commission. If the Kingdom were not as Jesus taught in His parables, then this would be a cruel, impossible assignment.

But the Kingdom of God was, and is, exactly as Jesus pictured it in these parables. It does have incredible power to multiply (parable of the Sower). Although it may start out small and insignificant, it will grow until it becomes the largest Kingdom (Parable of the Mustard Seed) and leavens and transforms all of the world everywhere (Parable of the Leaven).

This is exactly what the disciples discovered when they took Jesus at His word and trusted Him. After receiving the Baptism of the Holy Spirit on the Day of Pentecost, they burst forth from behind closed doors and watched the Kingdom of God begin to transform the world.

THEY SAW THE INCREDIBLE POWER OF THE KINGDOM TO MULTIPLY LIKE A SOWN SEED when 3,000 men believed and were baptized on Pentecost (Acts 2:41). But it didn't stop there. In the days, weeks and months to come the Kingdom kept spreading in Jerusalem.

The word of God kept on spreading; and the number of the disciples continued to increase greatly in Jerusalem, and a great many of the priests were becoming obedient to the faith.

Acts 6:7

However, it didn't stop there either, it multiplied beyond Jerusalem to the Hellenistic Jews (Acts 6:1), to the regions of Judea, and Samaria (Acts 8:1-12), Ethiopia (Acts 8:26-39), and finally Phoenicia, Cyprus and Antioch of Syria; which became such a great missionary church itself (Acts 11:19, see Acts 13:1).

And still the Kingdom grew and multiplied. At the end of the first section of Acts we read this summary statement:

But the Word of the Lord continued to grow and to be multiplied.

Acts 12:24

THEY FOUND THAT INDEED THE WORD WAS LIKE LEAVEN. Once it was released, it began to fill everywhere and begin to transform everything. This was exactly the charge of the anxious Jewish leaders and power brokers against the Apostles.

When they had brought them (the apostles), they stood them before the Council. The high priest questioned them, saying, "We gave you strict orders not to continue teaching in this name, and yet, YOU HAVE FILLED JERUSALEM WITH YOUR TEACHING and intend to bring this man's blood upon us."

Acts 5:28

But the leaven of the Kingdom message could not be contained. Paul took it to Ephesus and trained and sent out missionaries with the message of the triumph and rule of Jesus until the leaven was working throughout all of Asia.

And this took place for two years, so that ALL WHO LIVED IN ASIA HEARD THE WORD OF THE LORD, both Jews and Greeks.

Acts 19:9-10

The Word of the Lord was having its effect in Ephesus and Asia.

Many also of those who had believed kept coming, confessing and disclosing their practices. And many of those who practiced magic brought their books together and began burning them in the sight of all; and they counted up the price of them and found it fifty thousand pieces of silver. SO THE WORD OF THE LORD WAS GROWING AND MIGHTILY PREVAILING.

Acts 19:18-20

Everywhere the message and power of the Kingdom was filling and transforming individuals, families, villages, towns and whole cities. The mob, who dragged one of Paul's associates before the city authorities in Thessalonica, was correct in their charge:

And when they did not find them (Paul and Silas), they began dragging Jason and some brethren before the city authorities, crying out, "THESE MEN WHO HAVE

*TURNED THE WORLD UPSIDE DOWN have come here
also.*

Acts 17:6 (KJV)

HAVE YOU LOST YOUR SALTINESS?

The Kingdom of God indeed was and is exactly as Jesus pictured it.
It is invincible and charged with power and will displace every other
kingdom, philosophy or belief system it encounters. This is not only the
testimony of the Book of Acts but of history as well. ONLY WHERE
THE SUBJECTS OF THE KINGDOM (the church) HAVE GROWN
COMPROMISED, CORRUPTED AND UNBELIEVING CAN THE
KINGDOM FAIL TO ADVANCE. In those places, the church can even
suffer great setback. These are like the servant in the parable of the talents who was cast out. Jesus put it this way.

*You are the salt of the earth; BUT IF THE SALT HAS
BECOME TASTELESS, how shall it be made salty again?
IT IS GOOD FOR NOTHING ANYMORE, EXCEPT TO
BE TOSSED OUT AND TRAMPLED UNDER FOOT BY
MEN. You are the LIGHT of the world. A CITY SET ON A
HILL cannot be hidden.*

Matthew 5:13-14

Think about what Jesus is saying. Light displaces darkness and
darkness flees before it. Salt overcomes spoilage in meat. A city on a
hill rules over the countryside. From the walled city set on a hill a king
would rule over all the surrounding lands. These pictures underscore
that it is in the very nature of Kingdom people to transform and overcome. The Kingdom of God, and its King are greater than all. All
authority and power belong to Jesus.

But is salt still salt once it has lost its taste or saltiness? Only when
the church, through unbelief and disobedience, fails to have the savor
and light of the Kingdom does it lose its saltiness. In other words it has
lost its essence. It will be tossed out and trampled underfoot by other
movements and kingdoms until it recovers its saltiness.

The Kingdom is as Jesus described it. Even today its power and life
are on display around the globe. The Pentecostal/Charismatic and the
Evangelical forms of Christianity continue to be the fastest growing
movements on the planet. According to the U.S. Center for World Missions, they are growing annually at a rate of 7.3% and 5.6% respec-

tively. To compare, Islam is growing at 2.7%. The U.S. Center for World Missions further reports that Pentecostal and Evangelical Christianity are the only major religious groups in the world that are significantly expanding through conversions.

Even in your city the Kingdom is charged with power and life for any who have the faith to step out and believe God. It takes only faith, patience and obedience to see the Kingdom explode and grow.

In the next chapter I will introduce you to several of my friends. They are just ordinary people like you and me who made the discovery of the riches and power of God's Kingdom.

CHAPTER 9

THE MUSTARD SEED FACTOR

In our city is a wonderful woman named Mari Rothman. She is a wife, mother and hairdresser. Some years ago, Mari took up an exercise program of walking. A woman friend, who happened to be a teacher at a nearby elementary school, became her walking partner. Every morning they would talk as they walked. Mari's friend would often tell her of the disadvantaged children at the school where she taught. The school was in a poor neighborhood in our area and many of the parents had drug problems. Mari was shocked to hear such stories of neglect so close to her own home. A great compassion for these kids was being formed in her heart. She felt something needed to be done for these kids. *But what could she do?*

Although Mari didn't feel prepared or qualified to help, she and her friend began praying. As they talked and prayed, they came up with an idea. As a hair stylist, Mari did know about grooming. She would hold a six-week class with six students one hour a week on personal grooming. It didn't seem like a very big thing, but it was something she could do. They approached the principal with the idea. He was grateful for any help for these students.

Mari threw herself into the project. She completed several sessions of six students each. The students benefited from lessons on grooming, but even more from the love of this Christian woman who never lost an opportunity to tell them of God's love in Jesus Christ.

But there was a problem. The kids never wanted the six-week sessions to end. They continued to hang around Mari and she decided to add a once-a-week Bible club for these students at her hair-cutting store up the street. The first week 20 children showed up. The shop office had to be closed so that there would be room for all the students. Clearly they would have to move.

Mari and her friend approached the principal for a classroom to use after school. The principal agreed and the club began to meet on campus, staffed by Mari and her own children. The following year, the principal was transferred to a very troubled middle school in the same district. He asked his replacement to allow Mari to stay since she was having such a positive impact on the students.

At the new school, the principal encountered even greater problems. There was a stabbing of one student by another with scissors. Tensions were high. The principal remembered the effect Mari had on the students at his former school. Although he was not a Christian, he believed that her club, like the one at his former school, could help these students as well. He called Mari and asked her to start a club at the middle school.

After the club was established at the new school, God began to move on Mari's heart. She recruited a few friends from her church and approached a principal at a third school. Soon what had begun as a small class on grooming organized by a woman who simply wanted "to do something" grew into 3 weekly after-school clubs.

As we have seen, it is the nature of the Kingdom to continue to grow and multiply. Today, from that one small beginning, there are now over 200 volunteers working in 30 after-school Bible clubs and related ministries such as camps and a community teen center. And each step of the way, Jesus has supplied each need as He has built His Kingdom through the simple faith of those who will simply believe and obey.

The story of Mari Rothman is similar to the stories of so many others that I have known. They are ordinary people who make the discovery of the extraordinary Kingdom of which they have become a part. In gaining a vision of that Kingdom and its King, they realize that nothing is too difficult. They come to understand that if they will just trust God and begin, the Kingdom will continue to grow and expand. Certainly Mari had no idea that what began as such a small mustard seed would become such a big tree in the garden that would give shelter to so many children in the shade of its branches (Mark 4:30-32).

Mari could have never foreseen what would come of her willingness to step out and simply use what she had, to do what she could. She never could have imagined all the places from which help and support would come to her, or all the ways in which Jesus would solve problems, open doors and provide money. This is exactly part of the mystery of the Kingdom as Jesus Himself taught us.

And He (Jesus) was saying, "The Kingdom of God is like a man who casts seed upon the soil; and goes to bed at night and gets up by day, and THE SEED SPROUTS UP AND

GROWS – HOW, HE HIMSELF DOES NOT KNOW. THE SOIL PRODUCES CROPS BY ITSELF; first the blade, then the head, then the mature grain in the head. But when the crop permits, he immediately puts in the sickle, because the harvest has come."

Mark 4:26-29

Jesus is telling us that the power and the potential are in the seed. We do not understand all the mysterious ways of God's Kingdom. We can't always foresee how it will grow or triumph. We can't see the end from the beginning. Our part is simply to plant the seed and to believe in its potential and to be patient as it matures.

As this parable makes clear, we often will not recognize the growth of the Kingdom until it is ready for harvest. Our job is to remain faithful and believe in the wisdom of the One who created the seed and the soil. Just as life is locked within each seed, so the miracle of life is locked within each seed of the Kingdom. We must have faith to sow the seed and then reap the harvest at the right time.

JUST A BUNCH OF KIDS

In God's Kingdom wonderful things can come from seemingly unimportant and easily overlooked beginnings. Our church has always made camps for our youth one of its highest priorities. We believe in the importance of reaching and training youth. We also believe that camps and retreats are among the very best ways of doing this. For this reason, we put our very best into these camps. Even though I am a Senior Pastor, I attend every youth camp we hold. We also provide the best worship teams possible. Because of this commitment, our meetings at our youth camps are among the most dynamic of our church all year.

Two years ago at our Junior High Winter Camp, one group of eighth grade boys seemed to be especially affected. At each meeting, they would weep throughout the entire worship portion. One boy in particular would sob very loudly. I even considered taking him outside on several occasions, as I was concerned that it might be disruptive to others. I didn't know what was producing such an extreme response from this boy or this group. When I asked them, they couldn't tell me plainly, but several of them told me of visions they had.

When they got back home, they were gripped with a love for Jesus and a desire to worship Him. They began worshipping Jesus several nights a week at one boy's home. They decided to bring their guitars and worship before school at their public middle school. Soon they also began to gather after school for worship and were joined by a few others.

Just several months earlier, our community had gone through a horrible ordeal. We had experienced one of those horrible school shootings that had attracted worldwide media attention. Charles "Andy" Williams, a small, ninth grade boy who had been the recipient of much teasing and bullying, decided to get revenge. He brought a .22 caliber handgun to school in his backpack. At

9:20 in the morning, he entered a crowded boys bathroom and opened fire. Several boys collapsed to the ground in a pool of blood as the others ran out the door. Andy reloaded and emerged from the bathroom and began shooting at students and teachers in the small quad area outside, firing at least 30 shots. By the time it was over, less than ten minutes later, two students lay dead and thirteen other people were wounded. The surrounding community was in a state of shock.

No doubt this event and the shock it produced helped account for what happened next. As the small group of worshippers continued to meet, their numbers grew steadily. Soon they were meeting during lunch period as well. In the lunch court they were worshipping before the entire student body. Some students mocked and ridiculed them. Several times kids threw the fruit that their mothers had packed in their lunches at the group of worshippers, but this couldn't stop them. As more and more kids experienced God's presence in worship, the group continued to grow. Now they were meeting three times a day to worship. The group of worshippers continued to grow and crowds of up to eighty students would gather to worship. A number of students got saved. I baptized many students from this school and even one whole family that was reached because of the change in their middle school student.

What is so remarkable about this is that no adult had ever been involved. There had been no plan and no clear idea of what they wanted to happen. It had started out as nothing more than four boys, who had met God powerfully at camp, wanting to worship Him everywhere. Before it was over, a number of students had become Christians and a school had been changed. At the end of the school year these boys graduated and we planted an after-school Bible club to follow up the following year.

The next year these same boys entered a large public high school. They felt very small and intimidated as freshmen surrounded by several thousand upperclassmen. They started out as so many others do, by joining many extracurricular activities and began to be absorbed into the culture of a public high school. The first semester was passing quietly by, but then something happened. We held winter camp. These boys came once again and were once again mightily filled with the Holy Spirit during the worship. One of the boys had a vision. It was a vision of them worshipping God at the high school campus during lunch. They prayed about it and decided to do it.

Several days before they were to start, I had them come to my house. As we sat out in my Jacuzzi, I listened to them talk. They were afraid of what the other students would do to them, but they were committed to starting anyway. They expected not only to be ridiculed but to be physically beat up as well. I was impressed at the simple courage of these freshmen who were ready to face the rejection and opposition of an entire school.

The first day they were able to recruit nine other students, mainly from our church, to join them. The louder the catcalls and taunts became, the more they kept their eyes closed and focused on God. At one point some nearby students began chanting worship to Satan and a minute later an apple whizzed by one of their ears. The second day was much the same, except that two had dropped out and now there were only eleven. Once again, the taunting continued while they worshipped and silently prayed.

On the third day, the taunting mysteriously stopped. They found out later that the principal had stationed the campus police officer nearby to protect the circle of worshipping students. Once again, as students began to experience the presence of God in worship, the small group began to grow, from eleven to fifteen and then twenty, twenty-five and thirty. Once again, students were saved and baptized from that school as well.

The Kingdom is as Jesus portrayed it. It does multiply and grow like the mustard seed. It is charged with God's own power and riches, but it does work in mysterious ways, at times. A hairstylist discovered this, as did 4 fourteen-year-old boys. Are you ready to make the discovery as well?

SECTION TWO

Entering the Kingdom

...Truly, truly, I say to you, unless one is born of water and the Spirit he cannot enter into the Kingdom of God.

John 3:5

CHAPTER 10

THE AVAILABILITY OF
THE KINGDOM

A newlywed couple from a farm community were given, as a gift a night at a luxury suite at an expensive hotel in the city. Upon checking into the suite, the groom was somewhat surprised. Although the room was quite large and had beautiful furniture, a kitchenette, and sophisticated stereo and television equipment, it had no bed. The groom checked the sofa, and sure enough, it was a hide-a-bed. That night they did not sleep well on the uncomfortable hide-a-bed. The next morning, just as they were about to check out, the groom opened what he thought was a closet door and discovered a huge bedroom with an oversized bed, a hot tub, and on the dresser, a large fruit basket.

Although they had been given, a beautiful room with a luxurious bed, hot tub and large gift basket, they did not get to enjoy it because they realized it too late. They had been unaware of it because *they did not recognize the door into the greater room.*

This is how it will be for so many Christians. Upon arriving in heaven, they will realize how little of God's Kingdom they understood or enjoyed. They will recognize, then, that they were kept out by ignorance, unbelief and even certain teachings that told them that the Kingdom was not for them today.

Remember, Jesus' message was:

The time is fulfilled, and the Kingdom of God is at hand; repent and believe in the gospel.

Mark 1:14

Or as Matthew put it...

Repent, for the kingdom of heaven is at hand.

Matthew 4:17

This was the summary of Jesus' message. Let's break it down.

"The time is fulfilled." That is, the promised and long awaited time has arrived. That which the Old Testament Prophets promised is now beginning. I am bringing in a new state of affairs.

"Repent." To repent means to change the way you think and act. There are two main Greek words which are translated as "repent" in the New Testament. The first is *"metanoia,"* which means to change your mind or thinking. The second is *"epistrepho,"* which means to change your direction. Both of these meanings are contained in the idea of repentance. So He is saying, "Hold on, stop the presses, change the way you think and change the way you act because the Kingdom of God (that is, the realm of God's surpassing power, perfect love and infinite possibilities) is available now to change your life and world."

It's *"at hand."* That means it's within your grasp. I like the Bible translation I recently read that said, "The Kingdom of God is within reach." It's at hand. It's nearby. He is literally saying, "Wake up, the power and the love of God is *now* available to bring heaven to earth for anyone who will reach out and seize it."

Jesus' message to us is to enter that Kingdom. But it will require a change in the way we think and act. However, if we will do so, then the Kingdom will certainly open up to us. In fact, Jesus seems to be saying in Matthew 11:12, that if men would use great forcefulness they could overcome all obstacles and seize the Kingdom.

> *From the days of John the Baptist of John the Baptist until now, the Kingdom of Heaven has been forcefully advancing, and forceful men lay hold of it.*
>
> Matthew 11:12 (NIV)

A NIGHTTIME VISITOR

For many believers the Kingdom of God is just a mystery, like it was for the Pharisee Nicodemus. He came to Jesus by night to ask him questions. His religious training and teaching had blinded him from being able to understand Jesus, although He could not deny that God was at work through Him.

The third chapter of the gospel of John records the famous interchange between Nicodemus and Jesus. Although Nicodemus was a respected teacher of the Law, Jesus rocked his world (and ours) with the following words.

> *Truly, truly, I say to you, unless one is born again, he cannot see the Kingdom of God.*
>
> John 3:3

The Pharisees were faithfully waiting for the Kingdom of God, which they thought would be a future historical event in which the fortunes of Israel would turn and Israel would become the dominant nation on earth. Jesus points out to Nicodemus that he misunderstood. The coming of the Kingdom was not something that everyone would see. You could miss it.

Most of us have heard many sermons on this verse. Almost always the sermons stress the importance of being born again. That, of course, is absolutely true. However, look closely. *Being born again is not the main subject of the verse.* The main subject of the verse is the Kingdom of God. It's about *seeing* the Kingdom. We make being born again the end, instead of what it really is. It is the *means to the end.* You must be born again *so that you can see the Kingdom of God.* We stress the need to be born again, which is important, but we stop short of emphasizing the purpose of being born again, which is to see the Kingdom.

SEEING THE KINGDOM

The Kingdom of God is not evident to everyone. People who are not born again can't even perceive the Kingdom of God. They have not entered into the new dimension of Life that would allow them to see. That's why they don't understand why you do what you do or think like you think. *They can't see what you see.*

They ask, "Why do you give your money to the church?" "Why do you have to take this religious stuff so seriously?" They don't understand you because they can't see what you see. It can be frustrating not being understood.

It's similar to being in a room full of sleeping people. Those sleeping are not conscious of the fact that they are asleep or that you are awake. They are in a dream world of unreality and unawareness. You, however, are aware both that you are awake and that they are sleeping. This is how it can feel when you talk to those who are not born again.

It is a little like being Neo, the main character in the movie *The Matrix.* He discovers that the world he has been living in is an illusion. It is a mass-induced dream or hallucination. Their bodies are actually being held in suspended animation while their brains are being manipulated with images of this imaginary world. Yet only a few people realize that it is not reality. When told, the majority of people react the same way that some people react when you tell them that there is more to life than what they see and know, that you know God and are in contact with Jesus. They scoff and ridicule until it happens to them.

When a person is born again, their spirit is made spiritually alive by union with the Holy Spirit. They become alive to a whole new dimension of reality. Do you remember how it was with you? For me everything was new, because I now saw the reality of God and His ways in everything.

Nicodemus, because he was not born again, didn't have any idea what Jesus was talking about.

> *Nicodemus said to Him, "How can a man be born again when he is old? He cannot enter a second time into his mother's womb and be born, can he?"*

John 3:4

Jesus seizes upon Nicodemus' interest to give further teaching about the Kingdom.

> *Jesus answered, "Truly, truly, I say to you, unless one is born of water and the Spirit he cannot ENTER the Kingdom of God."*

John 3:5

Notice the secret that Jesus reveals to Nicodemus here. Beyond just seeing the Kingdom, you can enter it.

ENTERING THE KINGDOM

Remember what we have learned. The Kingdom of God is not known to the natural mind. The unregenerate (unsaved) person can't perceive it or understand it. You must be born again! But being born again only *qualifies* you to see the Kingdom. It doesn't guarantee that you will understand or enter the Kingdom. To be able to see the Kingdom is one thing, but to enter it is another.

This explains why some Christians live defeated lives. Rather than changing their world, they barely survive it. Other Christians, no matter how bad their circumstances, are never overcome by those circumstances. Instead, they change their world. These are the ones who have learned to enter the Kingdom, with all its power and potential.

These truly are Kingdom people. These are the ones who are following in the footsteps of Jesus, the Apostles and the first century church. These are the ones who learn that they do not have to be defeated or overcome by circumstances or difficulties.

Think about it. Jesus was a man just like us in every way (Hebrews 2:17-18 and 4:15). He surrendered all His miraculous powers and abilities when He came to earth and fully entered into our weaknesses and inabilities (Philippians 2:5-7). He could do no miraculous works except by faith and the leading of God (John 5:19; 30). He was dependent upon the power of the Holy Spirit to accomplish healings (Luke 5:17).

Although the Bible tells us that Jesus was just like us (except that He did not have a sin nature), the Bible also shows that He lived far differently from us. He was never limited by His circumstances. He was able to release God's blessing and provision into human need. He understood how to reach into the invisible realm, called the Kingdom of God, which was charged with God's power and superabundance. He taught His disciples this as well. The Book of Acts shows that the Apostles were not overcome by their circumstances. Instead, they were overcomers because they were taught to operate in the same Kingdom.

What you must understand is that these same Kingdom Truths will still open up the same Kingdom today. The Kingdom of God is still giving people victory today.

It is your destiny and heritage to overcome!

Look at this clear statement.

For whatever is born of God overcomes the world; and this is the victory that has overcome the world—our faith.

John 5:4

What could be clearer? Everything that is born of God overcomes the world. Now go and stand in front of the mirror and ask yourself this question. Are you born of God? Are you born again? If you are, then it is your nature to overcome!

Why? Because you have God's nature in you. And, because you are born again, you can see His Kingdom. And what is more, you can *enter* it because Jesus has given us the keys. And from within this Kingdom you can overcome anything because His Kingdom is greater than everything else.

Unfortunately, American society seems to produce in us unbelief and a busy distractedness. These work against our pressing into the Kingdom. Consequently, today we still have a way to go to recover New Testament Christianity. Nevertheless, I have personally seen the Kingdom of God powerfully at work.

I have witnessed people instantly delivered from years of powerful addictions to drugs and alcohol. I have seen the profoundly demonized delivered. I have seen people who had spent years in and out of mental institutions and on medications set free and go on to productive and stable *overcoming* lives

I have witnessed the power of God fall on dozens and even hundreds of people at a time. I have seen diseased organs restored and cancers healed. I have seen people raised up from their deathbeds. I have seen deaf ears hear. I have even seen a man get out of a wheel chair and walk.

I have seen lives changed, and impossible marriages restored. I have seen strongholds pulled down and injustice rectified. I have witnessed the most improbable coincidences. I have even seen money in a locked room multiply. I have witnessed things that I will not share publicly because many people would not believe them and I would merely be ridiculed.

It is easy to be skeptical, especially if you have been raised in our modern American society and educated in our schools. But who can argue that the New Testament presents Christianity as being decidedly supernatural? Who can deny what the first century church experienced in the Book of Acts? It is easy to be skeptical. It is easy to try and concoct doctrines or philosophies that make our subnormal Christian experience seem normal. But really, there is only one way to find out. Why not press into the Kingdom and find out for yourself?

Jesus is calling us to follow Him into His Kingdom. In the following chapters we will look at practical ways to lay hold of this Kingdom. All it takes is knowledge, faith and obedience. Oh yeah, and maybe a little courage.

CHAPTER 11

KINGDOM MYSTERIES AND KINGDOM KEYS

Norway produces the cheapest electricity in the world, so they never think of turning their lights off. They keep them on day and night. Their electricity is generated by the many rivers and waterfalls in their country. The Vikings lived in the same country years ago, but they used candles. They didn't use the power that was available because they were unaware of its potential (and the technology had not been invented yet).

In the same way, the church seems to be unaware of the potential of the Kingdom that surrounds us. When we come to understand it and its power and supply, we will change our world. Nothing is more common than for people to miss out on their opportunity to enter the Kingdom. How is it that some Christians enter the Kingdom while others fail to do so? Remember Jesus' words to His disciples?

*To you it has been granted to know **the mysteries** of the Kingdom of God, but to them it has not been granted.*
                                                              Matthew 13:11

The Kingdom of God is entered through knowing its mysteries. You don't enter the Kingdom of God because you figure it out with your natural mind. It can only be entered by knowing its secrets, which are revealed in the Bible, especially in the teachings of Jesus. These secrets actually go against the thinking of the natural mind. But even knowing these secrets is not enough. You must obey them and follow them in faith, or they are inactive and without power for you.

THE KEYS TO THE KINGDOM

Jesus spent His time with the disciples teaching them these secrets. After Peter's Great Confession that Jesus was in fact "the Christ, the Son of the Living God" (Matthew 16:16), Jesus made a promise to Him.

I will give you the keys to the Kingdom of Heaven; and whatever you bind on earth shall have been bound in heaven, and whatever you loose on earth shall have been bound in heaven.

Matthew 16:19

When Jesus promised Peter these keys, He was promising to give him the teaching that would allow him and others to enter the Kingdom and release its power and riches. They would be able to live in the Kingdom just as Jesus did. By following and using these Kingdom principles, just like Jesus, they would be able to link heaven's power to earth's situations. Heaven's power would be available to bring to pass Heaven's will.

Those things that were bound (forbidden) in heaven could be bound (forbidden) on earth, and those things that were allowed in heaven could be loosed upon the earth. By believing in and following these Kingdom principles they could help to be the answer to the prayer Jesus taught them to pray: *Thy Kingdom come.* ***Thy will be done on earth as it is in heaven*** (Matthew 6:10).

History records that this is just what happened. The Apostles and their converts in the first century were channels of Heaven's power. They changed their world. So have countless other followers of Jesus throughout history.

As you follow and practice the Kingdom truths and principles found in the Bible, you will find the Kingdom of God opens up to you. This book (and its companion, *Breakthrough Kingdom Living*) is dedicated to helping people to understand these mysteries and lay hold of the keys that will open up God's Kingdom.

In *Breakthrough Kingdom Living* we study 13 Kingdom Keys, or mysteries, in depth. We look at such Kingdom Keys as Thanksgiving and Praise, Diligence, Agreement, Overcoming Faith, Inspired Imagination and Displacement among others. These highly practical looks into the inner-workings of the Kingdom will change your life. (Information on ordering *Breakthrough Kingdom Living* is at the end of this book.)

If one is ignorant of the facts about God's Kingdom, or of the principles by which that Kingdom is entered and its power and riches supplied, then faith is precluded. A lack of knowledge or understanding can be devastating as God, through the prophet Hosea, pointed out many years ago.

My people are destroyed for lack of knowledge.

Hosea 4:6

It is absolutely critical for all of us who call ourselves Christians to become students of the teachings of our Master and of the Bible as a whole. Ignorance of the Bible and indifference to, what is contained in its pages is sin, just as surely as is stealing. The penalty for such ignorance or indifference is destruction of various types, as we just read from the prophet Hosea. It really, truly is a life and death matter.

I witness almost daily the tragedy and heartbreak that occurs in Christians' lives because they live ignorant, of or indifferent to the principles of life in God's Word. I watch them lose their health, finances, marriages, even their souls. I watch them lose something even more precious. I say this with unceasing sorrow. Many have lost their children to drugs, alcohol, sexual addiction, perversion, unbelief, atheism and even death.

All this because they treat the principles and commands in God's Word as nonessential things. That is, they treat them as an unimportant, optional part of life. But they are not optional. They are the key to success in life.

Moses understood the human inclination to ignore God's Word amidst all the busyness of life. He gave them a clear charge on the day He gave them God's Word.

Take to your heart all the words with which I am warning you today, which you shall command your sons to observe carefully, even all the words of this law. FOR IT IS NOT AN IDLE WORD FOR YOU; INDEED IT IS YOUR LIFE. AND BY THIS WORD YOU WILL PROLONG YOUR DAYS in the land which you are about to cross the Jordan to possess.

Deuteronomy 32:46-47

The hard truth is that *we are responsible to know God's principles for life* and to follow them. Without knowing His Word we cannot follow Jesus. Nor can we be delivered from the destructions of the world and be free as Jesus has indeed told us Himself.

If you continue in My Word, then you are truly disciples of Mine; and you will know the truth and the truth will make you free.

John 8:31-32

It is no excuse to say that you are too busy, or that you don't like to read or study. Like so many other things in life, *it is simply required.* Are you a student of God's Word? Do you truly study it, searching it for direction and seeking out its principles? When you go to a Bible study or sermon do you go prepared to work at listening and learning? Or do you go with a lazy, passive mind, requiring that the speaker entertain and amuse you? Look around next Sunday and you will see many people in this mindset.

My friend, Charles Simpson, likes to say that we have traded *Feelology* for *Theology*. We have traded feeling for thinking. Theology is the study of God and His Truth. Many people would rather just have religious feelings than to have to think, learn and understand. But it is not feelings that Jesus said would set you free, but truth. To be free, you must study and apply yourself to understand and to put it into practice. This is harder than just having religious "goosebumps," or some fantastic experience with the Holy Spirit.

If we do not know and follow God's promises and precepts, we cannot expect to get the promised results. Many people live careless lives, ignorant and indifferent to the very principles that God has given us to supply and protect us. Then, when failure or tragedy strikes, they are the first to blame God. It reminds me of a story about two women.

A woman named Betty had a very detailed recipe for a crabmeat casserole. Everyone who tasted it said it was the best dish they had ever tasted. Betty gave the recipe to her friend Eleanor, and some weeks later they were going to a potluck dinner and bringing their dishes. On the way, Eleanor said to Betty, "I'm serving your gorgeous crabmeat casserole tonight." But as they continued on their way to the dinner, Eleanor admitted that she had changed the recipe just a little bit. She didn't have any crab meat, so she substituted tuna. And canned mushroom soup had replaced the very delicate white sauce, because it was easier. And the sherry and the blanched almonds were left out because she had forgotten to put them in her shopping cart.

As Eleanor was dishing out her casserole to a friend at the potluck, she said, "Now, if you don't like this, don't blame me, blame Betty, it's her recipe."

Sometimes we are unwilling to live life God's way because we think this thing or that thing is too tough – or we don't like it, and so we ignore it or substitute our own wisdom and ways. But when something goes wrong, we want to blame God. After all, we say, He's in charge.

HOW FAR WILL YOU GO?

It is the right and duty of all born-again believers to not only see, but also to enter the Kingdom of God. God wants you to live in the power and supply of His invisible, yet ever advancing, Kingdom. Unfortunately, it is possible that a person can believe in the Kingdom, and even touch it, but never really enter it. Others may enter it but not advance very far.

Entering the Kingdom of God is progressive. One can gain entrance to more and more of the Kingdom. Greater entrance to the Kingdom is granted to those who have been faithful with what they have already received. Remember the words of Jesus in Matthew 13:11-12 we looked at earlier? Let's look at them again, because Jesus gives us the key to making further progress.

In the 13th chapter of Matthew, Jesus' disciples were confused. Why would He so often speak to the crowd in parables? Often these parables were like riddles that the people could not solve. Often the disciples could not understand them either. Later, Jesus would explain them privately to His disciples (Mark 4:33-34). The disciples came up to Jesus and asked Him, "Why do You speak to them in parables?" (Matthew 13:10) Jesus' answer reveals an important principle in understanding His Kingdom.

> *Jesus answered them, "TO YOU IT HAS BEEN GRANTED TO KNOW THE MYSTERIES OF THE KINGDOM OF HEAVEN, but to them it has not been granted. FOR WHOEVER HAS, TO HIM MORE SHALL BE GIVEN, and he shall have an abundance; but whoever does not have, even what he has shall be taken away from him."*
> Matthew 13:11-12

The disciples were qualified to receive further keys to enter the Kingdom because they had accepted the foundational truth of the Kingdom, that being, that Jesus was its King. They had believed in Jesus and become His followers. Having been faithful to believe and obey this first truth, they would have the chance to encounter further truth. Because they had accepted some Kingdom truth, they would receive more.

The crowds, however, had made no such commitment. They were there out of curiosity or to see some miracle. Perhaps in the future, some would choose to believe in Him and become His disciples as well. But for now, they had not accepted the foundational Kingdom truth that Jesus was the Messiah. They had nothing, so they would receive nothing. Eventually, even what they did have, the opportunity to hear and accept Jesus, would be lost to them.

How People Are Sorted Out

This is how the Kingdom of God works. People sort themselves out according to their willingness to accept and follow the Kingdom message. One of Jesus' favorite sayings was, "Let him who has ears to hear, hear." In fact, He says those words in the very verse before the ones we just quoted. People are at varying degrees of being *willing* to receive truth. Because of previous choices people have made, and even the environment that they grew up in, people are at varying degrees of being able to hear truth.

This is the main message of the Parable of the Sower (Matthew 13:3-23). There was nothing different with the seeds being sown. The difference was in the receptivity and productivity of the soil.

Many Christians today do not enter very far into the Kingdom, if they enter at all. They get stuck at some point where they will not accept Kingdom truth. They will not believe and obey God's Kingdom truth at some point. Perhaps they will not accept that all of the Bible is inspired by God and is authoritative over every dimension of their life. Perhaps they explain away parts they don't like. Perhaps they refuse the Kingdom at the point of their finances. They will not trust God. They will not tithe, nor sow extra seed for a harvest. Perhaps they refuse the Kingdom at the point of accepting complete forgiveness, or their identity in Christ, or how they conduct their marriage or family.

The truth is that people get stuck at some point because they are ignorant of Kingdom truth, or they won't accept or believe it. When you stop advancing, you don't get any more Truth until you accept the very point at which you are stuck. In this way people sort themselves out. Some people have a temporary glimpse of the Kingdom but soon become blind again. Others enter just a step or two, but are kept from advancing farther into its riches by unbelief or disobedience. Others, however, truly are followers or disciples of Jesus. They learn and obey His teachings. And through faith they enter into the riches, power and supply of His Kingdom.

The Kingdom of God is available to any who would learn its secrets. Those secrets are the principles by which it operates. They are the Keys to the Kingdom and they are found in the Bible. We have looked at a number of these already. The next several chapters will help you to enter through exploring some additional keys.

CHAPTER 12

KINGDOM PRIORITY

A story is told that one day long ago one of the Popes was showing St. Francis of Assisi the magnificence of the Cathedral in Rome and the opulence of the papal headquarters. As he showed Francis the treasure house, he jokingly remarked (quoting the Apostle Peter in Acts 3:6), "We can no longer say, '*Silver and gold have I none...*'" Francis responded by quoting the rest of the verse, "No, nor can we say, '*...but such as I have give I Thee, in the Name of Jesus Christ the Nazarene – get up and walk.*'"

The Pope in this story was enamored with the physical wealth of the church and therefore blind to the fact that it was poor where it really mattered. He was missing the riches of the Kingdom because of his preoccupation with this world's riches and value system.

This is a temptation and trap for us as well. We can become so preoccupied with the riches, values and pressures of our modern American society that we miss the Kingdom. Even without realizing it, we can adopt wrong agendas that keep us from entering the Kingdom. Jesus made it clear that the Kingdom of God must be sought above all other things.

The Kingdom of God will never belong to people who have not made up their minds that they want the Kingdom above everything else. The Kingdom of God is not something that we can acquire as an afterthought. It is not something that is "added" to us as we pursue first the necessities and pleasures of this life. In His great Sermon on the Mount, Jesus said just the opposite.

> *Do not worry then, saying, 'What shall we eat?' or 'What will we drink?' or 'What shall we wear for clothing?' For the Gentiles eagerly seek all these things; for your heavenly Father knows that you need all these things.* **But seek <u>first</u> His Kingdom and His righteousness, and all these things will be <u>added</u> to you.**
>
> Matthew 6:31-33

Jesus taught us that there is an invisible Kingdom or realm that is charged with God's love and power. He taught us that if we could gain access to this realm that it would bring with it every other thing. The Kingdom of God contains the riches of God. The Kingdom of God is unlimited and reflects all of the possibilities of God.

NO NATURAL ACCESS

There is a connection or interrelationship between this physical world and the Kingdom of God. It is, however, a one-way street. That is, the Kingdom of God can bring us everything we need in the physical world, but the physical world cannot bring us into the Kingdom.

No amount of money can buy our way into it. The rich man has no more access to it than the poor. Even Bill Gates is not rich enough to buy its treasures. He could not write a check big enough to buy the peace and joy that belongs to those in the Kingdom. Nor could he purchase a clear conscience or fellowship with God.

Likewise, no idol, potion, chant, crystal or good luck charm can give us access to its power and riches. To attempt to do so is to enter into witchcraft, idolatry or sorcery. Any such attempt will result in deception, delusion or worse yet, demonic control. For this reason, any such practices are strictly forbidden in Scripture.

God's Kingdom cannot be manipulated from the physical realm. The physical world was created by the spiritual world and not vice-a-versa. **God's Kingdom can only be entered through the doorway that God Himself has given us**. There is no other way. There is no natural access. The Bible makes this clear.

> *That which is born of the flesh is flesh and that which is born of the Spirit is spirit.*
>
> John 3:6

> *Now I say this, brethren, that flesh and blood cannot inherit* (obtain) *the Kingdom of God; nor does the perishable inherit the imperishable.*
>
> 1 Corinthians 15:50

God has granted us access into His Kingdom *only through Jesus and only when we seek that Kingdom as our first priority*. To do anything else is to dishonor Jesus, undervalue His Kingdom, and disqualify ourselves from entering it.

God directs us to seek *first* His Kingdom. If we do so, not only will we receive the Kingdom, but all other necessary things will be "added to us" as well. However, if you *reverse* this order you may get neither.

FIRST MEANS FIRST

First means first. It means that we attempt to establish the Kingdom, as our first priority, in all the affairs of our life. It means that we build our marriages, families, businesses and relationships with others on the principles of God's Word. It means that we depend upon the Holy Spirit's leading and enabling in all that we do. It means that we adopt the values and standards of God's Kingdom instead of those of the world. It means that our criteria for making decisions becomes, "Which choice will most increase the influence of the Kingdom in my life, family, workplace, church or community?"

This simple test would radically change the way we raise our children, spend our money and make decisions. The results would be profound and thrilling.

No other approach or strategy for living will give us access to God's all-powerful Kingdom. Many Christians shut themselves off from experiencing the victorious Kingdom life because their priorities do not reflect this simple admonition to "seek first His Kingdom."

We have sought many things over gaining the Kingdom. We have sought home ownership, job security, higher education and financial security, but we have not sought *first* the Kingdom. We have sought good health, exciting vacations, comfortable retirements, new cars, hobbies and entertainment, but we have not sought *first* the Kingdom. Surrounded by the abundance of American society, we have been content to live without the Kingdom of God.

Because we have not been seeking first the Kingdom of God, we have asked the wrong questions. We have asked, "Which decisions, according to my understanding, would allow me to become a homeowner? Which decisions would give me the most financial security? Which choices would allow my children the best chance at getting into the best universities? Which choice will make me happiest?"

These are the wrong questions. We make idols of houses, careers, families and personal happiness. The right question in every situation is always, "How do I seek first (and gain) the Kingdom of God? What is God leading me to do, regardless of my own understanding and desires?" Only then will we gain the Kingdom and (thrown in with it) every good and needful thing.

THE CHURCH AND THE KINGDOM

This requirement to seek first the Kingdom is true not only for individual Christians but for churches and even denominations as well. It is not only individual Christians who can miss the Kingdom in their entanglement with the ways of this world, but churches and whole denominations also.

In fact, it would be true to say that the failure of so many churches to seek first the Kingdom (and thereby gain it) is one of the primary reasons why so many individual Christians fail in turn.

Who can argue against the fact that the signs that Jesus said would accompany the Kingdom are lacking in many churches today? The picture we have of the early church in the New Testament shares little in common with what we find in so many of our churches today.

It would appear that many Christians, and even many congregations, are failing to truly gain the Kingdom. I believe that the primary reason for this is that we are not seeking first the Kingdom. The problem is certainly not that the Father is unwilling to give it to us. Jesus made this very clear as reflected in His comment recorded in the Gospel of Luke.

> *Do not be afraid, little flock, for your Father has chosen gladly to give you the Kingdom.*
>
> Luke 12:32

Jesus made it clear that the Father wants to give us the Kingdom. As a matter of fact, He taught us to pray for the Kingdom in the Lord's Prayer (Matthew 6:10). If we do not receive it, it is only because we do not, as individuals and churches, seek it first. *In every case, the reason for failing to gain the Kingdom is that we do not, on the whole, want it above everything else.*

As we have noted in an earlier chapter, we rarely preach or teach concerning the Kingdom of God. By all appearances many churches are quite content to continue on without the signs or evidences of the Kingdom. Seemingly, few people mourn the lack of spiritual power in the churches. Prayer meetings are non-existent or poorly attended. Few cry out to God for the outpouring of His Holy Spirit and for signs and wonders.

Where are the signs that marked the early church? Where are the multiplied salvations, deliverances and healings? Where is the radiant glory of His Presence? How can it be that most people associate the word "boring" with a worship service, which should be a meeting with God? It can only be because we have failed to lay hold of the Kingdom. I assure you that the power and glory of God is not boring. The anointing of the Holy Spirit is not boring.

In many churches, biblical practices are clearly ignored or even in some cases forbidden. Such New Testament practices as prayer for the sick with the laying on of hands, the ministry of deliverance to the demonized, prophecy and the display of spiritual gifts are considered unnecessary, if not downright frowned upon.

Many churches run from anything that is beyond our control or that might draw criticism from carnal people. Every minute of the service is planned and scripted. There is no room or need for the power and glory of the Holy Spirit to descend. We are content to have church without the Kingdom.

In our churches today we seem more interested in entertaining the flesh than in crucifying it. We seem more interested in winning man's approval than God's. In our "worship" services we court the attendance of man more than the Presence of God. **We spend more time counting attendance numbers on Monday morning than we spent praying Saturday night for God's attendance in the next morning's services**.

To any honest observer, we appear to be content to have church without God. A recent poll by George Barna revealed a distressing fact. The question was posed to people who attend church, "Do you experience God at church?" Fifty-nine percent of the respondents answered "Rarely or never." In fact, thirty-two percent reported that they had *never* experienced the Presence of God in a church service. This overwhelming testimony to the lack of God's presence in our services is a result of not gaining the Kingdom. The Kingdom can only be gained when it is sought first.

In our churches, we have sought attendance growth, the respect of our communities, and bigger and better buildings. We have sought to be the most successful and fastest growing church. We have not sought first the Kingdom. We have sought to make our churches places where we would feel loved and have our needs met, but we have not sought first the Kingdom.

If we seek first the Kingdom, then all the things that we need would be "added to us."

In our churches, our motives have often been church-centered rather than Kingdom-centered. Often our goals have been to get people to visit and join *our* church rather than that they should truly see and enter the Kingdom. Often our focus has been more on building up our own church to be successful (by worldly standards) rather than on building up the Kingdom of God. These are not the same thing. The church is not the Kingdom of God. It is a result of the Kingdom and it is an expression of the Kingdom, but it is not the Kingdom. The Kingdom of God is spiritual and invisible. The church is visible and tangible.

If we truly seek first the Kingdom, and our efforts are aimed at expanding the Kingdom, then healthy growing churches will result, or will be "added to us." If, however, our efforts are at building our church as our first priority, then we will not get the fullness of the Kingdom. It will not be added to us like some kind of "bonus." In fact, the "church" that results may be little more than a weak, powerless social club, a religious country club of sorts. What is worse, we will continue to lose our society to the kingdom of darkness.

Jesus came to destroy the works of the enemy. He came to destroy fear, bondage and oppression over all the people. He came that the world might be turned upside down and be transformed by His love, power and truth. We must join in this purpose if we would serve the King.

HARD QUESTIONS

All of us must ask ourselves this question, "Am I a Kingdom builder, or just a booster of some local church?" Every pastor and church leader must ask themselves these questions, "Am I truly working hard to build His Kingdom or my own? Am I working to see His Kingdom come among people, or am I working to gain the esteem of people, and a personal sense of identity and fulfillment? What is truly motivating me, a desire to appear to be successful or a hunger to see His Kingdom expand, no matter who gets the credit?"

After 25 years of ministry I must say candidly that many pastors I have encountered have little vision or interest in anything beyond the walls of their own church. Unless you can demonstrate to them how their participation in some event will directly benefit their Sunday morning attendance or weekly offering, they are not interested. They will not participate nor expend any effort no matter how much the thing might benefit the Kingdom of God or the cause of Christ in general. The truth is, we have often made our churches idols.

In the same way, we have made our families, houses and careers our idols. We, as American Christians, continually make decisions that reveal an unexamined adopting of our society's values and priorities. We value the same things they do. We have the same priorities that they do. It is these wrong values that end up shutting us out of the Kingdom.

The truth is that, surrounded by the relative abundance of modern American life, we have been content to live without the Kingdom. Most people think that they would be happy if they just had more "stuff," but the opposite is true. Our problem is not that we have too little, but too much. We have been anesthetized, hypnotized and drugged by possessions, opportunities and the busyness of life. People no longer understand their true selves or what they really need. **We have too much to live with and too little to live for**. People are drinking, drugging, and shopping themselves out of an awareness of their real need.

Most Americans, and even many Christians, fail to gain their deepest goals and satisfy their deepest needs. This is because they have been seduced into seeking the wrong things. They seek after things that cannot give them the Kingdom of God which, whether they understand it or not, is what they desperately want.

You can have a fat stock portfolio, tens of thousands of dollars of equity in your house and other real estate and still be bankrupt where it really matters. You can work hard in school and study hard to get all A's and still flunk life. *Jesus told us that we could gain the whole world and lose our soul, our marriage and our kids (everything that really matters)*.

DEVELOPING AN APPETITE

We must wake up and get on track. We must awaken in ourselves and in our kids a deep hunger for God and His Kingdom. *We must develop an appetite for the ways of God. Appetites and tastes are developed*.

We must simply stop *reacting* to the pressures, opportunities, fashions and allurements of our society. We must instead *plan* and *form* our life around developing an appetite for the things of God by seeking first His Kingdom and His righteousness. We must *consecrate* ourselves to this goal.

Perhaps the first and greatest reason for failing to enter and obtain the Kingdom is violating this simple principle given us by Jesus.

But seek first His Kingdom and His righteousness and all these things will be added to you as well.

Matthew 6:33

There it is again. Like a voice echoing in our head. We cannot gain the Kingdom unless we seek it first, above any other thing.

This would require a significant adjustment for most people. Most of us are distracted by so many things (even good things) that we cannot truly seek first the Kingdom. **We are seduced by the lie that "we can have it all."** *The truth is that we only have the time and resources to gain a limited amount of objectives*.

CHOOSING WHERE YOU WILL FAIL

Many people are trying to maintain a marriage, raise children, enlarge a business, coach a little league team, buy a bigger house, play the stock market, lower their golf score, be a sports fan, restore a classic car, go back to school, and seek the Kingdom of God.

The truth is they can't do it all. Does the above paragraph describe your life? Are you stressed out and torn apart with competing demands on your life? **If you cannot succeed at all these goals, which are you prepared to fail at**? Don't let other people's expectations or the pressures of society decide for you. You must decide which you are willing to fail at. Is it the success of your marriage? Is it in raising up your children to know and love God and succeed in life? Is it in gaining the Kingdom of God? Is it in truly loving and serving Jesus?

If you are not willing to fail in these things, then you must make some hard choices. What will you give up? What will you sacrifice to reach your non-negotiable goals?

My friend Mike Hagen played professional football for a number of years. For several of those years he played for the Michigan Panthers of the old U.S.F.L as a fullback. In 1983, the Panthers began the season with a playbook that was 4 inches thick. It was filled with lots of complicated plays and additional variations. In attempting to run these plays, the players were making many mistakes. Blocks were being missed, assignments fouled up, and players were running into each other.

The Panthers lost the first 5 games of that season. The offensive coordinator held a team meeting and threw out the playbook. From then on, they would have only 4 running plays and 4 passing plays. They drilled those plays until everyone knew their assignments and the team could run these plays flawlessly.

The Panthers won 10 of the remaining 11 games of the season and made the playoffs. Next, this team that everyone had written off took these same 8 plays into the playoffs and won both of their games.

In July of 1983 they faced the Philadelphia Stars in the USFL Championship game and won. This team that was winless in their first 5 games, that was written off by everybody, was now the champions because they had learned a simple lesson. They learned that having too much to think and worry about would lead to failure, but that concentrating on a few things can lead to excellence and success.

To seek first the Kingdom means that other things must be left unsought. The Kingdom of God will never be gained by those who only have time to dabble in it.

"Seek first His kingdom and His righteousness..." The Kingdom of God is offered to us if we will follow this simple yet uncompromising rule. But we must also seek His Kingdom where and how He has instructed us to. As we saw in Chapter 6, Jesus, like any other king, rules and brings supply through an administration. If one would fully enter the Kingdom, one must relate to Jesus' administration. We will look at this in the next chapter.

CHAPTER 13

THE ADMINISTRATION OF THE KINGDOM: RECEIVING THE KINGDOM SUPPLY

We have all read the tragic stories of children who have died because their well-meaning and otherwise loving parents refused them medical attention on religious grounds. These heartbreaking tragedies are caused by a costly presumption. That presumption is that it is unbelief to expect that God would limit Himself to working through a human instrument or representative such as a doctor. But the truth is, *while God may and does intervene directly in our lives, His most common way of supplying our needs is through channels or administrators. If we would enter the Kingdom, we must embrace Jesus' administration.*

In Chapter 6, we saw that just as a king, president, governor or mayor supplies us through an administration, so does Jesus. We have seen that Jesus began to set up His administration upon His ascension to Heaven. We have also noted that while the church is a primary component of His Kingdom, it is not the only one. Let us look closer at the administration of the Kingdom of God. Following is a list of some of the most important channels of God's grace and supply into our lives.

1. FAMILY (INCLUDING SPOUSE AND PARENTS)

The obvious truth is that God channels much of His love, care and support through our families. Whether the family is Christian or not, God the Creator has determined to largely care for His human creatures through the family.

Sometimes people give up on their marriage or family without realizing the cost of doing so. God's grace is available to help restore and heal our families. But when we disdain or lightly value our families, it shows we don't understand the gift that our family is. It is a channel of God's care to us.

This is especially true of parents who are clearly representatives for God. He protects, provides, and trains children through their parents. When parents fail in this duty, the consequences are serious indeed.

Parents are charged with:

- Providing for the physical needs of their children (1 Timothy 5:8).

- Nurturing and training their children (Ephesians 6:4).

- Disciplining their children when they act foolishly (Proverbs 22:15; 23:13-14).

- Teaching and them God's Word (Deuteronomy 6:6-7).

Because parents are God's agents and therefore represent Him, children are required to respect and obey them.

> *Children, obey your parents in the Lord* (i.e., in the Lord's administration), *for this is right. HONOR YOUR FATHER AND MOTHER (which is the first commandment with a promise), SO THAT IT MAY BE WELL WITH YOU, AND THAT YOU MAY LIVE LONG ON THE EARTH.*
>
> Ephesians 6:1-3

When a child disobeys, rebels, or lies to his parents, they cut themselves off from the wisdom, protection, and provision of God that He would supply through His agents, the parents. The effect of such dishonor will be to encounter destruction and danger. Family members must come to understand God's principle of delegated authority. A child or teenager must come to expect that God will direct and bless them as they submit to their parents for the Lord's sake. This is true even though the parents are far from perfect, for God is not limited by their shortcomings. It should be noted that when parents fail, God has given the church, and to a lesser degree, the government, a role in taking over the responsibilities of the parents.

Likewise, the wife must come to trust that God will bless and supply her as she honors her husband, because this is His plan and His administration, and by honoring it, we honor Him. Remember, God has said, "...Those who honor Me I will honor" (1 Samuel 2:30). A husband is honored not for his sake, but for God's. When the wife honors her husband as head of the family, she recognizes God's order and helps to release God's grace that will be dispensed through her husband. When this process breaks down, then the church, and failing that, the government intervenes.

2. CHURCH

The church is, of course, the primary administrative component of the Kingdom of God. Our growth into Christlikeness comes primarily as we receive the supply of grace that comes to us through the ministry of the Body of Christ.

> *...speaking the truth in love, WE ARE TO GROW UP IN ALL ASPECTS INTO HIM who is the head, even Christ, from whom the whole body, being fitted and held together BY WHAT EVERY JOINT SUPPLIES, according to the proper working of each individual part, CAUSES THE GROWTH OF THE BODY for the building up of itself in love.*
>
> Ephesians 4:15-16

God's mercy, provision, direction, guidance, support, protection and help come to us through the church as each member of Christ's Body exercises their gifts and fulfills their ministry. As this happens, we receive everything we need and grow in God's grace into the image of Jesus.

The truth is that 90% of everything that God does in our lives He will do through a member ("joint") in the Body of Christ.

- He will speak to us and give us personal direction through sermons and Bible studies (1 Timothy 4:13, 16; 1 Corinthians 1:21).

- He will protect us through counsel given us by more mature godly Christians (Proverbs 11:14).

- He will help us to "carry our burdens" through the love and support of other Christians (Galatians 6:2).

- He will inspire and encourage us so that we can inherit the blessing as we gather with other Christians (Hebrews 10:24-25).

- He will supply our physical needs through the love and generosity He puts in the hearts of our brothers and sisters in the body (Galatians 6:10; 1 John 3:17).

Many other examples could be multiplied to show that God's plan is to richly supply His followers with His grace, which is mediated through our fellow believers who are stewards of His gifts and mercy.

As each has received a special gift, employ it in serving one another as good stewards of the manifold (i.e., "many different forms") of God's grace.

1 Peter 4:10

While it is sometimes said by people, "You don't have to go to church to be a good Christian," that is a false statement. If you are not a vital part of a living local church, you cut yourself off from much of God's necessary grace in your life. You will suffer a serious "supply shortage."

You will be like a business that doesn't receive what it needs to properly operate because it has cut itself off from its suppliers. Body life (or church life) is God's plan to supply His followers.

When Christians isolate themselves and their personal lives and decisions from other Christians and hold themselves aloof from the church, they make a tragic mistake. They cut themselves off from the direction, protection, and supply of the Lord Jesus.

He who separates himself seeks his own desire. He quarrels against all sound wisdom.

Proverbs 18:1

3. PASTORS AND OTHER FIVE-FOLD MINISTERS

Part of the administration of the church deserves special notice. These are the special officers in the Body of Christ which are enumerated in Ephesians 4:11-12. These offices are Apostle, Prophet, Evangelist, Pastor, and Teacher. They carry special responsibility to care for and build up God's Kingdom and family. Listen to the charge that the Apostle Paul gave to the elders of Ephesus:

Be on guard for yourselves and for all the flock, among which the Holy Spirit has made you overseers, to shepherd the church of God which He purchased with His own blood.

Acts 20:28

One of God's favorite ways to refer to His followers is as a flock. Individually we are sheep of that flock and Jesus is the Great Shepherd (Hebrews 13:20, John 10:16, 1 Peter 2:25). Jesus shepherds the flock by appointing under-shepherds that carry His Spirit and empowerment.

SHEPHERD THE FLOCK OF GOD AMONG YOU, exercising oversight not under compulsion, but voluntarily, ACCORDING TO THE WILL OF GOD; and not for sordid

*gain, but with eagerness; nor yet as lording it over THOSE
ALLOTED TO YOUR CHARGE, but proving to be examples
to the flock. And when the Chief Shepherd appears, you will
receive the unfading crown of glory.*

1 Peter 5:2-4

As the above verse makes clear, it is God's will and plan that Jesus
delegate men to represent Him and care for the flock for His sake.
Jesus Himself made this very clear when He spoke to John the Apostle following His resurrection and before His ascension in the twenty-first chapter of John.

*So when they had finished breakfast, Jesus said to Simon
Peter, "Simon, son of John, do you love Me more than these?"
He said to Him, "Yes, Lord; You know that I love You." He
(Jesus) said to him, "Tend My lambs."*

John 21:15

The word translated "tend" here is translated as "feed" in the KJV.
It is the Greek word "bosko" which comes from a root word meaning "to
nourish."The human shepherds, such as John, are Jesus' instruments
to feed and nourish His flock. Apart from a commitment from these
shepherds to faithfully carry out that charge, and a corresponding commitment from the flock to honor and receive the shepherds, the flock
cannot be fed or nurtured.

A sheep without a shepherd is in trouble. It is not a terribly flattering picture to think of oneself as a sheep. Many of us balk at the
thought of being part of a flock and needing shepherds to watch over
us. Flattering or not, this is the picture that God reveals of the reality
of our situation. We are vulnerable and need care and protection in the
world in which we live. Without shepherds, we are ill fed, unprotected,
and liable to wander off and get lost. THE TRUTH IS THAT EVERYBODY NEEDS SHEPHERDS, EVEN THE FIVE-FOLD MINISTERS.

Many people pray to Jesus for guidance and protection and then
disregard the leaders and overseers, the very ones that Jesus has
appointed, trained and gifted to supply what they are praying for. If we
want Jesus' spiritual guidance and protection, we must submit to their
direction.

*Obey your leaders and submit to them, for THEY KEEP
WATCH OVER YOUR SOULS AS THOSE WHO WILL
GIVE AN ACCOUNT. Let them do this with joy and not
with grief, for this would be unprofitable for you.*

Hebrews 13:17

Do you want Jesus to watch over your soul? Do you want Jesus to guard your family? If so, then you must submit to the ministry of the leaders Jesus has placed over your life. This cannot be avoided because this is a vital part of how He administrates His protection and guidance.

Why does the Scripture above state that leaders must give an account for others? This is because they have received supernatural enabling from the Chief Shepherd to be able to sense danger and discern the way of escape and victory. They have received a spiritual gift and anointing to be the instruments of Jesus in fulfilling His ministry of shepherding you. When we despise the delegated office, we cut ourselves off from much protection and direction. In discussing this issue with other church leaders, we have agreed that the number one reason why Christian marriages break up and children are lost to drugs or rebellion is because the ministry and counsel of church leaders is not heeded.

Our job is to submit to and obey these representatives. When we submit to and obey pastors and other five-fold ministers, we help activate the gift and anointing on our behalf. I know this from my own experience. When people in my church look to me as a shepherd representing Christ's care in their life, I feel great anointing of the Holy Spirit flow through me. Many times in these settings, great wisdom and understanding, not of my own, has flowed through me to those seeking counsel. Their faith and obedience to Christ's administration, and their willingness to honor the office I have been appointed to, has released Jesus' ministry through me. This is the meaning of the following verse:

He who receives a prophet in the name of a prophet shall receive a prophet's reward; and he who receives a righteous man in the name of a righteous man shall receive a righteous man's reward.

Matthew 10:41

The reward of receiving a prophet, because you recognize and honor the office of a prophet, is that you receive the flow of ministry that Jesus allows to flow through a prophet. By receiving the prophet according to his office, and not viewing him merely from human considerations, you allow Jesus to encourage and upbuild you, and confirm His direction for you. The same is true for a righteous man, or an apostle, an evangelist, a pastor or a teacher. Each carries a blessing (or reward) from God for us if we receive them as being sent and appointed by the Lord.

4. THE HOLY SPIRIT

When Jesus was about to finish His earthly mission, He told the disciples that His departure was near. Of course they worried about what life would be like without Jesus. After all, their lives had revolved around Him for the past three years. They had served Him and taken their directions from Him. At this point, Jesus revealed that He would not leave them alone. He had a very special part of His administration that would make up for His absence.

> *But I tell you the truth, IT IS TO YOUR ADVANTAGE THAT I GO AWAY; for if I do not go away, the Helper will not come to you; but if I go, I will send Him to you.*
> *I have many more things to say to you but you cannot bear them now.*
> *BUT WHEN HE, THE SPIRIT OF TRUTH COMES, HE WILL GUIDE YOU INTO ALL HE TRUTH; for He will not speak on His own initiative, but whatever He hears, He will speak; and He will disclose to you what is to come.*
> *He will glorify Me, for HE WILL TAKE OF MINE AND WILL DISCLOSE IT TO YOU.*
>
> John 16:7,12-14

Jesus promised them that under His new Kingdom administration, they would be in a better situation. When He was no longer able to be with them, He would be able to be within them through the Holy Spirit sent from heaven. No more standing in line to talk to Jesus. No more waiting for Jesus to wake up to ask Him a question. From now on, a new Helper would be with them to instruct and guide them. He would distribute among them the far greater gifts and blessings that would be available to people after Jesus reconciled us to God through His crucifixion and resurrection.

The Holy Spirit is the Chief Administrator of Christ's Kingdom. The riches of Christ Jesus are available to us through the Holy Spirit.

As we have seen from the verse above, it is through the agency of the Holy Spirit that we will be guided into the truth. It is through His ministry that Jesus will disclose and reveal things to us. It is He that will distribute to us the far greater riches that became available once Jesus had reconciled us to God the Father.

The righteousness, peace and joy that people seek are available through the Holy Spirit.

For the Kingdom of God is not eating and drinking, but righteousness, peace and joy IN THE HOLY SPIRIT.

Romans 14:17

The power and joy of true religion is to be found through the agency of the Holy Spirit. It is only through our vital union with the Holy Spirit that the character of Jesus can actually become an experienced reality in our lives. The Holy Spirit brings the very life of Jesus into our lives.

But the fruit of the Spirit is love, joy, peace, patience, kindness, goodness, faithfulness, gentleness, and self-control; against such things there is no law. Now those who belong to Christ Jesus have crucified the flesh with its passions and desires. If we live by the Spirit, let us also walk by the Spirit.

Galatians 5:22-25

In other words, it is by welcoming the Holy Spirit for Jesus' sake, and yielding to His influences, that Jesus is made real to us and we receive of His riches. This is a principle that is true for all of Christ's administrators.

It is through welcoming the baptism in the Holy Spirit and abiding in His anointing that we receive the power for victorious living and effective Christian witness that Jesus promised us.

But YOU WILL RECEIVE POWER WHEN THE HOLY SPIRIT HAS COME UPON YOU; and you shall be my witnesses both in Jerusalem, and in all Judea and Samaria, and even to the remotest part of the earth.

Acts 1:8

The power that we so desperately need to be overcoming Christians and fruitful and effective Kingdom workers can't be found apart from the anointing of the Holy Spirit. Likewise, the spiritual gifts that multiply the availability of Jesus' riches and guidance to us can only be found through the agency of the Holy Spirit.

Now there are varieties of (spiritual) gifts, but the same Spirit... But to each one is given the manifestation of the Spirit for the common good. For to one is given the word of wisdom through the Spirit, and to another the word of knowledge according to the same Spirit; to another faith by the same

Spirit, and to another gifts of healing by the one Spirit, and to another the effecting of miracles, and to another prophecy, and to another the distinguishing of spirits, to another various kinds of tongues, and to another the interpretation of tongues. But ONE AND THE SAME SPIRIT WORKS ALL THESE THINGS, DISTRIBUTING TO EACH ONE INDIVIDUALLY just as He wills.

1 Corinthians 12:4, 7-11

When you consider the absolutely crucial and key role that the Holy Spirit plays in the Kingdom of God, it is amazing how little respect He gets from so many Christians. How much of the defeat that so many Christians seem to suffer in their lives come from this one fact? How much of the powerlessness and ineffectiveness of much of the church comes from its neglecting the Chief Administrator of the Kingdom of God? If we dishonor the Holy Spirit by neglect, we impoverish our world and ourselves.

We must go beyond merely having an abstract doctrine of the Holy Spirit. We must go beyond giving mere lip service to the Holy Spirit. We must truly give the Holy Spirit back His rightful place in our lives and in the church. We must repent of resisting His sovereign movement because we have wanted to remain in control.

We must repent of despising His gifts, such as tongues or prophecy, because we think they are beneath our dignity. In our private lives we must come to love, honor and worship the Holy Spirit as part of the Holy Trinity. We need to begin to cultivate a daily walk with Him, depending upon His leadership, assurance, comfort and guidance. We need to pray daily, no, hourly, for Him to lead and empower our lives through all of His gifts and enabling.

If we want our churches to know the fullness of the Kingdom of God, we need to realize that the Holy Spirit is its Chief Administrator. We need to stop "resisting" the Holy Spirit because of our stiff necks and hard hearts (Acts 7:51). We must cease from "grieving" the Holy Spirit by our selfishness and ungodliness (Ephesians 4:30). And we must stop "quenching" Him by neglecting and treating with contempt the spiritual gifts, such as prophecy (1 Thessalonians 5:19-21). Instead, we must pray for these gifts and "earnestly desire" them (1 Corinthians 14:1).

5. Scripture

God assures us, reveals His will to us, and instructs us out of His Word, which is contained in the Bible. If we want to know the truth about things, if we want spiritual illumination and understanding, we cannot neglect the Bible. The Bible itself is very clear on its central importance in our life.

> *How can a young man keep His way pure? By keeping it according to Your word. If Your law had not been my delight, then I would have perished in my affliction. Your commandments make me wiser than my enemies. Your word is a lamp to my feet and a light to my path. Those who love Your law have great peace, and nothing causes them to stumble.*
>
> Psalm 119:9, 92, 98, 105, 165

People ask God to prosper them and make them successful. They ask for wisdom, direction, and peace. They pray to Him and ask Him to keep them from danger and destruction. They seek His favor and blessing on their life, not realizing that none of this will happen apart from them knowing, honoring and obeying His Word.

> *The one who despises the Word will be in debt to it, but the one who fears the commandment will be rewarded.*
>
> Proverbs 13:13

> *This book of the law shall not depart from your mouth, but you shall meditate on it day and night, so that you may be careful to do according to all that is written in it; for then you will make your way prosperous and then you will have success.*
>
> Joshua 1:8

How does God bring about His blessing, favor and increase into our lives to make us prosperous and successful? When we are diligent to study, meditate, understand and obey His Word, we honor the administration of Jesus and allow His blessing to overtake us.

6. Prayer

The Bible is very clear that God requires that we seek His face in prayer and make our requests known to Him, if we are to obtain what He has promised us.

> *You are envious and cannot obtain; so you fight and quarrel. You do not have because you do not ask.*
>
> James 4:2

*Be anxious for nothing, but in everything by prayer and sup-
plication with thanksgiving let your requests be made
known to God. And the peace of God, which surpasses all
comprehension will guard your hearts and your minds in
Christ Jesus... And my God will supply all your needs
according to His riches in glory in Christ Jesus.*

Philippians 4:6-7, 19

Jesus has tied the supply and miracle power of His Kingdom to
prayer. Our part is that we must pray to receive the full riches. Failure
to understand and practice this will leave us defeated and impover-
ished.

7. GOVERNMENT

Another important administrator for Christ is civil government. The
Bible is very clear that civil government is God's minister or administrator.

*Every person is to be in subjection to the governing authori-
ties. For there is no authority except from God, and those
which exist are established by God. Therefore whoever resists
authority has opposed the ordinance of God; and they who
oppose will receive condemnation upon themselves. For rulers
are not a cause of fear for good behavior, but for evil. Do you
want to have no fear of authority? Do what is good and you
will have praise from the same; FOR IT IS A MINISTER OF
GOD TO YOU FOR GOOD. But if you do what is evil, be
afraid; FOR IT DOES NOT BEAR THE SWORD FOR
NOTHING; for IT IS A MINISTER OF GOD, AN
AVENGER who brings wrath on the one who practices evil.*

Romans 13:1-4

In verse four, government is twice called "a minister of God" (see also
verse 6, where rulers are referred to as "servants" of God). The word
translated "minister" here is the Greek word "diakonos." It is the same
word that is transliterated as "deacon" when referring to those in the
church who serve the body with practical helps ministry.

Government serves two main functions. First, it is intended by God
for our good, and second, it is meant to avenge evil. The Greek word
translated "good" is the word "agathos" which means "beneficial." Government is meant by God to benefit us by promoting public safety and
rules by which we can conduct commerce and orderly living. Secondly,
civil government is meant to "avenge evil." It is to protect people from
being victimized by lawbreakers.

God will most often answer our prayers for the protection of ourselves and our possessions through the police force. If we dishonor them and reject them, then we dishonor God and cut ourselves off from protection. This is because God works in our lives through administrators. For this reason God has given them "the sword" or coercive power. This is an authorization that God has not given to you, or to the church for that matter, but has reserved for the police and the nation's military.

8. EMPLOYERS

Many times people forget that employers are God's agents and suppliers to us. Christ is faithful to bring our needed provision to us. *He has determined to do that, however, through our own labor.*

2 Thessalonians 3:10 is very clear; *"...If anyone is not willing to work, then he is not to eat either."* Often God channels this provision to us through an employer.

> *Slaves, in all things obey those who are your masters on earth, not with external service, as those who merely please men, but with sincerity of heart, fearing the Lord. Whatever you do, do your work heartily, as for the Lord rather than for men, knowing that from the Lord you will receive the reward of the inheritance. It is the Lord Christ whom you serve.*
> Ephesians 3:22-24

The ancient economic system that the early Christians found themselves in was based on slavery. Thankfully, that is not a system we live in, however, the principles in God's Kingdom are the same. Note some of the truths we learn from this passage:

1. God is our provider. This is true no matter who employer or how we receive our provision. It is Christ whom we serve and from Him we receive the "reward," which includes our daily bread. Even when we are laid off, God is still our supply. In whatever condition we are in, we simply try to serve Christ because He is our rewarder. Our employer is merely Christ's administrator.

2. Therefore, we must respect our employer for God's sake, since they represent His provision for us. To disrespect them is to disrespect God.

3. If we steal from our employer or do shoddy work, we can disrupt God's supply for us and suffer His discipline. We

must serve and honor those who employ us for Christ's sake. If an employer or job requires us to dishonor Jesus, then we must quit. Remember, Jesus is our supplier, not our boss or job. If we cannot honor Jesus in the job, then we must quit and trust Jesus to work out the details of providing for us.

9. ANGELS

One final agent of the Administration of the Kingdom of God requires a brief mention. They are angels. Although the Bible does not give us great detail about angels, they do appear prominently through-out the history of God's dealings with men. They help us as fellow ser-vants of God. Concerning angels the Bible teaches us:

Are they not all ministering spirits, sent out to render service for the sake of those who will inherit salvation?

Hebrews 1:14

The Bible pictures angels as spiritual beings who are sent on assignments to assist and help God's people. In most cases, the human recipients are unaware of the angelic helpers. Although they have a place as part of the administration of God's Kingdom, the Triune God alone directs their movements. We are given no directions concerning them except that we are not to mock or dishonor them since they are representatives of God's authority (Jude 8-10). It is enough for us to be encouraged and grateful knowing that angels are sent to assist us.

In closing this chapter on the agents of the Administration of the Kingdom of God, *we must stress again that failure to honor, esteem, obey and receive from these agents means that we will not receive the promised benefits of the Kingdom of God.* We can't say that we believe in and love Jesus if we are not submitted to His administration.

CHAPTER 14

RESTORING KINGDOM PREACHING AND TEACHING

A famous Theologian, Paul Althaus, once addressed a group of Pastors who were complaining that people were unwilling to listen to preaching anymore. He said to them, "It's not that they are bored of preaching, it is just that they are bored of *our* preaching."

I do not believe that people today are unwilling to listen to preaching, if it is preaching that shows them how they can solve the critical issues facing them and experience the reality of God's wonderful presence in every dimension of life.

As we have seen, one of the biggest reasons that Christians are not pressing into the Kingdom is that they are largely ignorant of its principles. A large part of the reason for this lies in our pulpits. It is the gospel we preach and teach.

As we pointed out in Chapter 3, we often preach a shrunk-down gospel of forgiveness and heaven, rather than the fuller gospel or "good news" about the dawning of the Kingdom of God. The present message that is largely preached by the church is *an edited and watered-down version* of what Jesus taught and what the Bible reveals.

People can only have faith to enter into the promises that they know and understand are for them. Therefore, when the message is compromised or deficient, overcoming faith becomes impossible.

In all honesty, even though I love God and hunger after His Kingdom and His righteousness, I am often bored listening to much of the preaching and teaching on our Christian radio stations. The truth is that we have shrunk down the gospel message. We have reduced our teaching of the precepts of God to a safe, tame and manageable few. Our message and teaching doesn't offend or shock anybody. No one is accusing us of being revolutionary!

This certainly could not be said of our Founder or those who followed after Him. They were opposed, arrested and even killed because their message and teaching was a threat to the status quo.

TAKING AWAY THE KEYS

The scribes or lawyers of Jesus' time were those who were the experts in the laws of the Bible, since these were the laws that governed Israel. They knew more of the Bible than anyone else. Yet they did not listen to Jesus or enter His Kingdom.

Jesus condemned the scribes and lawyers not only for failing to recognize and enter the Kingdom but also for hindering others from doing so. They were not fully and accurately teaching the Word of God. If they had been, then the people would have had the keys to enter the Kingdom.

Woe to you lawyers! For you have taken away the key of knowledge, you yourselves did not enter, and you hindered those who were entering.

Luke 11:52

Notice that Jesus said that the key was "knowledge." This is the knowledge provided by God's Word concerning the Kingdom. These are the keys that open up the Kingdom that we might enter. Although Jesus came to reveal more about the Kingdom of God, the Jewish lawyers already had the keys that were revealed in the Old Testament.

No one had greater knowledge of the Old Testament material than them. This should have helped them to recognize and enter Christ's Kingdom. But, they did not enter. Instead they had reduced the message of the Old Testament to a legalistic code of do's and don'ts. Further, by their interpretations of the Bible and their teachings, they made it more difficult for others who wanted to enter in.

Remember that in Jesus' time, very few people could own a copy of the Scriptures. They were hand copied and therefore very expensive. The people, therefore, were very dependent upon the teaching and counsel of the scribes and their interpretations of the Scriptures. They had "taken away the keys" by twisting God's Word until the true teachings and principles, by which people might enter, were lost or perverted.

Even today, great care must be taken by those who would teach God's Word, since it provides the doorway that allows entrance into the Kingdom of God. Teaching God's Word is a tremendous responsibility. We are warned not to do it carelessly, since teachers will be judged more strictly (see James 3:1). Even today, Christian leaders, by their teaching, can either open up the Kingdom to people or hinder people from entering. I must appeal to my fellow ministers and ask the question, "Are we not in some way doing the same thing as the scribes and lawyers of Jesus time? Are we regularly teaching the whole counsel of God? Are we fearlessly proclaiming all the truths and principles of the Bible without diluting or conforming them to the socially acceptable ideas and theories of our day?"

For instance, I sometimes ask people when was the last time that they heard a sermon on the Kingdom of God. Most people cannot answer that question. Many people cannot remember ever having heard a sermon on that topic. This is not right. How can we not preach and teach about that which was the main message of Jesus?

Jesus said that if we sought first His Kingdom, that all necessary earthly things would become ours as well (Matthew 6:33). It is through His Kingdom that Jesus wants to supply the needs of His followers. Unless we teach specifically the principles of living in and drawing from the resources of that Kingdom, then those in our churches will suffer great lack.

John Maxwell tells the following story. A man was told that if he worked the very hardest he could, he would become rich. The hardest work he knew was digging holes, so he set about digging great holes in his backyard. He didn't get rich; he only got a backache. The poor man. Although he was willing to work hard, he didn't realize that there was no profit to be made from digging holes in his backyard. In the same way, many of God's children are laboring to achieve blessedness and increase and yet are working in vain because they are ignorant of the keys and principles that lead to blessedness.

In order to enter into God's supply, God's children must know where to dig. We must follow the teachings of God's Word in every area of life. This means that the Bible's teachings must be expounded on concerning every area of life, such as how to conduct business, how to discipline children, how to maintain good health, and how a government should function.

Instead, too often we simply preach an old tired variation of the same safe, simplistic message week after week. Our preaching and teaching is often of such limited scope. Often we do not really address the critical issues that our people are facing with a clear, anointed Word from God. Perhaps it is because we do not know how to, or maybe it is because we are reluctant to rock the boat and really challenge people with the Biblical solution.

For instance, many preachers are either unable or unwilling to fully and faithfully teach what the Bible says about marriage roles, gender differences, sexual practices, education, child rearing, materialism, politics or financial practices. Perhaps they themselves have never been taught. Or perhaps they are unwilling because the Bible's teaching on these subjects is "politically incorrect" and out of fashion. They are afraid of offending someone who might then stop attending church. And yet problems will not be solved unless they are Biblically addressed.

No doubt, both of these are reasons for the inadequacy of what is being taught in churches today. On the one hand, pastors themselves (as well as their congregations) are not being adequately instructed. And on the other hand, there is a clear tendency to not want to take unpopular stands and risk offending people.

RESTORING THE MESSAGE

In order to bring a full spectrum of teaching that will allow and encourage Christians to lay hold of the Kingdom two things must happen. **First, we must restore the balance of the five ministry gifts, and second, we must restore courage and boldness to the pulpits**.

Remember when we were studying that Jesus set up His administration to minister to the saints. We saw that Jesus gave five officers to the church to instruct it and bring its members to maturity.

> *And **He gave** some as **apostles**, and some as **prophets**, and some as **evangelists**, and some as **pastors** and **teachers**, **for the equipping of the saints** for the work of service, to the building up of the Body of Christ; **until we all attain to** the unity of the faith, and of the knowledge of the Son of God, to **a mature man, to the measure of the stature which belongs to the fullness of Christ**.*
>
> Ephesians 4:11-13

By reading only the emboldened letters in the verse above you can see clearly what is God's plan to bring His people into maturity and fullness. The supply to the Body will be inadequate unless all five ministry gifts are impacting (directly or indirectly) every local church fellowship. Until that time the teaching and preaching going on in churches will be deficient.

We must restore the ministry of the five-fold offices to the churches. Each of these five ministry gifts brings a needed and unique dimension and insight to the Body. Each sees from a different perspective. Each carries a different anointing and commission. Only when all are functioning does the full ministry of Jesus come to the church. When any are lacking, then the teaching and ministry the saints receive is deficient and unbalanced. In many of the churches today, we do not see all five of the gifts functioning in a balanced way. Therefore, Christians, including most pastors, are being fed a diet that is lacking. This is one reason why people are failing to enter the Kingdom.

Most churches are receiving only the ministry of a pastor or perhaps a teacher. Ministry by an apostle, prophet, or evangelist is rare or completely lacking. *The ministry by a pastor or teacher is good, but by itself it is inadequate. This is by the design of God.* He has set five offices in the church, not just one or two. A pastor or teacher needs the ministry of a prophet or apostle in his life to fully release his own gift. Likewise, his congregation needs their ministry as well.

If we would enter the Kingdom we must open up our churches and pulpits to the ministry of all of the five ministry gifts. They are all functioning in the Church today, although they may not always be known by their proper name. Some ministers are trying to function as pastors who are actually more properly apostles, prophets or evangelists (This is because our present church structure or wineskin does not fully recognize and give proper place to all five of the gifts). We must recognize their true function and then invite them to minister their gift in our churches.

The second thing we must do is to restore boldness and a prophetic edge to our pulpits. Part of the solution to this is, of course, to open up our pulpits to apostles and prophets. When this happens it will also help release a greater boldness in the pastors.

Pastors, due to their gifting, are motivated and oriented inward to the church to nurture and gather the flock. This orientation is the proper one for their assignment. However, it works against having outward-looking prophetic insight and perception into trends affecting society which in turn affect the church. Such insight comes naturally to prophets and apostles whose assignment and gifting is different.

Likewise, a pastor's anointing is to bind up the wounds of the sheep and to shepherd them through the dangers of everyday life. His basic orientation is on the problems of today. This is proper. However, it means that a true pastor will be weak in long-term strategic thinking and providing bold leadership for the church.

Church pollster George Barna conducted a study of over 600 Protestant pastors in 1997. One of the questions he asked them was to list what they believed their spiritual gifts were. Only 5% checked the spiritual gift of leadership. A second finding was that less than one in ten pastors could articulate what he believed was God's vision for the church he was pastoring (cited in *The Second Coming of the Church* by George Barna). This explains why so many churches seem to lack direction and vision.

The clear truth is that most pastors are not gifted with leadership. This is because leadership is a spiritual anointing that usually goes with one of the other ministry offices like apostle or prophet. If leadership is going to be restored to our churches, then we must restore the ministry of all five of the ministry gifts to the church.

PULPITS AFLAME

The church today greatly needs boldness, insight and strategic leadership restored to its pulpits. Until this happens, our message will be deficient and only partially effective.

Too often we have been reluctant to challenge the status quo. Someone told me once in jest that "status quo" was French for "the mess we are currently in." This is certainly true for our day. And yet many pulpits are not saying much that is revolutionary or truly counter-cultural to the present "mess we are currently in."

Is it true that we really have nothing new to say and no real answers to challenge people with? Are we really searching the Scriptures and digging deeply enough? Have we "taken away the keys" and lost them through neglect or timidity? Are our seminaries and Bible colleges teaching our ministers how to forcefully enter the Kingdom (Matthew 11:12)? Are all five ministry gifts bringing supply to your church?

Are we ready to preach and teach the full truth of the Kingdom of God?

CHAPTER 15

ENTER THE KINGDOM

In order to enter the Kingdom of God, you must remember this simple truth: **Every Kingdom has a King**. Without a King, there would be no Kingdom. The King, therefore, is obviously the key to every Kingdom.

Jesus reigns as King over the Kingdom of God. Jesus made it clear that He is the only way into the Kingdom. He is the access point into the blessings and grace of the Kingdom of God.

I am the door; if anyone enters through Me, he will be saved.
John 10:9

I am the way, and the truth, and the life; no one comes to the Father but through Me.
John 14:6

The Bible is steadfast in its insistence that Jesus is the only way to God and the only entrance into the Heavenly Kingdom. This truth must be firmly grasped by those wishing to enter into the Kingdom, even though it flies in the face of the current politically correct notions of relativism, pluralism and so-called multiculturalism. The Bible is very clear on this.

For there is one God, and one mediator also between God and men, the man Christ Jesus.
1 Timothy 2:5

And there is salvation in no one else; for there is no other name under heaven that has been given among men by which we must be saved.
Acts 4:12

In other words, there is no other way in except through accepting the forgiveness that comes through Jesus and then being born again in His name. There is no other religion, philosophy or practice that will allow one to enter the Kingdom of God.

JESUS IMPOSTORS

Furthermore, the only Jesus you can enter by is the one that is witnessed to in the Bible. That is, Jesus as He is defined by Himself and others in the sacred pages of Holy Scripture. The *biblical* Jesus is distinct from the various "Jesus *Impostors*" which many other groups speak of.

Because Jesus was the most famous and influential person of all history, He cannot be ignored. Since He can't be ignored, various movements and groups try to recreate Him in their own image.

The New Age gurus and teachers falsely describe Jesus as a sort of pluralistic eastern-style guru who tapped into universal consciousness. Some even claim that during Jesus' years before He was thirty, He traveled the Orient and studied with Eastern spiritual Masters. Such claims are, of course, false and lack any credible evidence.

Nor is He the "Jesus" spoken of in the Koran, the holy book of the Muslims. There, Jesus is just one more prophet among others, inferior to Mohammed. Nor is He like the Jesus, described by the liberals, who just wants everyone to be happy and have good self-esteem.

The only Jesus that will gain us access is Jesus as the Bible describes Him. *However, this is a Jesus that many people reject*. This is not surprising because Jesus upsets many people. He was not politically correct and pluralistic. In fact, Jesus was a threat to the status quo and so they crucified Him. He stood for very definite things.

He still does today!

When people try to transform Jesus into something other than how the New Testament describes Him, they are creating a false idol that will not give them access into the Kingdom. This is what Paul warned us about when he wrote that people would come and *"proclaim another Jesus whom we have not preached"* (2 Corinthians 11:4). These same people would therefore be proclaiming a *"different gospel"* (see 2 Corinthians 11:4 and Galatians 1:6-9).

This is why Jesus said that we must enter through the "narrow gate."

> *Enter through the narrow gate; for the gate is wide and the way is broad that leads to destruction, and there are many who enter through it. For the gate is small and the way is narrow that leads to life, and there are few who find it.*
> Matthew 7:13-14

Jesus did not mean that the narrowness of the gate was caused by how hard it is to live a "totally righteous" life, because as we know, salvation is given to us as a gift. He meant that the way was narrow because He was the only door. Out of all the religions, philosophies and different "ways," He was the only way in.

DESIGNER RELIGION

There simply is not a lot of room for personal interpretation. Salvation does not come from going down the buffet line and creating your own personalized "designer religion" or "custom Jesus." Many are shut out of the Kingdom at just this point.

I once worked at an office where a secretary had moved in to live with a man who was not yet divorced from his wife. Since we were friends, and she was a professing Christian, I asked her how she felt Jesus viewed this. She responded, "My God is a God of love and He loves me and wants me to be happy. I am happy living with this man."

Like many others today, she had created her own "personalized" version of Jesus, which in the end means she had no Jesus at all. Many are like her today. They make up a Jesus that fits in with their desires. They are shut out of the Kingdom and, sadly, it will be for many just as Jesus said:

> *Strive to enter through the narrow door;* ***for many, I tell you, will seek to enter and will not be able.***
>
> Luke 13:24

Having accepted King Jesus, one has gained the doorway into the Kingdom. However, to fully enter into the fullness and riches of the Kingdom, one must accept and embrace all of Jesus.

This means that you must embrace Jesus in all four of His roles. There are four great titles given to Jesus, or we might say, He occupies four offices. Those offices are: Savior, Teacher, Lord and Christ (or Messiah).

1. JESUS AS SAVIOR

As Savior, Jesus died on a cross for us and offers us forgiveness as a gift. It is He who saves us from the penalty of our sins. There is a famous old saying that goes like this: "Jesus paid a debt He didn't owe because we owed a debt we could never pay."

The angel Gabriel told Joseph that the Virgin Mary, to whom he was engaged, was pregnant, with these words:

> *She will bear a Son, and you shall call His name Jesus, for* ***He will save His people from their sins***.
>
> Matthew 1:21

Mary would bring forth a child who would be their Savior. They were to name Him Jesus because in the original Hebrew "Jesus" (or "Joshua") means "God saves."

Jesus is our Savior. It is just as the angel said to the shepherds on the day that Jesus was born.

> *But the angel said to them, "Do not be afraid; for behold, I bring you good news of great joy which will be for all the people; for today in the city of David there has been born for you a Savior, who is Christ the Lord."*
>
> Luke 2:10-11

To accept Jesus we must first accept and embrace Him as our Savior. *A savior saves you. He does for you what you could not do for yourself.* None of us could earn forgiveness, eternal salvation or reconciliation with God. Jesus did for us what we could not do for ourselves. We must admit that we were helpless and accept salvation as a gift.

> *For while we were still helpless, at the right time Christ died for the ungodly.*
>
> Romans 5:6

Unless we accept salvation as a gift given to us, though we were helpless and undeserving, we cannot receive forgiveness and enter into the Kingdom. If we try to earn it we are cut off.

> *You have been severed from Christ, you who are seeking to be justified by law; you have fallen from grace.*
>
> Galatians 5:4

Think about what this means. **Just as we had to relate to Jesus as a Savior to get our introduction to the Kingdom, we must continue to relate to Jesus as Savior in order to make further progress into the Kingdom**.

Jesus' relationship to us remains as a Savior throughout all the challenges and opportunities of our lives. His role as Savior doesn't end with dying on the cross for our sins. Think about what this means. *It means that if we are to progress into the Kingdom, we must become comfortable with a life in which we are continually being put into situations where we are helpless and unable to save ourselves.*

Remember, a Savior does for you that which you cannot do for yourself.

Many people shut themselves off from the riches and glory of the Kingdom because they refuse to live this way. It takes courage and faith to live a life that requires not being in control and not having visible guarantees. That is the life that is required if you will continually relate to Jesus as Savior. Remember, Jesus, as Savior, is the only door into the Kingdom.

Our flesh revolts at having to live in daily dependence. We draw back from the thought of putting ourselves in a place where we must depend upon Divine intervention, or even a miracle.

We want to live feeling like we are "in control," where we have it all figured out. We want to live in a place where we don't need to be saved. Even when we are in trouble, we long for the day when we get out of trouble and don't have to depend upon God. *We want to have enough faith today that we get so much that we don't have to trust God tomorrow.* The truth is, once we get in that position, then we no longer are embracing Jesus in His role as Savior and we are blocked from entering further into the Kingdom.

When Jesus has so blessed you that you have all your needs met and even more set aside, it is only so that you will extend yourself into greater challenges. Having trusted God in the area of your own personal needs, your faith has been built up and now God will lead you to greater Kingdom challenges. You will be ready to do your part to change the world.

Believe me, and I speak from experience, He will take you to a place where you will need a Savior. The Savior will lead you deeper into His Kingdom.

Ask yourself right now, "Where in my life am I being forced to live beyond my ability and resources? Where am I attempting something that requires faith and courage? Where am I forced to depend upon a Savior?"

If we are truly walking with Jesus as our Savior and venturing deeper into His Kingdom, then we are familiar with having to depend upon Jesus showing up and doing that of which we are not capable. We should know the feeling of, *"If Jesus doesn't come through then I am in big trouble,"* and if not, then perhaps we have backed away from Jesus and His Kingdom.

2. JESUS AS TEACHER

But Jesus is more than simply a Savior. The New Testament also reveals that He is our great Teacher. In fact, the most common title for Jesus in the New Testament is Rabbi. Rabbi is simply the Aramaic word for teacher.

A teacher is a different role than a savior. A savior does for you that which you cannot do for yourself. A teacher, on the other hand, teaches you knowledge and truth so that you might act wisely and succeed.

On September 11, 2001, many injured were carried out of the World Trade Center by rescue workers who put their own lives at risk. Many of these people would not have made it out of the building without the help of the police and firemen. They would rightly call them their "saviors," but not their teachers. In the same way, I have had many teachers who have never saved my life. They were to me teachers but not saviors. They are two different things.

We must know Jesus as Teacher as well as Savior. As Savior, Jesus removed the penalty of death for my sins and removed the barrier between myself and God. *As Teacher, He instructs me in the principles by which I can walk in fellowship with God and experience the fullness of His Kingdom.*

Many believers today have been introduced to Jesus as Savior, but have not gone far into knowing and embracing Him as Teacher. They have felt His freely given love and felt the forgiveness that is theirs as a gift. They have felt His joy and had tremendous emotional experiences at church or retreats. However, their lives show limited victory and little fruit. Often the reason is because they are ignorant of the teaching of Jesus that would lead them into success and victory.

Many people shun Jesus as Teacher. They love to feel good and have the wonderful emotional experiences with Jesus, but they don't like to read, study or think hard. They don't want to take notes during sermons, which would allow them to review and master the material later. It seems too much like work.

They sit in church listening passively. During the sermon, when the concepts get difficult, their eyes glaze over. They wake up only when a joke or emotional story is told. They came to church to be entertained or emotionally moved but not to think hard about life.

They excuse themselves from reading books or studying by simply saying, "I've never been much of a reader." What they do not understand is that they are refusing Jesus as Teacher and shutting themselves off from the Kingdom. They are ensuring defeat and heartache for themselves and their loved ones.

We have noted before the Kingdom is gained largely by knowing the keys to the Kingdom, that is, the knowledge of its secrets and the principles by which it operates.[1] When you are ignorant of these principles, or forget them, the riches and power of the Kingdom is shut off from you. You will need grace and help, but it will seem far from you. Instead of deliverance and victory, you and your children will experience defeat.

> ***My people are destroyed for lack of knowledge.*** *Because you have rejected knowledge, I also will reject you from being My priests. Since you have forgotten the Law of God, I also will forget your children.*
>
> Hosea 4:6

There is a heavy price for not knowing God's Word. It can cost us and our families very dearly. Laziness and excuses may come very easy to us, however this doesn't change the fact that ignorance of God's counsel and precepts leads to heartache and devastation.

Like breathing or working, studying and knowing God's Word is simply one of those things that we must do. *This is reality that we must adapt ourselves to.* Principles in the spiritual world are like the laws of nature. They are unforgiving.

> *Wisdom shouts in the street, she lifts her voice in the square; at the head of the noisy streets she cries out; at the entrance of the gates in the city she utters her sayings: "How long, O naive ones, will you love being simple-minded? And scoffers delight themselves in scoffing and fools hate knowledge? Turn to my reproof, behold, I will pour out my spirit on you; I will make my words known to you.* ***Because I called and you refused, I stretched out my hand and no one paid attention; and you neglected all my counsel and did not want my reproof;*** *I will also laugh at your calamity; I will mock when your dread comes, when your dread comes like a storm and your calamity comes like a whirlwind, when distress and anguish come upon you. Then they will call on me, but I will not answer; they will seek me dili-*

---

[1] My companion book *Breakthrough Kingdom Living* deals with many of these key Kingdom principles and is available at the end of this book.

*gently but they will not find me, because they hated knowledge and did not choose the fear of the Lord. They would not accept my counsel, they spurned all my reproof. So they shall eat of the fruit of their own way and be satiated with their own devices. **For the waywardness of the naive will kill them, and the complacency of fools will destroy them**. But he who listens to me shall live securely and will be at ease from the dread of evil.*

Proverbs 1:20-33

It cannot be any clearer than it states in verse 32. Being naive and complacent can bring destruction. We must become students of our great Teacher. If we do, then the riches of the Kingdom are ours no matter what the difficulty.

Do you know what the Bible instructs you to do when you face opposition or are in financial difficulties or are experiencing marriage difficulties? The Bible will teach you how to release God's power and love into each situation to bring victory. Jesus will teach you how to have lasting peace. He will teach you how to raise godly children. None of these things will happen just by praying and wishing.

As a pastor I witness every day God's people placing themselves and their children outside of the realm of God's blessing and protection. In their ignorance of God's principles, they make choices that place themselves and their loved ones under the influence, oppression and curse of Satan. The result is that they often lose their children to drugs, unbelief and other destructions. Perhaps they themselves end up losing their own souls.

Many of God's children do not actively seek wisdom from God's word for daily decisions. Fewer still seek pastoral counsel before making major life decisions. God's people must come to realize that warm religious feelings and good intentions will not make up for the lack of understanding God's precepts.

I study the principles of the Kingdom because I want them to become second nature to me so that in whatever circumstances I find myself, I can receive God's Kingdom power and supply. I want to renew my mind to respond with a Kingdom mentality rather than with my natural mind.

3. JESUS AS LORD

Other people know Jesus as Savior and Teacher, but not as Lord. They have been born again and heard much teaching, but their lives remain largely unchanged. They may live defeated lives. They may think that it is enough to know the truth. However, knowing the truth accomplishes nothing. You must *do* the truth.

But prove yourselves to be doers of the Word and not merely hearers who delude themselves.

James 1:22

Some people have heard much teaching on the importance of forgiveness, for instance. They may even be able to counsel others on this topic. However, if there are people that they won't forgive, they will live under a curse no matter how much they know.

Other people could give Bible studies on how prayer changes things, but if they will not persevere in prayer, they will see no breakthroughs.

All of these are like people playing a virtual reality game. You have seen them in the arcade, with their helmets, goggles and electronic gloves on; they are lost in a make-believe world, flying a plane, surfing a wave, or fighting a dragon. They are totally caught up in the experience. They are gesturing wildly and are even emotionally engaged, letting out groans and gasps. It is quite humorous to watch.

There is only one problem, though. It is not a real experience. They aren't flying, surfing or fighting a dragon. It is all make-believe in their mind. Their senses and imagination are engaged, but there is no reality. The danger is not real; nor is the prize they hope to gain. So it is with those who are hearers, but not doers of the Word.

As teacher, Jesus instructs us in the principles that lead to victory and life, but as Lord, He commands us to walk in them.

Many people have heard great teaching about water baptism, but they shy away from receiving baptism because they don't want to make a spectacle of themselves, standing in front of people dripping wet. Perhaps they are worried about their figure or how their hair would look wet. Therefore, they excuse themselves from what Jesus and the Bible has directed them to do (Matthew 28:19; Acts 2:38).

Others read about being baptized in the Holy Spirit. They read how we need the power that comes from the Holy Spirit to be effective witnesses for Jesus. However, they are worried about losing control or embarrassed about speaking in tongues, so they excuse themselves. After all, what would their friends say? They don't want to be identified with those crazy Pentecostals. So they ignore Christ's command (Acts 1:4-5; Ephesians 5:18).

Because people won't obey, they can't enter in. They will live out their lives in weakness and defeat. And all because they trust in their own understanding rather than obeying their Lord Jesus. They are rejecting Jesus in His role of Lord.

Why do you call Me 'Lord, Lord,' and do not do what I say?
Luke 6:46

You cannot pick and choose what part of Jesus you want to embrace. If you will not have Jesus as your Lord, you can't have Him as your Savior. If you want Jesus to be your Savior in the financial realm, you must make Him your Lord in the financial realm. You can't trust God to meet your every financial need if you are refusing to obey Him by paying the tithe. How can you say that you are trusting Him with your soul for eternity if you can't trust Him for this month's rent money after paying the tithe?

Dear friends, we are missing out on such growth in Jesus and such joy and victory in His Kingdom because we won't move forward by obeying Him over our fears or emotions. If we would set these aside and simply obey what He has said, we would see the Kingdom open up to us. What has he told you to do? Do it.

PRINCIPLE VERSUS EMOTION-BASED LIVING

In order to follow Jesus as Teacher and Lord, we must make one critically important change. We must switch from *emotion-based* living to *principle-based* living.

Most people's lives and decisions are based upon their emotions. They won't forgive someone who has hurt them because they *feel* hurt and angry. They won't act in the moment of opportunity because they *feel* anxious or afraid. They violate their value system because they *feel* great desire or envy. This is not only caused by immaturity but also by socialization. We are taught to live by our feelings.

You see, in our culture we are no longer asked what we believe or think about something, we are asked how we feel about it. People shy away from saying, "I believe that it is wrong," or "I think that it is untrue." To do so would be to invite censure from the relativistic crowd. Instead we say, "I *feel* uncomfortable with it."

This is not surprising since our popular culture is emotion-driven. This is because industries such as entertainment, advertising, marketing and pop psychology depend upon manipulating emotions. **However, a victor and overcomer must learn to act on the basis of principles, not emotions or feelings**. Only then can he or she walk in obedience to our Lord and reap the benefits of following His counsel and precepts.

In order to do this, one must swim against the tide. Popular culture tends to ridicule and stigmatize those who do not indulge their feelings and desires. They are called "puritanical." It is said of them that they are "missing out on the fun," and that it is "unhealthy" to be "repressed."

Instead, we are told to "obey your thirst" and "just do it." This is because it is believed that we are nothing more than highly-evolved animals who have no higher purpose than to indulge our pleasures.

Hollywood movies and television, as well as the music industry, seek to inflame our lusts and passions for their profit. They lead us to think that by indulging our passions and emotions we will become free, sophisticated and happy. Only by acting on our emotions can we be "true to ourselves," they imply.

The results of this huge social experiment are in and the opposite is, in fact, true. Living to satisfy lusts and feelings leads not to freedom and happiness but to boredom, emptiness, unhappiness, sickness, and even death. It does not help us to "find ourselves." Even more importantly, by listening to this lie we can be robbed of our God-given freedom and kept from going deeper into the Kingdom.

A look into the private lives of contemporary rock stars, movie stars, producers and popular authors will reveal the accuracy of the following Scripture:

> *For speaking out arrogant words of vanity they entice by fleshly desire, by sensuality, those who barely escape from those who live in error, **promising them freedom while they themselves are slaves of corruption; for by what a man is overcome** (i.e., sexual perversion, drugs, alcohol, sensuality, emptiness and frustration, etc.), **by this he is enslaved**.*
>
> 2 Peter 2:18-19

Living out our feelings and desires does not lead to freedom and happiness. In fact, it leads to physical, intellectual and emotional self-destruction. To live that way is to live with a death wish.

Beloved, I urge you as aliens and strangers to abstain from
fleshly lusts which wage war against the soul.

1 Peter 2:11

Instead, we must become convinced that blessedness and happiness come not from obeying our emotions and desires but from following God's Word.

How blessed is the man who does not walk in the counsel of the wicked, nor stand in the path of sinners, nor sit in the seat of scoffers! But his delight is in the Law of the Lord, and in His law he meditates day and night.

Psalm 1:1-2

This Book of the Law shall not depart from your mouth, but you shall meditate on it day and night, so that you may be careful to do according to all that is written in it; for then you will make your way prosperous and then you will have success.

Joshua 1:8

But He (Jesus) said, "On the contrary, blessed are they that hear the Word of God and observe it."

Luke 11:28

Principle-based living, in which we act on the basis of God's promises and principles over any conflicting emotion or feeling, is essential if we are to follow Jesus into the Kingdom. Failure to do this will keep us from the power and riches of His Kingdom.

Emotions and feelings may be good or bad. They may be false or true. They are not to be our barometer or our master. If a person cannot overcome his feelings and emotions in order to act on principle, he is blocked from the Kingdom.

One final note on living with Jesus as your Lord. This can only happen when you are in fellowship with other believers. Jesus exercises His authority through delegated authorities. He gives the church His authority. If you will not submit to the Body of Christ and its authorities then you are deceiving yourself. *Your true submissiveness to Jesus is tested and proven by the quality of your submission to the church and its leadership.*

4. JESUS AS THE CHRIST (MESSIAH)

A fourth title for Jesus is Christ or Messiah. Christ is the Greek translation of the Hebrew Old Testament word Messiah. They both mean "Anointed One." It refers to one who has been anointed with oil (i.e., had oil poured or placed on them). In the Old Testament oil was a clear symbol of the Holy Spirit. Prophets, priests and kings were anointed with holy anointing oil. It was meant to symbolize their receiving a specific measure of God's Holy Sprit to enable them to perform their new function. *The anointing of God's Spirit is a supernatural enabling to accomplish something by God's power.*

In the Old Testament prophecies, the Messiah was to be a figure who would uniquely bear the Spirit of God in a way that none had before. The Messiah would usher in a new age of the Spirit being poured out among God's people. All of God's followers would receive the anointing power of God that previously was reserved for prophets, priests and kings.

> *It will come about after this that I will pour out my Spirit on all mankind. And your sons and daughters will prophesy, your old men will dream dreams, your young men will see visions. Even on the male and female servants I will pour out My Spirit in those days.*

> Joel 2:28-29

Jesus' fourth important role was and is to pour out the anointing of God's Spirit on people. This is what the Bible refers to as "the Baptism of the Holy Spirit." John the Baptist prepared the people for the arrival of the Messiah Jesus (in the Greek "Jesus the Christ") with the following words:

> *After me One is coming who is mightier than I, and I am not fit to stoop down and untie the thong of His sandals. I baptized you with water; but **He will baptize you with the Holy Spirit**.*

> Mark 1:7-8

It was this that Jesus instructed His disciples to wait for after His resurrection. Shortly before His triumphant, final ascension to Heaven, Jesus gave his disciples an important directive.

> *Gathering them together, He commanded them not to leave Jerusalem, but to wait for what the Father had promised, "Which," He said, "you heard of from Me; for John baptized with water, but you will be baptized with the Holy Spirit not many days from now."*

> Acts 1:4-5

We see that Jesus actually gave to His disciples two commandments before leaving them. The first we refer to as the *"Great Com-*

mission" which is to *"Go therefore and make disciples of all the nations..."* (Matthew 28:19-20). The second commission, however, is listed above. They were to wait to receive the Baptism of the Holy Spirit.

This event took place some days later on the Jewish Feast Day of Pentecost. You can read about it in the second chapter of Acts. In that account, Peter specifically relates that event as the fulfillment of the passage in Joel, Chapter 2 that we quoted above (Acts 2:14-18).

To enter into the Kingdom, you must receive and relate to Jesus as the Christ, the Baptizer in the Holy Spirit. It is not enough to know and embrace Jesus as Savior, Teacher, and Lord to fully gain access to His Kingdom. You must embrace Him as the one who anoints with the Holy Spirit. You must walk in His Anointing.

It is not enough to know God's will (Jesus as Teacher), it is not even enough to be committed to obeying His will (Jesus as Lord), if you lack the power to live it out. To follow Jesus in a victorious Christian walk is not humanly possible for unaided men and women. *The Christian walk must be a supernatural walk. It must be lived out in the power and gifts of the Holy Spirit.*

God's great works are accomplished through His Spirit. The promises of God become realized by those who walk by faith in the power and illumination of the Holy Spirit. In fact, *all of the blessings of the Kingdom are found in the Holy Spirit.*

> *For the Kingdom of God is not eating and drinking* (i.e., it's not about what you eat and drink) *but righteousness, peace and joy* **in the Holy Spirit**.
>
> Romans 14:17

The blessings and power of the Kingdom of God are in the realm of the Holy Spirit. The Holy Spirit is the agent of the Kingdom of God.

If you would live in the Kingdom you must receive the initial introduction to the power and gifts of the Holy Spirit, which is known by the phrase, "the Baptism with the Holy Spirit." *This is something more than merely being born again or being made regenerate by the Holy Spirit.*

MORE THAN BEING BORN AGAIN

On the first evening following Jesus' resurrection from the dead, He appeared to His disciples. His disciples rejoiced and were overcome with joy to see Jesus alive. Jesus did something very significant at that first reunion.

> *And when He had said this,* **He breathed on them and said, "Receive the Holy Spirit**. *If you forgive the sins of any, their sins are forgiven them; if you retain the sins of any, they have been retained."*

> John 20:22-23

Jesus, by His death, had paid the penalty for their sins, which were now forgiven. By His resurrection from the dead, He had become an eternal life-giving Spirit (1 Corinthians 15: 20-21,45). Now the wall of sin and guilt dividing the disciples from God had been removed. The disciples could receive the Spirit of God into their spirit and be born again. When Jesus breathed upon them they became regenerate by the Holy Spirit. Now they could extend to others the same forgiveness they had just received.

What a glorious day. What a glorious truth. *But there was more. There was more beyond forgiveness and being born again.* For forty days He continued to teach and instruct them to prepare them for their future ministry (Acts 1:3). Remember the charge that Jesus gave them on His final day with them, as He was about to ascend to Heaven for good?

> *And behold, I am sending forth the promise of My Father upon you; but* **you are to stay in the city until you are clothed with power from on high**.

> Luke 24:49

Although they had received the Holy Spirit in regeneration in John 20:22-23, there was more to come. Jesus warned them not to leave Jerusalem and try to fulfill their calling until they received this power. Jesus knew that being forgiven and born again was not enough. He knew that it didn't matter how much they knew, how well they had been trained or how sincere they were. They were not prepared until they received the Baptism with the Holy Spirit. Acts Chapter 2 records their baptism with the Spirit on the Day of Pentecost.

It is the same today. There is more than being forgiven and born again. We are not prepared to represent Christ until we receive the promised Baptism in the Holy Spirit. It was true for the Apostles, it was true for the believers in Ephesus (Acts 19:1-6), it was true for the early church leader, Apollos (Acts 18:24-26), and it is true for you and me as well.

MY STORY

Although I was raised in a mainline denominational church and had a love for God as a child, it was not until I was 15 that it was clearly explained to me that I had to receive Jesus personally as my Savior and be born again. I remember the night I gave my life to Jesus. A friend had invited me to visit a different church for an evening service. I went forward at an altar call and prayed with a man from that church. I was born again.

I knew inside that something had changed. I was quite sincere and for two years honestly tried to please Jesus. However, I was not acquainted with the power of the Holy Spirit. I was not able to affect my circle of friends for Christ. I often lacked the power to deal with the intimidation and temptation of the public high school campus.

By the time I was seventeen, I had succumbed to the pressure and was beginning to make small compromises that led to larger compromises. Gradually, I was sucked deeper and deeper into the world's ways. By the time I was nineteen I was abusing drugs and alcohol regularly and had completely dropped out of church. I continued to spiral downhill for the next 4 years. I became a full-blown alcoholic. I was completely lost without any direction or purpose. I was timid, passive and aimless. I began to be suicidal.

At age 23 I made one of my very, very rare appearances at a Christian event. A friend from high school had become a Christian and was playing in a Christian band. I went to see him play a concert. During the concert he shared about Christ. As he spoke, the power of the Holy Spirit fell upon me. I felt the demonic darkness and oppression broken off of me as the fire of God's Spirit filled me. I left that meeting completely changed. I was literally burning with the Baptism of God's Spirit.

Within several days I was busy serving God. Immediately I began leading people to Jesus. I was beginning to move in the gifts of the Holy Spirit. People were attracted to the anointing on my life and my ministry grew. In little more than a year I was speaking to large groups and then I was placed in charge of a ministry that began to grow dramatically.

From that day until this, wherever I have gone people have gotten saved and the Kingdom of God has advanced by virtue of the anointing of God's Spirit.

How About You?

Have you been baptized in the Holy Spirit? Are you aware of this dimension of power and supernatural life that is available to you? Christ has commanded you to receive it before you venture forth. **You must know Him as the Baptizer in the Holy Spirit.**

Ask Jesus to baptize you in the Holy Spirit. Seek to learn how to grow in understanding this part of Jesus' ministry. If this is new to you, then get books and tapes to help you grow. Go to places where the anointing of the Spirit is flowing. Begin to be around places and people who are familiar with this dimension of the Christian walk. Just like everything else in the Christian walk, association is important. We gain much by transference. As the old saying goes, "More is caught than taught." If you would grow in this dimension of the Christian life, you must make it a priority to be in an atmosphere and among people where the activity of the Holy Spirit is courted.

Some years ago I used to attend a church that was over one hundred miles from my house. Every week for nearly two years I would drive up for church. Often my wife and I and several friends would also drive up for special seminars, classes and even home fellowships during the week. God's Holy Spirit was operating in that church in a uniquely powerful way and I wanted to learn and absorb as much as possible.

Further, realize that being filled with the Holy Spirit is repeatable in the believer's life. Because we leak, we must seek for multiple fillings of His Spirit. Peter who was first filled on the Day of Pentecost (Acts 2:4), was subsequently filled in Acts 4:8, and then again in Acts 4:31. This is a pattern seen throughout the Book of Acts. Do not think that having been baptized once you are done.

After receiving the Baptism with the Holy Spirit, you must seek to cultivate a walk in the Holy Spirit. You must develop a life that is dependent upon the Holy Spirit. You must seek to live in a daily, conscious partnership with Him. Victorious Kingdom living will never be attained by those who are unfamiliar with the power and anointing of the Holy Spirit.

You must daily seek and pray for fresh anointing, illumination and empowerment by the Holy Spirit. You must endeavor to have continual fellowship with the Holy Spirit. Remember, the Holy Spirit is a present reality for those who daily seek Him with all their hearts.

As you go through your day, pray such things as,"Fill me afresh, Spirit of God, lead me Blessed Spirit, empower me Holy Spirit." Turn off the radio and spend a few minutes talking to your Divine Companion and Enabler. Walk away from the conversation at the water cooler and seek the Holy Spirit for fresh anointing. Honor Him throughout the day and He will honor you. Turn off the T.V. at night and go for a walk and seek His companionship. In this way you honor Him. Seek Him regularly and He will anoint you. Learn to stay attuned to the Spirit and Glory of God. They surround you at all times.

Do not be as those who only give occasional lip service to the Holy Spirit but who ignore Him as they go through their day. In this way they both "quench" and "grieve" Him and His activity in their lives. Remember, the Christian life can only be lived as a supernatural life, or as a life lived by His Spirit.

CHAPTER 16

GIVE THE HOLY SPIRIT BACK HIS SPACE

Think about it. What is it that can set the Christian apart from all other people and the Church apart from all other clubs, social organizations and religious groups?

Is it that we sincerely believe in what we say and give testimony of how it has changed our lives? No, many people sincerely believe other philosophies and religions and are ready to give testimony of how meaningful it is to them and how they believe it has helped them.

Is it that we have meetings? Certainly not, all groups have meetings. Is it that we have membership and camaraderie among our members? No, certainly we witness this among many groups. Is it that we have a Holy Book, say prayers and sings songs of worship to God? No, every religion does this.

What sets us apart is found right in our name. We are "Christians" or literally, "little anointed ones." *It is the anointing of the Holy Spirit that sets us apart. It is the presence and power of God among us that makes us unique.* We alone are baptized in His Holy Spirit and are a temple of that Spirit (1 Corinthians 3:16-17; 6:19).

It is this that, above all, sets us apart from the Old Testament believer as well. They had much of the Bible, they had a relationship with God by grace based on covenants. They had forgiveness of sins through a sacrifice. They had faith in a promised Savior/Deliverer. The biggest difference between them and us is Pentecost.

We stand out and are unique among all other groups, organizations and religions to the extent that the Holy Spirit is expressing Himself among us and through us. To the extent that God's love, power and gifts are evident, to that extent we shine amidst all other counterfeit religions and movements.

We must be, first and foremost, people of God's Spirit. Without this anointing we appear as just another religion or, worse yet, one of many "special interest groups" alongside others like the environ-mental movement or gays rights lobby. This is largely how the world sees us today.

THE TESTIMONY OF GOD

What we need is the testimony of God or the authentication by Him that this is the true way. This is God's plan. The accompanying signs of His presence and anointing have always been meant to be a part of our testimony. This partially explains the explosive growth of the early church.

*After it (the gospel of the Kingdom) was at the first spoken through the Lord, it was confirmed to us by those who heard, and **God also testifying with them, both by signs and wonders by various miracles and by gifts of the Holy Spirit** according to His own will.*

Hebrews 2:3-4

But if all prophesy, and an unbeliever or an ungifted man enters, he is convicted by all, he is called to account by all; the secrets of his heart are disclosed; and so he will fall on his face and worship God, declaring that God is certainly among you.

1 Corinthians 14: 24-25

The signs and manifestations of the Holy Spirit cause people to cry out, "God is certainly among you." It is God's witness concerning our message and us. It was largely this that set Jesus apart from all other "rabbis" or false messiah figures of His time. After all, the title most associated with Jesus is "Christ." Jesus Himself pointed to the signs and wonders He did by the power of the Holy Spirit as the evidence that He spoke the Truth of God.

If I do not do the works of My Father, do not believe Me; but if I do them, though you do not believe Me, believe the works, so that you may know and understand that the Father is in Me, and I in the Father.

John 10:37-38

But the testimony which I have is greater than the testimony of John; for the works which the Father has given Me to accomplish – the very works that I do – testify about Me that the Father has sent Me.

John 5:36

There was a greater testimony than even that given by John the Baptist. It was the testimony of God Himself through the miracles and signs and wonders given to Jesus to do. The mere testimony of man was to be backed up by the testimony of God Himself. Peter, on his great speech on the Day of Pentecost, stated:

> *Men of Israel, listen to these words: Jesus the Nazarene, **a man attested to you by God with miracles and wonders and signs** which God performed through Him in your midst, just as you yourselves know...*
>
> Acts 2:22

In fact, it was the testimony of the signs and wonders and healings that confounded the enemies of Christ. They were unable to compete with the signs that the Holy Spirit was accomplishing through the ministry of Jesus.

> *Therefore the chief priests and the Pharisees convened a council, and said, "What are we doing? For this man (Jesus) is performing many signs. If we let Him go on like this, all men will believe in Him, and the Romans will come and take away both our place and our nation."*
>
> John 11:47-48

Likewise the Pharisees and the Jewish leaders were also confounded in their attempts to stop the growth of the early fledgling church by the signs God was giving on behalf of it. They were able to arrest the Apostles and church leaders, but not to stop their message.

> *What shall we do with these men? For the fact that a noteworthy miracle has taken place through them is apparent to all who live in Jerusalem, and we cannot deny it.*
>
> Acts 4:16

God wants to bear His testimony to our witness, which is why Jesus promised that we would do the same works that He did (John 14:12). If we are to be effective witnesses for Christ, we must have the manifestations of His Holy Spirit. We must have His testimony. We must have the anointing of the Holy Spirit on our churches. It is this which will also set us apart from all the other voices and movements of our day.

THE WORD AND THE POWER

We must restore the works of the Holy Spirit to our churches. It is not enough for us to proclaim God's Word if we do not have the testimony of God through the Holy Spirit's works to go with it. God wants a balance in the church between the proclaimed Word and the power of the Holy Spirit. It takes both of these to establish God's Kingdom.

God's Kingdom is found where God's Word and God's Power operate in union.

We have already seen that only that which conforms to God's will (and therefore His Word) can be within His Kingdom. A Kingdom consists of the realm where a King's will is in force. That is why when a person's lifestyle is outside the blueprints of the Kingdom (God's will as revealed in the Bible), they are living outside of His Kingdom and its blessings.

At the same time however, *God's will can never be accomplished by human effort alone*. The opposition of our sinful flesh, a wicked world's system, and the powers of Hell itself are such that only the anointing of God's Spirit will enable us to overcome and gain victory.

PUT THE TRAIN ON THE TRACK

Baptists, Evangelicals and Fundamentalists have placed a strong emphasis on Bible study. Pentecostals have placed a strong emphasis on the Holy Spirit. Sometimes they have criticized each other. But the truth is, they need each other. It has been noted that the Evangelicals have a track but no train, and the Pentecostals have a train but no track. When they get together, then we will get somewhere. There is an old saying that goes like this, "If a church only has the Bible, they dry up; if they only have the Holy Spirit, they blow up, but when they have both, they grow up."

The Kingdom of God can never be established by human strength. This principle remains the same as it did when Israel faced the rebuilding of Jerusalem and the Temple after they were completely destroyed. For many years they sat in ruins while the people lived in exile in Babylon. The returning exiles faced the seemingly impossible job of rebuilding Jerusalem, which was then the center of God's Kingdom activity. They were greatly discouraged, because while they had the good intentions of rebuilding the city and Temple, they were unable to do it. That lacked the strength. Through the prophet, Zechariah, God told the people the secret to their victory and success.

Not by (human) might, nor by (human) power, but by my Spirit," says the Lord.

Zechariah 4:6

They would succeed in this great venture, not on the basis of their own strength or power, but by the power and anointing of God's Spirit. It is the same today.

Many churches seemingly ignore this reality. Consequently, many Christians are unfamiliar with this power. Their lives are not marked with victory. They have never led anyone to Christ, nor cast out a demon, nor seen a sick person healed. They are not bold in the face of opposition. They do not overcome.

Jesus promised that we would do the same works that He did. Jesus did all His works by depending upon the Holy Spirit. We will never see these works until we learn to live in the daily empowerment of the Holy Spirit. Our churches will never transform our society until they are ablaze with the power and manifestations of the Holy Spirit.

When people are anointed with the Holy Spirit, nothing can stop them. Nothing else is equal to the creativity, boldness and wisdom that the anointing brings people. For years I have witnessed the power of God's anointing to win the lost, heal the sick, cast out demons, and deliver those afflicted by despair and hopelessness.

We must once again do the works that the early church did by the power of the Holy Spirit. *We must not be afraid of the supernatural. It belongs to Jesus. Our guide into it is the Bible.* Christians who remember Jesus' words will be encouraged as they seek for the anointing of God's Spirit.

> *Now suppose one of you fathers is asked by his son for a fish; he will not give him a snake instead of a fish, will he? Or if he asks for an egg, he will not give him a scorpion, will he? If you then, being evil (compared to God) know how to give good gifts to your children,* ***how much more will your heavenly Father give the Holy Spirit to those who ask Him?***

Luke 11:11-13

Our Heavenly Father is more willing to give us the Holy Spirit than we are to give our children food. Further, the symbols mentioned here are significant. Fish and eggs had significance for the early church.

Eggs were a symbol of the new resurrection life because, just like Jesus (and now all of us), the new life of the egg burst forth from a shell (in our case, a flesh and blood body). This is why eggs were associated with Easter. The fish was significant because, in the Greek, the word for fish "icthus" is an acronym (a word formed by taking the first letter from each word in a phrase) for the phrase, "Jesus Christ, God's Son, Savior."

Likewise, throughout the Bible and the New Testament in particular, the snake was a symbol for Satan and scorpions for demons (Luke 10:19, etc.).

Jesus is clearly trying to encourage His followers about not being timid in seeking the supernatural power of the Holy Spirit. If you seek with a right heart and spirit, and *if* you are living within the counsel of God's Word, and *if* you are in true submission to the Body of Christ and its leadership, then you have no fear of being led astray by demons. God wants you to prepare yourself and then seek for His anointing.

PROVOKING THE HOLY SPIRIT

The church must boldly seek Jesus for the power of the Holy Spirit. We must make this a priority. We can no longer treat the Baptism of the Holy Spirit as something that is merely an option for a Christian. We dare not be *indifferent* to His gifts and anointing. We must no longer say, "Well, I guess that if God wants to baptize me in His Holy Spirit and give me gifts, He can."

Instead, we are told to "earnestly desire spiritual gifts, and especially that you may prophesy" (1 Corinthians 14:1), and to "earnestly desire the greater gifts" (1 Corinthians 12:31). This means that we must not be passive. We must earnestly seek for that which God wants to give us. To do anything less is unbelief and disobedience.

If we are to see the work and activity of the Holy Spirit restored to the church, we must remember something. The Holy Spirit is not a force, but a Person. He has a personality and responds to our actions and motives.

Therefore, the Bible tells us that He can be both "grieved" (Ephesians 4:30) and "quenched" (1 Thessalonians 5:19). If we do either of these, we will diminish His activity and works among us. On the other hand, we are also told that we can "kindle afresh" or "fan into flame" (2 Timothy 1:6) the gift of the Spirit. *This means that we are always provoking a response by the Holy Spirit. We are either "quenching" or "fanning into flame" His activity.*

Our attitude and manner toward Him provokes a response. If we ignore Him or treat Him as an afterthought, we are grieving Him. If we live as though His gifts and power are unneeded in our life then we are grieving Him. If we ignore His convictions and promptings and instead follow our own wisdom and ways, then we are quenching Him. If we ignore or are ignorant of God's Word, then we are quenching His activity because the Spirit of God and the Word of God always act in agreement.

Likewise, in our church meetings we are always provoking a response in the Holy Spirit. *Why is it that so many people associate the word "boring" with church? It is because we have quenched and grieved the Holy Spirit in our meetings.* How have we done this?

When we try to entertain people rather than God in our "worship" services, then we are grieving the Holy Spirit. When we preach our sermons to please man rather than God, then we are grieving the Holy Spirit. When we court and solicit the presence of people more than the Presence of God in our meetings, then we grieve the Holy Spirit. And when we fear offending people in our meetings more than we fear offending God, then we grieve Him as well.

When we carefully schedule every minute of the service and do not leave room that requires us to "wait" on the Holy Spirit, then we quench Him. When we have services that are built *primarily* upon our talents rather than His gifts, then we quench the Holy Spirit.

If we would see the manifestations of God's Spirit in our services, then we must cultivate an environment for the Holy Spirit, one that honors Him rather than grieving and quenching Him. We must prepare so that we can entertain and host the presence of God. After all, our highest calling is to be a temple of the Holy Spirit (1 Corinthians 3:16-17).

When the Holy Spirit is given back the proper place, He will bring with Him a powerful expression of the presence of our Heavenly Father and His Son, Jesus, into our services. Many people have given testimony to experiencing God's presence upon entering the front doors of our church. In fact, many of the most impressive testimonies in our church are of people who were converted by the presence of God before one word of the sermon was preached.

Among these were some of the most "lost" people in our community. Former alcoholics, drug addicts, mental patients and homosexuals have told us how simply by entering the building and then listening to the first worship songs, they were overcome by God's wonderful glory and love, and gave their lives to Him. In many cases, these people had come to church reluctantly and yet God had overwhelmed them. Years later, they are still living righteously for Jesus and involved in ministry.

Recently, a man I had known very casually for many years came up to me. I knew that he had been a Christian all his life, and had been brought to church ever since he was a baby. He had been faithful in going to church and had lived a moral Christian life. He said to me, "My brother told me for years about your church but I never visited until several months ago. The first time I attended I left very unsettled. Although I had gone to church all my life, I had never experienced the presence of God in church; I had never experienced the reality of the Holy Spirit like that. When I left, I wasn't sure that I wanted to return and have my little world turned upside down. But something brought me back and now I am excited about Jesus and I can't wait to get here and worship God."

We will have to rethink how we conduct out meetings if we want to see the power and manifestations of the Holy Spirit returning to more of our churches. No longer can we continue to have services that are so scheduled and predictable that they do not require the leading and activity of the Holy Spirit. We must learn to have services that give place to the unpredictable and surprising work of the Holy Spirit. We must learn how to wait upon the leading of the Holy Spirit in our service times.

In addition, remember that church is not just a one-hour a week meeting, but rather it's a body that functions 24/7. *This means that we are provoking a response 7 days a week.* Sunday morning is a reflection of the response that the body has been provoking for the past six days. If we would see God's glory back in the house, we must be serious and sanctify ourselves at home, work, and leisure. We must be a people prepared to meet with God.

It is time for the church to awaken and reclaim our inheritance of the Baptism and Anointing of the Holy Spirit.

CHAPTER 17

KINGDOM COURAGE

Jerry Falwell made much news in the early eighties with an organization he began which he called "The Moral Majority." After a number of early victories, Falwell came under merciless attack in the press. Because he was such a public figure, he was an easy target. He and his followers were marginalized and demonized in the press. The humanists and secularists instinctively realized the danger of an active church.

I was never a part of his organization, nor even on his mailing list. But I certainly know what some Christians have apparently forgotten. You can never let your impression of someone be formed by that person's ideological enemies. Too many times Christians turn against their brothers and natural ideological allies. They accept the distorted caricatures of Christian leaders which are portrayed in the humanistic, secular media. They wilt before the disapproval of the nice, attractive "talking heads" that we invite into our living rooms each evening for the six o'clock news.

Such was the fate of Jerry Falwell's Moral Majority. After some years, Jerry disbanded his organization. The issue that I wish to address here is not whether you agreed with his politics or even his methods. I wish to focus on the reason Jerry Falwell gave for disbanding his organization and withdrawing from such a prominent place of leadership among Christians.

When asked for the reasons that he had disbanded his organization and stepped back from such visible public leadership, he candidly admitted to being disillusioned in trying to lead Christians. This veteran of so many cultural battles made the following remark:

"The thing about Christians is that they quit. When they win they quit, and when they lose they quit. They just quit." (Reed, Ralph. *Politically Incorrect*, Word, 1994. p. 253)

In the experience of many Christian leaders, this statement is on the mark. Many Christians are afraid of controversy and the criticism and rejection that can come with it. We often run from the hard work and sacrifice that is required to see victory and advance.

This helps explain the often tepid and ineffectual preaching and teaching in today's church which we noted in a previous chapter. It helps explain why so much of the radical message of the Bible is left unsaid.

Nice Guys Flunk Out

Christians, it seems, just want to be thought of as nice guys. They want lives that are comfortable. They do not want conflict. However, this presents a real problem to entering the Kingdom of God.

Unless you are willing to be radically counter-cultural, you cannot follow Christ into the fullness of His Kingdom. Christ has radically different values, goals, and customs than does the world. Therefore, it requires great determination to press into the Kingdom while living in the world. The world is constantly trying to intimidate, pressure, tempt and distract us from entering the Kingdom.

The Kingdom of God is not for those who can't make up their minds about what they want. If you do not seek first the Kingdom, then you will certainly fail to gain it. Although the door into the Kingdom is open, one must violently push past everyone and everything that would oppose or distract you from entering.

The preaching of John the Baptist signaled a change in the availability of the Kingdom to people. His ministry marked the dawn of the Kingdom of God being accessible to the very bold. Jesus challenged a crowd with these words.

From the days of John the Baptist until now, the kingdom of heaven has been forcefully advancing, and forceful men lay hold of it.

Matthew 11:12 (NIV)

"From the days of John the Baptist..." John became a model for a new era. He became the model for a follower of Jesus in the era of the available Kingdom.

John was a forceful man. He was a man of forceful action, even violent action. He is a model for us. There is a violence, a war, surrounding the Kingdom of God. Only people of determination and forceful action will overcome the opposition to their entering the Kingdom of God.

Unless Christians are willing to welcome and embrace conflict they cannot enter the Kingdom of God. When it comes to the Kingdom of God, it's not just true that nice guys finish last; for the most part they don't even get started. You can't truly follow Jesus if you are reluctant to embrace conflict. Conflict was central to the reason that Jesus came.

> *The Son of God appeared for this purpose, **to destroy** the works of the devil.*
>
> 1 John 3:8

> *And consider these words of Jesus Himself. Do not think I came to bring peace to the earth. I did not come to bring peace, but a sword.*
>
> Matthew 10:34

Jesus' arrival on earth was an invasion that was violently opposed. From the slaughter of all of the male children under two years in Bethlehem and its vicinity (Matthew 2:16), to Jesus' crucifixion and the subsequent persecution of His followers, this was a most violent phase of an ongoing war between two kingdoms.

THE PRESENCE OF THE KINGDOM

The Kingdom of God is present wherever the works of Satan are being destroyed and his kingdom is being driven back. This is a ceaseless war between these two kingdoms that has never known a ceasefire, and never will. There will be no peace nor ceasefires until Jesus' final, total victory. Jesus' followers are not allowed to live in peaceful co-existence with Satan's kingdom. If they do, they are living outside of the Kingdom of God.

This conflict with, and victory over the kingdom of darkness is a primary evidence of the presence of God's Kingdom. Jesus Himself made this clear:

> *But if I cast out demons by the finger of God, then the Kingdom of God has come upon you.*
>
> Luke 11:20

John the Baptist sent his followers to Jesus to inquire whether He was the Messiah, the King of the Kingdom of God. In answering them, Jesus did not take them to the many messianic prophecies of the Old Testament to show how He fulfilled them. Instead, He simply pointed out He was destroying the works of Satan and his kingdom. This proved that He was the King and that He had brought in His Kingdom.

Jesus answered and said to them, "Go and report to John what you hear and see. The blind receive sight and the lame walk, the lepers are cleansed and the deaf hear, the dead are raised up, and the poor have the gospel preached to them."

Matthew 11:4-5

The primary evidence, Jesus was saying, of the presence of the King and His Kingdom, is conflict. It is the destruction of the works of Satan. Wherever Jesus' Kingdom is present, there will be a power encounter with the kingdom of darkness. This is why demons would always cry out in Jesus' presence.

If there is not a clear conflict with the devil and his system, then the Kingdom is not clearly present. If a church is not seeing the lost saved, the demonized delivered, the sick healed, and the unjust social structures around them being unseated, then the Kingdom is not decisively present in that church.

Some churches are not Kingdom centers, but just religious clubs.

CALLED TO CONFLICT

To embrace Christ means to enter into conflict with Satan and with his systems. God's way and Satan's way are never going to agree. God's ways and the ways of unregenerate man are never going to agree. To follow Christ will mean that you must constantly swim against the stream. To do that means to face misunderstanding, criticism and opposition.

As His followers, we are committed to living under His values. Even more, according to His commission to us, we are committed to establishing them over the whole world.

Think about what this means. God's Kingdom and His culture and values cannot be established unless others are rejected and opposed. This will always mean conflict. If you follow Christ, then controversy, criticism and opposition will be inevitable. You will be called "crazy," "fanatical," and "dangerous." *You will be called this because they will rightly perceive that you are a threat to the status quo.* Relatives and neighbors will, at times, misunderstand you. Sometimes it will hurt you very much. It is a painful but inevitable part of following Jesus.

If we are always well regarded and well spoken of by the world, if we are not at least occasionally vilified in the press and slandered, it can only mean one thing. We are not really following Jesus and are far from His Kingdom. This Jesus Himself has taught us:

If you were of the world, the world would love its own; but because you are not of the world, but I chose you out of the world, because of this the world hates you. Remember the word that I said to you, 'A slave is not greater than his master.' If they persecuted Me, they will also persecute you.

John 15:20

If the world does not hate us, but embraces us, it can only mean that we are of the world more than of Jesus. If the world persecutes us, it may well mean that we are indeed following Jesus. When our churches are patronized by society, it can only mean we are not following Jesus or, worse yet, are inconsequential. When we become effective like Him we will truly be vilified until the wicked status quo has been replaced by a more godly order.

A disciple is not above his teacher, nor a slave above his master. It is enough for the disciple that he become like his teacher, and the slave his master. IF THEY HAVE CALLED THE HEAD OF THE HOUSE BEELZEBUB, HOW MUCH MORE WILL THEY MALIGN THE MEMBERS OF HIS HOUSEHOLD!

Matthew 10:24

The world will little notice nor care if we gather in our comfortable little churches and sing hymns. This will not earn persecution or opposition. But just go out and begin to successfully engage society on Jesus' behalf and you will be violently opposed. For instance, if you become a school board member and attempt to implement Jesus' values, then you will see great hostility and persecution. If we effectively operate as salt and light in the world, then we will be treated as He was. If we truly enter the Kingdom we will see the war firsthand.

Jesus points out that the response of the unregenerate world and its systems to us can serve as a barometer of our faithfulness to Him and His mission. Therefore, we are to fear not the world's rejection and hatred, but its acceptance!

Woe to you when all men speak well of you, for their fathers used to treat the false prophets in the same way.

Luke 6:26

Blessed are you when men hate you and ostracize you, and

insult you, and scorn your name as evil, for the sake of the Son of Man

Luke 6:22

Anyone who will not embrace conflict as a part of their lifestyle is blocked from following the King into His Kingdom. Jesus' Kingdom is a Kingdom at war. When Jesus and His apostles began the invasion of Satan's kingdom, Satan ruled the world. The Apostle John reminded the small band of followers of Jesus:

We know that we are of God, and that THE WHOLE WORLD LIES IN THE POWER OF THE EVIL ONE.

1 John 5:19

The mission of Jesus was to free people from the hold of the kingdom of Satan, and to transfer them to His Kingdom (Colossians 1:13). This is now our mission. However, Satan will not abdicate his power nor release people without a fight. Therefore, Jesus has prepared us for just such a fight. There is a harvest to be reaped, but we must battle for it.

Jesus sent seventy of His followers out into the countryside of Israel. They healed the sick and cast out demons and preached the good news of the Kingdom. After they returned, flush with their success, Jesus spoke to them. He had trained them well, and in their success He was watching Satan's being driven from his position of power.

And He said to them, "Behold, I was watching Satan fall from heaven like lightning. Behold I have given you authority to tread on serpents and scorpions, and over all the power of the enemy, and nothing shall injure you."

Luke 10:18-19

Serpents and scorpions are a clear allusion to the power of demons and are found in many places in Scripture. In the effective ministry of the seventy, Jesus saw the inevitable defeat of Satan. *It would be an army of His followers, foreshadowed by the seventy, that would defeat Satan's power on earth.*

TRUE RIGHTEOUSNESS BY GOD'S STANDARDS

Courage and bold confidence are indispensable to entering the Kingdom. We use a different standard in assessing someone's Christianity than does God. We look for people who are nice and don't curse or ever have a moral failing. God looks for people who have enough faith to act. He values courage and bold faith over faultless moral behavior. True faith and knowledge of God results in bold action.

> *But the people who know their God will display strength and take action.*
>
> Daniel 11:32

We must rethink what the word "righteousness" means. It means much more than moral living and good manners. It means the courage and conviction to believe God and fully obey Him. It means trusting in God's provision and strength so much that we obey His commands completely. The life of Abraham, known as the Father of the Faith, illustrates this.

God appeared to Abraham and told him to leave his extended family, clan, homeland and city, and go to a distant land whose location was not disclosed to him. He must simply leave and trust that God would bless, protect and guide him. He knew nothing more. Abraham chose to believe and obey God, and set off for a life of nomadic journeying. He continued to live in a foreign land, apart from his kin, because God had promised to give him many descendants and to give them the land. This was righteousness by God's standard.

> *Then he (Abraham) believed God, and He reckoned it to him as righteousness.*
>
> Genesis 15:6

> *But My righteous one shall live by faith; and if he shrinks back, my soul has no pleasure in him.*
>
> Hebrews 10:38

A righteous person endeavors to fully obey God through living by faith. Living by faith means trusting in His provision and strength, rather than our own calculations. Only in this way are we lifted above the fear and intimidation of the world's opposition. Only then can we fully obey Him.

Every true follower of Jesus is committed to obeying Him. Simply going to church is not a substitute for obedience. Jesus told us to go out into all the world and make disciples of all nations. He promised that the gates of hell would not prevail against us. He told us to heal the sick and cast out demons.

Righteousness means that we do not let discomfort, difficulty, insecurity, timidity or unbelief keep us from fulfilling these commands. We cannot fully enter the Kingdom unless we have the courage and determination to not only face conflict, but also overcome it. Jesus has not called us to win a popularity contest. He has called us to be agents of His Kingdom. His Kingdom is at war and is violently opposed. You cannot serve Him and not offend people or encounter hostility.

Look at society around us. Look at the great suffering that sin is causing. Look at the destruction of the young and naive that is brought about by those who are manipulating and exploiting them. Do you think that Jesus is pleased with a church that is not strenuously battling these destructive forces? Do you think He is pleased with the "live and let live" attitude of many congregations? I tell you no. He will spit them out of His mouth. Jesus demands that His followers overcome these forces.

POSSESSING THE PROMISE LAND

When God fulfilled His promise to Moses by bringing His descendants to the edge of the Promised Land, it was not unoccupied. *The land that God promised them could only be theirs if they were willing to drive out the Canaanites who had been appointed by God for destruction.* Because the first generation was afraid of the conflict, they failed to enter. The next generation displayed more courage and therefore possessed the land with God's help.

Likewise, God has a Kingdom for us with its many promises. We will not enter it without a fight, however. God would give us great blessings, but only if we claim them by driving back the darkness of Satan's reign.

Does it seem too difficult? Does the job seem too large? This is why we must live by faith. True faith will result in courage and boldness. True faith will say to a mountain: *"Be taken up and be thrown in the sea"* (Mark 11:23). In this way the Kingdom will open wide to you.

CHAPTER 18

KINGDOM LEADERS

In the late 1930's, western civilization was coming under the shadow of a dark cloud, although many did not want to acknowledge it. Adolph Hitler became Chancellor and his Nazi party assumed power in Germany in January of 1933. Quickly, Hitler began to move toward his goal of world domination. He built a huge war machine in Germany and began to set the stage for his first conquests. In 1938, he annexed Austria and began to threaten an invasion of Czechoslovakia.

In England, Winston Churchill was vainly trying to warn his countrymen of the danger that was brewing in Germany. But times were good. England was in an economic upswing and did not want to hear about it. Churchill was dismissed in the press, and by most other government officials, as an alarmist and a war monger. His strong will and uncompromising manner caused him to be characterized as a "bulldog."

They chose instead Neville Chamberlain as Prime Minister. Chamberlain was an affable and popular man. He did not take strong stands nor offend people. He worked rather to make compromises and build coalitions. He was a consummate politician.

England was in no mood for the truth about the threat of Hitler's Germany and so Chamberlain and his government told the people what they wanted to hear. They seemingly ignored the facts of the situation. Chamberlain's policy toward Hitler was to appease Hitler by giving him what he wanted, believing that such concessions would satisfy Hitler. History would show that Chamberlain was very wrong.

In order to keep Hitler from going to war, Chamberlain signed a pact with Hitler in Munich in early 1939 that in essence granted Hitler the right to large portions of Czechoslovakia, in return for not invading the rest of the nation.

Chamberlain returned triumphant to England to the adulation of the press and public, holding in his hand a copy of the pact and declaring that he had achieved "peace in our time." The peace, however, was to be short-lived.

In March of 1939, Adolph Hitler seized the rest of Czechoslovakia and six months later, on September 1, he invaded Poland. Almost immediately France and England declared war on Germany. But the appeasements to Hitler and the failure to heed Churchill's warnings to build up their military would prove very costly indeed.

Neville Chamberlain left office in disgrace and Winston Churchill was elected as the new Prime Minister. By 1940, all of Europe, including France, had fallen to Adolph Hitler. Only England remained; her army had been defeated in France and had to be rescued at Dunkirk, and evacuated across the English Channel back to Britain. The fate of western civilization seemed grim.

The greatest weapon that England had was Winston Churchill. It seems as though he had been divinely prepared for such a moment. By his courage, faith, and vision he rallied a defeated and discouraged nation. He held the nation together with his will and inspired sacrifice from the fighting soldier and the civilian at home alike.

He stood before the House of Commons and addressed the nation, saying that he could only offer "blood, toil, tears and sweat." He went on, "You ask, 'What is our aim?' I can answer in one word: Victory. It is victory. Victory at all costs. Victory in spite of all terror. Victory, however long and hard the road may be."

He rallied the nation with these words, "We shall go on to the end... we shall defend our island, whatever the cost may be. We shall fight on the landing-grounds; we shall fight in the fields and in the streets...we shall never surrender."

He helped the people to grasp the greatness of the task before them and the necessity of the sacrifices they were being called to make. "If we can stand up to Hitler, all Europe may be free, and the way of the world may move forward into broad, sunlit uplands. But if we fail, then the whole world, including the United States, including all that we have known and cared for, will sink into the abyss of a new Dark Age. Let us therefore brace ourselves to our duties and so bear ourselves that if Britain and the Commonwealth last for a thousand years, many will say,'This was their finest hour.'"

Under Churchill's leadership, Britain fought on. In the United States the pacifists continued to tell Americans that we were not at risk. That it was not our war. That we could sit this one out. The bombing of Pearl Harbor by Germany's ally, Japan, changed all that. Together, the United States and England defeated Hitler in Europe and saved it.

During the war, Churchill was much loved. His strengths were appreciated. But the year following victory, Churchill's Conservative party was defeated and the Liberal party gained control of Parliament. Churchill yielded the position of Prime Minister to Clement Richard Atlee. The war was over and so the political climate had changed.

In times of peace, people look for leaders who build coalitions by blurring truth and avoiding controversy. They want leaders who will protect their personal comfort and affluence.

Wartime demands a different kind of leader than does peacetime. Wartime demands a type of leader who can motivate people to action and sacrifice in order to win the war.

WARTIME LEADERSHIP

The Christian life is one that is lived out in the context of a great war.

And there was war in heaven, Michael and his angels waging war with the dragon. The dragon and his angels waged war, and they were not strong enough, and there was no longer a place found for them in heaven. And the great dragon was thrown down, the serpent of old who is called the devil and Satan, who deceives the whole world; and he was thrown down to the earth, and his angels with him.
Revelation 12:7-9

The Book of Revelation shows us that earth is part of a much larger reality. We are part of a great war that includes and transcends our world. Each of us was born into a war for which there is no neutrality. It doesn't matter whether we wish to be in this war or not. It simply is.

Think about your life. Do you live as one who lives in wartime or peacetime? Those who lived during our country's great wars lived quite differently then those who live in peacetime. The generations who lived during the first and second wars made great sacrifices. People have different goals and value systems during wartime. People sacrifice for the greater national goal of victory.

I ask you. Do we live in wartime or peacetime? Are we in a state of war or a state of peace?

If we are at war, do we not need wartime leadership? People value different qualities in their leaders in a time of war than a time of peace. During war, they look for leaders who display courage, decisiveness and the will to win despite the personal cost.

Until we realize that we are at war, we will neither be the kind of people, nor follow the kind of leaders who will allow us to enter the Kingdom of God.

THE MAN GOD CHOOSES

What kind of people does Jesus value on his side? What are the values that He most seeks in His leaders? What type of person did He choose to surround Himself with and build His Church upon? Consider first John the Baptist.

Jesus paid the highest compliment to John the Baptist. He said of him:

> *Truly I say to you, among those born of women there has not arisen anyone greater than John the Baptist.*
>
> Matthew 11:11

What a statement! Think of it! Of all the heroes of the Old Testament, none were greater than John in Jesus' estimation. What were the qualities of John that elicited such praise from his Master? Jesus, Himself, lists them in the same passage:

> *As these men were going away, Jesus began to speak to the crowds about John, "What did you go out into the wilderness to see? A reed shaken by the wind? But what did you go out to see? A man dressed in soft clothing? Those who wear soft clothing are in King's palaces."*
>
> Matthew 11:7-8

Jesus tells us the kind of man that John was by telling us what he was not.

First, he was not a "reed shaken by the wind." That is, he was not a spineless blade of grass that blew with the wind. He was not swayed by hardship, difficulties or popular opinion. He was not distracted by trends, fashions or fame.

He was not afraid of conflict, and would not run from a fight. He would not surrender the truth just because of the cost involved. He went to jail for opposing a king. He was not a quitter, a complainer or a wimp. He was not a man of excuses. He suffered whatever came his way, endured what he had to and overcame every obstacle that rose up before him in order to fulfill his mission.

Nor was he a man "dressed in soft clothing" and living in a king's palace. He was not a politician or a court bureaucrat. He did not court power or approval. He did not pander nor play the game to get his "share of the pie." He could not be lulled to sleep by the promise of wealth and success.

He was a man who could not be bought or intimidated. He was one of the most able men of his generation. He was, perhaps, except for Jesus, the most influential individual of his generation. He could have been wealthy, comfortable and politically powerful.

Instead, he lived out in the wilderness, dressed in animal skins, seeking God for a word for his generation. He was a prophet.

> *But what did you go out to see? A prophet? Yes, I tell you, and one who is more than a prophet.*
>
> Matthew 11:9

John was faithful as a prophet. He had a message to deliver and he lived to deliver that message. He understood that his mission was more important than his comfort or even his safety. But he was even more, according to Jesus.

He was the forerunner. He came to prepare the way for the Messiah and His Kingdom.

> *This is the One about Whom it is written 'Behold I send My Messenger ahead of You, who will prepare your way before You.'*
>
> Matthew 11:10

John prepared the way for the coming King by preparing the people to enter His Kingdom. He did this by preaching His message of repentance and by becoming a model of those who would enter it. As we stated in an earlier chapter, He served as a model of the new era. He demonstrated how forceful people could now bring the blessings and the reign of the Kingdom to earth by forceful actions (Matthew 11:12).

John was the type of person that Jesus values most as a follower. These are the ones that He chooses for special favor and friendship.

Look at the men He chose to become apostles. Not a *single* well-respected religious leader among them. They were men of action. Look at His three closest followers, Peter, James and John.

JESUS' INNER CIRCLE

Peter was a bold, strong-willed man. He would argue with Jesus (Mark 8:32-33). He would boast to Jesus (Matthew 26:33-35). When they came to arrest Jesus, he pulled out a sword and cut off the ear of one of them (and that's only because the fellow dodged out of the way – no doubt Peter was going for his head).

Peter would never last as a pastor of one of our churches today. Jesus made him a leader over the whole church.

James and John were zealous and men of action as well. Their temperament was such that Jesus gave them the nickname "the Sons of Thunder" (Mark 3:17). Once, when a town insulted Jesus, they requested permission and authority to call fire down from heaven to destroy the town (Luke 9:54).

These were the three men that Jesus selected to be His closest friends, and most trusted associates.

THE APOSTLE PAUL

Who did Jesus choose to be the Apostle to the Gentiles? He chose a ruthless man named Saul (later called Paul). The Book of Acts portrays Saul as one of the chief persecutors of the early church. Acts 26:11 describes Saul as "furiously enraged" against the church. Acts 9:1 vividly pictures Saul as "breathing threats and murder against the disciples." He was a Doberman Pincher of a man who traveled far to persecute the church. Jesus looked at perhaps the worst enemy that the church had and said, "He has what it takes to be my greatest follower."

Paul could be your worst enemy, but also your greatest comrade. Jesus loved him because he had what it would take to invade the darkness and advance Jesus' Kingdom.

The Apostle Paul may have been a little intense, a little opinionated, and a little too confrontative. He may have been a little bit hard to take. You might not want to invite him to your tea party, but he was a great guy to have in your corner in a fight. And, after all, Jesus knows this is a fight, not a tea party. In fact, it is more than that, it is war.

OLD TESTAMENT HEROES

If you check the heroes of the Old Testament, you will see the same characteristics in those men. Look at the lives of men like Moses,

Joshua, Samson, King David, and many others. Some of these men did horrible things, including murder and adultery. Yet they are among the greatest of the heroes of the Bible. What they had in common is that they were great warriors and men of courage.

In fact, if you study Hebrews, Chapter 11, the chapter with the so-called *"Old Testament Hall of Fame,"* you may be in for a surprise. Although some of those listed lived righteous and moral lives without compromise, many others had quite a checkered history. There is even a prostitute listed. And yet they are listed side by side as heroes.

How can this be? The answer is that what made them heroes was not their morality, but their courage. *Those listed are not there for their perfect behavior, but for their daring behavior.*

In a war, moral failings can be forgiven and mistakes can be rectified, but fear, timidity and apathy are fatal to your cause.

King David committed adultery, and in order to cover up this sin, conspired to see that the woman's husband was killed in battle. King Saul only partially obeyed a direct order because he feared the people and then tried to justify his actions before Samuel the prophet (1 Samuel 15:1-26). Most people would say that David's sin was worse than Saul's.

Today, we would kick David out of the church and consider putting Saul into leadership. However, God forgave David and allowed him to remain on the throne, and his sons after him. Saul however, was rejected.

To God, Saul was unfit for leadership because his fear of the people made full obedience impossible. Further, his unwillingness to be honest with himself and God disqualified him from receiving from God.

David, although he failed greatly, demonstrated his courage and faith in God on many occasions and was therefore able to obey God's commands completely. Courage is often necessary in order to completely obey God. Further, his psalms (especially Psalm 51) reflect how deeply honest and repentant he was for his sin.

RESTORING JESUS' STANDARD FOR LEADERSHIP

It is time that we re-evaluate what are the most important qualities in our leaders. If our churches truly want to serve our Lord and Master Jesus Christ, we must strive to be more than simply "nice people;" we must strive to be bold and courageous.

STORY OF JOHN CONRAD

In future chapters I will tell of how our city of El Cajon is changing. But let me give you a foretaste by telling you the story of one of the pastors in our community who is a "wartime leader." As I go to press, this is one of the most recent victories and is still unfolding...

We need the most courageous and bold of our young people to grow up and go in to full-time Christian service. We need our most creative people serving the church. We need to make our young people see the challenge and adventure of following Jesus into a life of destroying strongholds. It's a tragedy when our kids grow up in church thinking that the sum of the Christian life is to dress up and sit quietly.

We need a new yardstick by which to measure a church. We obviously need to rethink what we look for and expect in our leaders.

We must realize that the church needs the kind of leaders that are held up in the Bible. We must choose the type of person to lead that Jesus chose.

They were men of courage, vigor, force and passion. They were fully committed and even sometimes ruthless in their mission. Jesus knew that only such people would be able to advance His Kingdom. The same is true today.

Too often such leaders are not found in the church. Rather, we content ourselves with leaders that make us feel good. We want a pastor who will remember our names and birthdays, have us over for dinner and play softball with us. *We want religious politicians who will court us for our membership.* It is good to have pastors who are kind, loving and gentle. But this is not enough.

Too often we think that the church exists for us, as a social club to ease our stress and make us feel good about ourselves. But the Church exists first for Jesus. It must first fulfill His purposes. It must serve His Kingdom.

This means that we must have, at the head of the church, the type of leaders that Jesus put at the head. We need to follow the kind of leaders who, though imperfect in many other ways, are able to advance Jesus' Kingdom.

This will not happen until we use a new standard to evaluate leadership. *Even more importantly it will not take place until we restore the whole five-fold leadership team over our churches.* Apostles, prophets and teachers must be restored to help guide the church. More than the gift of pastor, these offices are anointed for boldness and vision. Whereas pastors give care to the flock, apostles and prophets provide strategic leadership and vision.

Any church or pastor that is functioning without the input of prophets and apostles will be frustrated. This is one reason why such a large percentage of pastors contemplate quitting. If you are frustrated in the ministry, or if your church is not growing or knowing victory, quite likely the reason is that you are functioning only on one cylinder instead of five. Pastors must begin to seek out ministry relationships with those whom they identify as having one of the other ministry gifts.

Many growing churches seem to be flourishing without the acknowledged ministry of an apostle, prophet or teacher. However, in many of these cases, the Senior Pastor is actually not a pastor at all but one of the other ministry offices functioning under the title of Senior Pastor. The church may also have the ministry of one or more of the ministry gifts functioning through an itinerate ministry that has relationship with the church, whether they rightly identify the correct office of the person or not.

The new wine that Jesus wants to pour out must be poured into new wineskins. This will require a new paradigm for church leadership. In these days, we must restore the type of leaders that led the church in the First Century.

SECTION THREE

Laying Hold of the Kingdom

From the days of John the Baptist until now, the Kingdom of Heaven has been forcefully advancing, and forceful men lay hold of it.

Matthew 11:12 (NIV)

CHAPTER 19

CHIEF OF THE MOUNTAINS

The Kingdom of God was inaugurated during the reign of what was perhaps the greatest and most powerful empire that the world has ever known, the Roman Empire. King Jesus faced Caesar for supremacy of the world.

Rome outlawed Christianity in 64A.D. The two greatest leaders of the church, Peter and Paul, were executed in Rome during the 60's. In fact, of the 12 disciples, only John escaped martyrdom to die a natural death. For the next two and one-half centuries, Christianity would remain illegal. But that didn't stop the Kingdom of God from advancing.

Before 200A.D., Tertullian, an influential church leader, would write in his book, *Apologeticum: An Impassioned Defense*, addressing the pagan Roman ruling class, "We (Christians) have filled everything you have, cities, tenements, forts, towns, exchanges, yes, and army camps, tribes, palace, senate, forum. All we have left you is the (pagan) temples." (*Apologeticum* 37.4-5)

Even before that, Pliny, the Roman provincial governor of Bithynia, wrote to Emperor Trajan reporting that under the onslaught of Christianity even the pagan temples were deserted (*Letters* 10:96). In several centuries, the Roman Empire would be converted to Christianity.

How did this happen? And more importantly, could it happen again? To answer this, we must understand the governmental nature of the Kingdom of God.

COULD IT HAPPEN AGAIN?

Remember the passage from Daniel 2 that we looked at in Chapter 2? It showed the stone being cut from the mountain and destroying the image that represented the great world empires. The stone, of course, represented the Kingdom of God that would supersede the previous world rulers and empires. Do you remember from that passage, however, what the stone grew into? Let's look at it again.

You continued looking until a stone was cut out without hands, and it struck the statue on its feet of iron and clay, and crushed them. Then the iron, the clay, the bronze, the silver and the gold were crushed all at the same time, and became like chaff from the summer threshing floors; and the wind carried them away so that not a trace of them was found. BUT THE STONE WHICH STRUCK THE STATUE BECAME A GREAT MOUNTAIN AND FILLED THE WHOLE EARTH.

Daniel 2:34-35

As we have already shown in the previous chapter, this passage clearly states that this stone that grows into a mountain is the Kingdom of God that Jesus established. But what is the significance of it growing into a mountain?

The stone is a clear reference to Jesus. He was the "chief cornerstone" and the "stone that the builders rejected" (Acts 4:11; 1 Peter 2:6-8). In that it was "cut out without hands" refers to the fact that Jesus was not born of human will or action, but was conceived of the Holy Spirit (Matthew 1:18). That it grew into a mountain that filled the whole earth is significant.

In the Bible, mountains are often symbolic of government. This may have come from the fact that great and powerful cities were generally built on mountains for better defense. Or it may have come from the fact that Jerusalem, the seat of government for Israel and the place where the Temple was found (which represented the seat of God's Kingdom on earth), was built on Mount Zion.

King David thanks God for establishing his Kingdom preeminent among his foes with these words:

O Lord, by Thy favor Thou hast made my mountain to stand strong.

Psalm 30:7

Likewise, Satan is pictured in his rebellion against God and his attempt to establish himself as a rival government to God with these words:

But you (Satan) said in your heart, "I will ascend to heaven; I WILL RAISE MY THRONE above the stars of God (i.e., the other angels), AND I WILL SIT ON THE MOUNT OF ASSEMBLY... I will make myself like the Most High."

Isaiah 14:13-14

In Nebuchadnezzar's dream, when the stone grows into a mountain that fills the whole earth, it refers to the fact that the government of Jesus would grow and grow until it came to rule over all. This fulfills a prophecy made many centuries earlier through Isaiah the prophet.

Now it will come about that in the last days, THE MOUN-TAIN OF THE HOUSE OF THE LORD WILL BE ESTAB-LISHED AS THE CHIEF OF THE MOUNTAINS, and will be raised above the hills, and all the nations will stream to it.

Isaiah 2:2

It clearly states here that one of the features of the last days is that the government of Jesus would become stronger and stronger until it was chief among all governments and all other governments would somehow "come" to it.

Isaiah, as we have seen, clearly stated this same principle several chapters later in speaking of the birth of the Messiah.

For a child will be born to us and a son will be given to us; AND THE GOVERNMENT WILL REST ON HIS SHOUL-DERS; And His name will be called Wonderful, Counselor, Mighty God, Eternal Father, Prince of Peace. THERE WILL BE <u>NO END TO THE INCREASE</u> OF HIS GOVERN-MENT or of peace.

Isaiah 9:6-7

Now, we can't escape the fact that the Bible clearly teaches us that the Kingdom of God involves government, and not just government over the church, but government over all things. It teaches that this government will grow until it becomes pre-eminent. God's plan clearly involves more than just personal salvation and happiness for individuals. God has come not just to reconcile individuals to Himself, but all of His creation.

For it was the Father's good pleasure for all the fullness to dwell in Him (Christ Jesus), AND THROUGH HIM TO RECONCILE ALL THINGS TO HIMSELF, having made peace through the blood of the cross; through Him, I say, WHETHER THINGS ON EARTH OR THINGS IN HEAV-EN.

Colossians 1:19-20

Now this verse doesn't mean that all people will eventually be saved, but rather that all rebellion will be overcome; either through the salvation offered, Jesus, or the judgment and defeat of those who resist Him. However, before final judgment, peace is first offered to all.

If we are to understand the Kingdom of God, we must understand God's government on earth. We can't avoid this subject because of some mistakes that have been made in the past by the church or some of its leaders. In addition, we must overcome our understandable reluctance to consider this subject brought about by observing the Islamic model of tyranny and oppression. The Kingdom of God differs from "dar es Islam" (the realm of Islam) as day differs from night.

We must not be reactionary in our thinking and strategies but biblical. *We must remember that it is Satan's strategy to keep the church reluctant to talk about government, because only then will his* (Satan's) *government* (rule) *be safe.* When Christians, through indifference, ignorance or misunderstanding fail to exercise their Kingdom authority, then Satan's kingdom is unmolested and much suffering follows.

REVISIONING THE FUTURE

Many Christians today see themselves as powerless. They look around at their city and nation and see much that distresses them. They feel, however, that there is little or nothing that they can do to change it. They say things like, " Well, we know things are going to get worse and worse."

Tell me, how do we know this? Where does it state this in the Bible? *If you have read this book to this point, do you still believe that Jesus and the Bible teach defeat, powerlessness and the inevitability of the triumph of wickedness in history?* Perhaps this sense of powerlessness comes because they have been taken in by a man-made doctrine of the end times that contradicts the overall teaching of Scripture. It ignores the flow of history as well. It focuses instead on some very symbolic, ambiguous and hard to understand passages, which are wrongly interpreted and applied in a very dogmatic fashion. This leads to an *eschatology* (doctrine of the end times), which is very pessimistic and discouraging.

If this particular interpretation of these Scriptures is all you have ever heard, and if this is the only eschatology you have ever been taught, then it probably makes sense to you and seems correct. I know it did to me for many years. However, you need to be aware that it has not been the dominant understanding of these passages or of eschatology throughout history. All the prophecies of the Bible can be best understood in such a way that rather than contradicting the overall message of the Bible, there is harmony and agreement.

The great advances in Christian civilization have been made primarily when people believed something much different about the future than do many Christians in America today.

The view of the last days held by many evangelical Christians today, and made popular in recent books and movies, was not the view of such men as Martin Luther, John Calvin, St. Augustine, Charles Spurgeon, Charles Finney, or most other Christian leaders throughout history.

A fuller discussion of eschatology or an in-depth analysis of various apocalyptic Bible passages popularly believed to apply to the end times is beyond the scope of this book. Such books are available, and several are listed at the end of this chapter.

My point is simply this. What people believe about the future determines how they act. Do they believe that evil is destined to triumph in human history and they can only sit back largely powerless and watch it unfold? Or do they believe that they are citizens and ministers of a Kingdom that has, and continues to displace all other kingdoms? What authority has been given to them? What is their assignment and commission? What is their duty as disciples of Jesus Christ? Wrong ideas on these questions can have disastrous consequences.

Leo Tolstoy, the famous Russian author of *War and Peace,* was the owner of a huge estate that employed hundreds of workers. Tolstoy was a fair and generous man and the peasants enjoyed the benefits and treatment of living on his estate. He cared for their needs and provided decent housing and enough food.

In adult life, Tolstoy became an ardent Christian. He earnestly desired inner peace and assurance of salvation. Upon studying the Sermon on the Mount, he decided that this would require selling everything he owned and giving the money to the poor. He believed that this would make him a better disciple and would please God.

Unfortunately, the estate he sold came into the possession of greedy and cruel owners who mistreated the peasants and took great advantage of them. In their plight, the peasants cried out to Tolstoy to deliver them, but he was no longer in a position to help. Because of his misunderstanding of Scripture, he had surrendered authority and power to the wicked. He had misunderstood his call to be a disciple and surrendered the authority granted to him by God. The result was great suffering and oppression.

Likewise, when we believe things that prevent us from understanding our authority granted us by Jesus, we surrender our realm of influence to Satan and oppression. What do you see when you look out at your neighborhood and city and into the eyes of the young who are growing up in it? What is your role? What is your responsibility? Are you really powerless to change it or are you, like Tolstoy, surrendering your authority to the godless because of ignorance and misunderstanding? What do you think? Let's consider this question in depth. A key to answering it will be to understand how God's authority functions.

References used in the writing of this chapter include:

1. Chilton, David. *Paradise Restored: An Eschatology of Dominion*. Tyler, Texas: Dominion Press, 1999.

2. De Mar, Gary. *Last Days Madness: Obsession of the Modern Church*. 3rd ed. Atlanta: American Vision, 1997.

3. Kik, J. Marcellus. *An Eschatology of Victory*. Nutley, NJ: The Presbyterian and Reformed Publishing Co., 1971.

CHAPTER 20

KINGDOM POWER AND AUTHORITY

If you want to experience God's power and increase, you must have the authority to release it. In understanding how Jesus delegates the authority and power of His Kingdom, it is necessary to understand one more concept. *When Jesus delegates His authority to His administration, He also defines the scope and limits of that authority.* Jesus divides up His power and authority and distributes it throughout His administration.

The different parts of the administration of His Kingdom carry different assignments. It is only when we stay within these particular assignments that we carry legitimate authority and can expect God to back us up.

SPHERES OF AUTHORITY

I call these "appointed spheres of authority." We all experience this in many different ways. For instance, if you are a parent, you have authority over your children but not my children. Your children are under your "sphere of authority" but mine are not. This is why you can depend upon God to work on your behalf and back up your authority as you parent your children. Likewise, your house and home are under your authority as are your finances, etc. God has, however, not granted you to be in authority over your neighbor's home or finances.

In your God-given "sphere of authority," you have more power and authority than anyone else. This is because God's Kingdom will back you up, since He has appointed you to represent Him there. This is why you have more impact and influence (for better or worse) over your children than does anyone else. God has determined that parents have the primary responsibility, influence, and authority over their children. They have authority and power to bless or curse their children above that of anyone else.

Whenever you are standing in the place that Jesus has sent and appointed you, you are the most important person there. Others may be smarter or more gifted, but if you are the "appointed one," then your power and authority is the greatest. This puts a tremendous responsibility on your shoulders if you are, for instance, a parent, a pastor, a business owner, or a mayor.

The other side of this is also true. When you exceed your "sphere of authority" and try to exercise authority in someone else's sphere, then you are no longer a legitimate authority. You can't expect God's help and supernatural assistance.

The Apostle Paul realized the importance of knowing what God had given him to be responsible for. He realized that, within the sphere that God had appointed for him, he did not have to back down before anyone. He also understood, however, not to exceed what Jesus had appointed him to.

> *But we will not boast beyond our measure, but WITHIN THE MEASURE OF THE SPHERE WHICH GOD APPORTIONED TO US as a measure, to reach even as far as you. For we are not overextending ourselves, as if we did not reach to you, for we were the first to come even as far as you in the gospel of Christ; NOT BOASTING BEYOND OUR MEASURE that is, in other men's labors, but with the hope that as your faith grows, we will be, WITHIN OUR SPHERE, enlarged even more by you.*
>
> 2 Corinthians 10:13-15

Paul knew that he had been appointed as apostle over the church of Corinth. That was within his sphere as an administrator of God's Kingdom. Therefore he was bold in exercising his authority and confident that God would supply all the grace he would need to be effective and successful. He was wise enough to realize, however, that his authority and divine enabling did not extend beyond the sphere of his appointment. That is why he was careful not to overextend himself and "boast beyond his measure."

Paul was meek enough to realize that the power and grace that flowed through his life was not of himself, but was a result of standing in the position that God had appointed him for in his Kingdom administration. Therefore, he would not presume upon them beyond the clear limits of God's appointment. However, Paul was bold in God within the sphere of his appointment because of his confidence in God's grace. Paul knew that God had placed the Corinthian church in his sphere and given him a special place over it that he could not relinquish.

I do not write these things to shame you, but to admonish you AS MY BELOVED CHILDREN. FOR IF YOU WERE TO HAVE COUNTLESS TUTORS IN CHRIST, YET YOU WOULD NOT HAVE MANY FATHERS for IN CHRIST JESUS, I BECAME YOUR FATHER through the gospel therefore, I exhort you, BE IMITATORS OF ME.

1 Corinthians 5:14-16

Paul serves as a good example of how we should operate our personal lives and responsibilities within God's Kingdom. We need to be confident of God's backing and supply within the sphere of our own responsibilities, and not be critical or worry about areas that are not our responsibility. (This frees us from having to be the world's sheriff.) If we look humbly to God, then we should be confident to operate in whatever assignments we have received (i.e., parents, pastors, teachers, elected officials, policemen, etc.), knowing that God will supply us and stand behind us.

THE SOURCE OF ALL AUTHORITY

It is important to remember that there is no authority apart from God. He is Creator and Lord over all. All authority must be derived from Him.

Every person is to be in subjection to the governing authorities. FOR THERE IS NO AUTHORITY EXCEPT FROM GOD, AND THOSE WHICH EXIST ARE ESTABLISHED BY GOD.

Romans 13:1

This is the meaning behind the words that Jesus spoke to Pilate, the Roman governor of Judea. Jesus was telling him that his authority came, ultimately, not from Rome, but from God.

You would have no authority over Me, unless it had been granted you from above.

John 19:11

All authority is to be derived from God. All who are in authority are therefore accountable and answerable to Him.

Obey your leaders and submit to them, for they keep watch over your souls AS THOSE WHO WILL GIVE AN ACCOUNT.

Hebrews 3:17

Since all authority is God's, and all in authority are merely His delegated authorities that will have to give Him an account, then we must limit our exercise of authority to what God directs. If we exceed the limits of authority God gives us, or exercise that authority in a way that is not consistent with the principles in the Bible, then we become illegitimate authority. We become rogue tyrants whom God will now oppose rather than back.

THE LIMITS OF AUTHORITY

Any time an administrator of God's Kingdom exceeds the commission or assignment given them, they begin to be opposed by God. WITHIN THE BOUNDARIES OF THEIR COMMISSION, GOD ASSISTS THEM AND BLESSES THEM, BUT WHEN THEY ATTEMPT TO GO BEYOND THE BOUNDARIES OF THEIR COMMISSION, GOD OPPOSES OR CURSES THEM. This is a reflection of a basic principle in Scripture that is listed in several places.

God is opposed to the proud, but gives grace to the humble.
James 4:6
(see also Matthew 23:12; 1 Peter 5:5;
Psalm 138:6 and Proverbs 3:34)

One important aspect of pride is to think more highly of yourself than you should, or to take too much onto yourself (Romans 12:3). When a person or institution attempts to take for himself or herself more than God has granted, they are acting in pride and presumption. They are trying to act beyond the limits of God's call and therefore beyond the provision of grace for them. It is pride because they believe they can be effective beyond what God has gifted and given them grace for.

On the other hand, the opposite is also true. When we are unwilling or hesitant to take responsibility for all that God has granted us, then we are operating in fear and unbelief. We are limiting ourselves by our own abilities and insecurities rather than trusting in God's wise appointment of us and His empowering help. It is reported that Moody's farewell words to his sons as he lay on his deathbed were, "If God be your partner – make your plans large."

True humility, that which receives God's grace, neither attempts to go beyond what God has called us to nor does it doubt God's promise to enable us to function effectively in our God-given role. Institutions, as well as individuals, must remember this rule.

CHAPTER 21

THE SWORD AND THE KEYS

God's government on the earth operates through four basic institutions or realms. These are:

- Human conscience/self government
- The family
- The church
- Civil government

God has assigned certain responsibilities and authority to each of the four. This is God's plan for governing and caring for the world.

The first level is that of self-government or self-control through the human conscience. God's plan is that individuals would govern their own actions according to their conscience which is instructed by the Word of God. In this way God's righteousness and peace is advanced and society enjoys great freedom and justice. Leaving this level of God's government aside, let us look at the proper balance of the other three, that of the family, the church and civil government.

When each of these three spheres of authority operates within its God-given boundaries, He gives it power and grace to be effective. The problem comes when one of those spheres will not take responsibility for the area that God has given it (this is often the case with the family), or when one of the spheres attempts to overstep its bounds and trespass on that which has been assigned to another (this is typically the problem with civil government).

CHURCH AND STATE

But how can we know what areas of life God has assigned to each of the human agents of His government? The answer is, of course, to be found in the Bible. God's government on earth operates through two distinct spheres: the civil government and the church. (Ideally, the family, God's third main agent of His rule, operates as a subset of the church. The Christian family is the smallest unit of the church, and the church is the largest expression of the Christian family, which is the redeemed family of God).

The Bible gives us keys to dividing up the different areas of responsibility between the civil government and the church. We read that God has given the sword to the civil government and the keys to the church.

For (civil) rulers are not a cause of fear for good behavior, but for evil. Do you want to have no fear of authority? Do what is good and you will have praise from the same; for it is a minister of God to you for good. BUT IF YOU DO WHAT IS EVIL, BE AFRAID; FOR IT DOES NOT BEAR THE SWORD FOR NOTHING; FOR IT IS A MINISTER OF GOD, AN AVENGER WHO BRINGS WRATH ON THE ONE WHO PRACTICES EVIL.

Romans 13:3-4

Here we have the purpose and role of civil government laid out. Its symbol is the sword, which is the symbol of COERCIVE POWER. Coercive power is power that is great enough to force someone to comply. Civil government's main purpose is to use force to restrain and punish evil and therefore protect that which is good.

Jesus gives quite a different symbol for the authority of the church. This symbol also will define its purpose and role in God's government.

I also say to you that you are Peter, and upon this rock I WILL BUILD MY CHURCH; and the gates of Hades will not overpower it. I WILL GIVE YOU THE KEYS TO THE KINGDOM OF HEAVEN; and whatever you bind on earth shall have been bound in heaven, and whatever you loose on earth shall have been loosed in heaven.

Matthew 16:18-19

Here you have it, the state has the sword and the church has the keys. These define the differing roles for the two.

The state or civil authorities have been granted the right and authority to use coercive power to restrain evil and punish wrongdoers. This includes the right to arrest, detain, and even exercise capital punishment (Genesis 9:6). This also includes the right to raise an army and fight wars, and to have sanctioned regulatory powers that ensure public safety. This is what is implied in God giving the state the sword. These are powers that are specifically denied the church. The church is forbidden from using coercive force.

Never pay back evil for evil to anyone.

Romans 12:17

Never take your own revenge, beloved, but leave room for the wrath of God, for it is written, "VENGEANCE IS MINE, I WILL REPAY," says the Lord. "BUT IF YOUR ENEMY IS HUNGRY, FEED HIM, AND IF HE IS THIRSTY, GIVE HIM SOMETHING TO DRINK; FOR IN SO DOING YOU WILL HEAP BURNING COALS ON HIS HEAD." Do not be overcome by evil but overcome evil with good.

Romans 12:19-21

These verses address the church and forbid us from seeking vengeance or using violence. Several verses later, we read that God has given the state the sword to punish evil and act as His avenger (Romans 13:3-4). The above-cited verses are for the church and not the state. A Christian cannot serve as a policeman nor as a serviceman in the military if he does not understand the difference. He can serve God's Kingdom in both the sphere of the church and the sphere of civil government, but he has different God-given roles in each.

The church is specifically forbidden the sword. Jesus forbade Peter, the first member of the church, to use his sword. Peter had drawn out his sword and struck at one who had come to arrest Jesus. Jesus said to him:

Put your sword back into its place, for all who live by the sword shall perish by the sword.

Matthew 26:52

RESPECTING GOD'S BOUNDARIES

The darkest hours in church history have come when the church has forgotten its place and has tried to take up the sword. We are still trying to live down the dishonor earned by the Inquisition and the Crusades many centuries later. The church is not allowed to use force in fulfilling her mission.

Islam has no prohibition on the religious community taking up the sword and the result has been fanatical violence and unspeakable horror. This underscores for us the necessity for honoring the clear biblical injunction against the church taking up the sword or using coercive power.

What the church has been given is far more powerful than the sword. The church has been given keys to the Kingdom. Whereas the sword represents the coercive power to punish and restrain evil, the keys represent the truth, love and grace that can open up men's hearts and transform them from the inside.

When that same Peter who had been told to put away his sword stood up just weeks later on the Day of Pentecost and preached, he opened up eternal life and the Kingdom of God to three thousand men plus an unknown amount of women and children (Acts 2:37-42). On that day, a power was released that has changed the world more than any other force. Hundreds of millions of lives have been transformed, families have been restored, and whole societies have been raised to new levels of justice and mercy. No sword, no coercive power, no civil government on earth has the authority to do this. Only the church can do this, because only the church has been given keys.

Think about it. What do keys do? Keys unlock things. Keys open doors and chests full of treasure. A sword cannot do this. And understanding this helps us to separate what belongs to the realm of the church and what belongs to the realm the state.

The sword represents the power of man, but the keys represent the limitless supernatural power of God. Only the church can unlock the kingdom of God to people and release the transforming power of God into their lives. It is a well-observed fact that prison, for instance, does not rehabilitate people. The vast majority of those released from prisons return to a life of crime. Government does not have the proper tool to change a person's heart – they have not been given the keys.

This is the reason for the popular saying, "You can't legislate morality." This is true because you cannot change people's hearts and morals simply by changing laws. What laws can do is to help create a just society by restraining evil. Or as Martin Luther King put it so graphically many years ago, "The law may not be able to make a man love me, but it can stop him from lynching me, and I think that is pretty important." Laws can play a part in encouraging moral behavior by punishing immoral behavior, but by themselves they can never change a human heart.

Civil government has not been commissioned to transform or reform individuals or to bring forth the perfect society (otherwise known as the Kingdom of God) and they should not try to. You can't change a human heart with a sword.

You can't make people good by threatening them. The sword is only to restrain and punish evil. It can never give people the spiritual power to be transformed.

The civil government's job is to offer its citizens protection against violence, criminal behavior and injustice. It can protect us from invasion by menacing foreign powers. It can pass laws and sanctions to force people to act in such a way (even against their will) as to promote public safety and basic human rights. But coercive power cannot make men or societies good. It cannot open up heaven to mankind or even create a "heaven on earth." Not understanding this has led to unimaginable horror.

The greatest horrors of the 20th century came from political leaders trying to create the "good society" or "heaven on earth" through political and military force. From Adolph Hitler's attempts to create the "Third Reich" in Germany, to Lenin's and Stalin's efforts in the Soviet Union to create a "workers paradise," to Chairman Mao's bloody "cultural revolution," political leaders have tried to create the ideal society by using the power of the sword.

Political demagogues like Pol Pot in Cambodia, Fidel Castro in Cuba, and many others have joined them in this delusion. The result is that together they have killed hundreds of millions of their own civilian population trying to create a paradise on earth with the power of man. The sad truth is that, in the past century, *more people were killed by their own governments than died in all the wars fought in that century*.

In each of the above situations, the church was banned by the state and the state attempted to take upon itself that which God had reserved for the church. The result was suffering and horror. The state, because it possesses coercive power, is always a threat of overrunning its God-given boundaries. This is especially true when unregenerate people who do not fear God nor respect the Bible come into power. This is a truth that we must never forget, even in our own country.

When the state seizes areas not assigned to it, or robs from the family or church what has been given them by God, it becomes a thief. Further, it becomes illegitimate in its authority. It may exercise power, but it is without authority to do so. God will therefore oppose it. Denis de Rougemont, in his book, *The Devil's Share*, makes the point clear, "One does not become a father by stealing a child. One can steal the child, not paternity. One can steal power, not authority."

CHAPTER 22

NO TRESPASSING

When our Founding Fathers created a new nation, they did so as students of the Bible. Their writings reveal a heavy dependence upon the worldview of the Bible and, in fact, they quote from and allude to it far more than to any other book. They understood the divinely ordained, unique roles and limitations placed upon the church and civil government. This understanding is clearly seen in the Constitution and its amendments as well as other formative documents. In them the role of civil government is strictly limited.

The Founders further sought to limit the growth of the reach of government by establishing the balance of powers. They set the Judicial Branch (the courts), the Executive Branch and the Legislative Branch in balance against each other. Each was meant to restrict the power and slow down the growth of the other branches. They understood from history civil government's appetite to trespass into areas not assigned it.

Perhaps their concern is most clearly seen in the First Amendment to the Constitution, which attempts to limit government's incursion into the area reserved for the church. It reads, "Congress shall make no law respecting an establishment of religion, or prohibiting the free exercise thereof..."

Despite what some people might try to get you to believe, the First Amendment was not written to limit the church, but the state. The early founders of this nation knew that it was the state, because it holds coercive power, that was the real danger of overrunning its boundaries and trespassing into the realms not assigned to it by God. And despite the genius of our Founding Fathers, this is exactly what has been gradually happening in our country.

The secular critics and enemies of the church often raise the cry of "separation of church and state." They do this in an attempt to limit the influence of the church in society. They are correct that religion and the state must be separate. Each has its proper, beneficial, God-given role in the government or rule of God.

The problem is that the state has overrun its boundaries and has stepped into areas that are reserved by God for the family and the church. *And it is precisely in these areas where the conflicts arise.* The truth is, there is almost no area of life where the state has not or is not attempting to rule.

The church and state should not be in competition but should complement one another. The conflict comes because of the insatiable appetite of the humanist state. It wants to grow until it is all encompassing. Just like in the days of the caesars of ancient Rome, it wants to be worshipped as god.

BLESSING OR CURSE?

Remember, the state is only one of four basic realms of God's government. We saw earlier that God apportions and commissions the areas of responsibility to each. We also stated the principle that: WITHIN THE BOUNDARIES OF THEIR COMMISSION GOD BLESSES AND ASSISTS THEM, BUT WHEN THEY ATTEMPT TO GO BEYOND THOSE BOUNDARIES GOD OPPOSES THEM.

This can be clearly seen in the performance of our government. In those areas where it is rightly operating it does remarkably well and receives generally high marks from its citizens. This is because within its appointed assignments, God blesses and assists it.

For instance, who can deny that our military has been remarkably blessed and successful in its history? Our military enjoys high respect by our citizens. Likewise, our police and fire are very good at what they have been called to do and are looked upon as heroes by many of their fellow citizens. Governmental laws promoting public safety, such as building and fire codes, have made this the safest nation in history. Regulations which prohibit unjust and unrighteous business practices and which ensure honest measurements, weights and standards have helped create the environment in which the strongest economy in world history could develop.

While some might argue that government goes too far in some of its regulations, it must be admitted that, in the areas that are its proper domain, it has succeeded and enjoys the respect of its citizens. What all of these have in common is that they are properly within the civil government's realm, the realm of the sword or coercive power. But in other areas the government does not fare so well.

How can we explain the fact that the same government that can win the Gulf War and the war in Afghanistan so easily, that can develop our highway system, that can so efficiently protect the life and health of its citizens living in large urban areas, can also produce our permanent welfare underclass through its welfare programs, fail so miserably to rehabilitate criminals through its penal system, and produce an education system that scores near dead last of all developed nations, despite spending more per student. The failure of public education, for instance, is so stunning as to prompt a government study of it to title itself "A Nation at Risk." That study made the following striking assessment of government's educational performance:

> If an unfriendly foreign power had attempted to impose on America the mediocre educational performance that exists today, we might well have viewed it as an act of war. As it stands, we have allowed this to happen to ourselves...we have, in effect, been committing an act of unthinking, unilateral educational disarmament.
>
> National Commission on
> Excellence in Education
> *A Nation At Risk* 1983

Nationally syndicated columnist Don Feder wrote, "Public education is hopeless. A society with even a minimal survival instinct would be moving as quickly as possible toward private schooling."

In each of these above areas, the government is not respected but criticized, and its record is clearly one of failure and not success. That is because these are areas that require something that the civil government is not equipped to supply. To succeed in these areas requires the ability to produce change in people by spiritual transformation and the development of faith, hope and love. The church has been given the keys to the Kingdom by the King and is therefore equipped to do just that; the government is not. It is against God's will for the government to be in these areas. He opposes the incursion into what He has properly assigned to another. Rather than blessing it, He opposes it. It will therefore not prosper. Christians are naïve to ask God to bless what is outside His will.

Whereas the state has largely failed in these areas, we see the church producing great results among the same populations. Prison Fellowship, a Christian ministry headed up by former White House aide and ex-felon, Charles Colson, works with inmates in some of

America's toughest prisons. Recent studies have shown the effectiveness of Prison Fellowship's Christ-centered and Bible-centered approach. For instance, in a South Carolina study at Lieber Medium Security Men's Prison, only 10% of the inmates who participated in the Prison Fellowship program committed prison infractions, compared to 23% of those who did not participate, or nearly two and a half times less. And the more involved an inmate was with PF's program, the less likely they were to commit an infraction.

Likewise, in a New York study of recidivism among former inmates of New York prisons, Prison Fellowship participants greatly outperformed those who were in other programs or no programs at all. Only 14% of those who had been involved in Prison Fellowship programs were rearrested during the 12 months following their release, compared to 41%, or three times the percentage, of a matched comparison group of inmates who did not attend PF programs. No doubt, the results would be even more dramatic if Prison Fellowship could oversee the entire correctional program, using Biblical keys and principles, rather than just be a part of the state-run process.

Teen Challenge, another evangelical Christian organization, for years has had a far, far greater success rate with drug addicts than government or secular programs. A recent study compared the effectiveness of Teen Challenge with several state-funded secular therapeutic programs. It revealed that after one year, 28% of the graduates of the secular state-funded programs were listed as "highly favorable" outcomes (i.e., no arrests or incarcerations and no drug use apart from occasional marijuana use), compared to 86% of the graduates of Teen Challenge who scored as "highly favorable."

Likewise, home schooling parents and Christian schools produce far superior outcomes with just a fraction of the resources. Columnist Don Feder recently gave some grim statistics in comparing state-run and church-run education.

> Want to know why the establishment dreads private schooling? Compare the records of the two systems which educate Chicago's children. In the Windy City's public schools, the drop out rate is between 43% and 53%. In its Catholic school, whose enrollment is mostly black and Hispanic, less than 1% drop out, more than 70% go on to college. It costs roughly four times as much to educate a student in Chicago's public schools as in their parochial counterparts.

When we say that the church has been given the keys, we mean the keys that open the Kingdom and its grace and blessing to people. These are the keys that unlock the benefits that come from Christ's death on the cross, His resurrection, and sending of the Holy Spirit. It is the gospel of the Kingdom that transforms people through the very power of God.

> *For I am not ashamed of the gospel, FOR IT IS THE POWER OF GOD FOR SALVATION to everyone who believes, to the Jew first and also to the Greek.*
>
> Romans 1:16

> *For the WORD OF THE CROSS is foolishness to those who are perishing, but to those who are being saved IT IS THE POWER OF GOD*
>
> 1 Corinthians 1:18

When Jesus promised Peter to give him the keys to the Kingdom (Matthew 16:18-19), He was promising to give him the principles and truths that would allow people to enter into the blessings and power of that Kingdom. It begins with the principles of repentance and faith toward Jesus and continues with the many other Biblical principles that enlarge the Kingdom's power and influence into our lives, families and world. Some of these principles are in this book and many more are included in the companion book *Breakthrough Kingdom Living.*

THE WRONG FIGHT

Many Christians, recognizing the great destructiveness that has come from the removal of God from public life and the marginalizing of religion, are desperately trying to find a way for government to accommodate religion in its institutions. Their opponents fight them, arguing that the state must stay neutral in areas of religion due to the Constitution (as they interpret it) and the need to protect the rights of all citizens in a pluralistic society. And so we have battlegrounds over prayer in school, religious displays on public property, and tax subsidies to certain organizations. *But this fight is on the wrong battlefield.* Christians can agree that civil government should stay neutral. The battleground should be over the proper role and domain of government.

In all areas of the sword's realm we must have religious tolerance or else we would risk the tyranny and oppression found in Islamic societies. And after all, why would a particular religion need to come into play in fighting a war, arresting a burglar, checking weights and measures or fixing potholes in streets? There is no need for conflict with religion in these areas. It is enough that the public officials follow the general standards of righteousness and justice to which the human conscience, the Bible, and even many other religions point to. But specific religious doctrines are not at issue in these functions. The conflict is caused because the sword is constantly trespassing into the realm of the keys.

You see, religion is not properly at stake in the building of a highway but it certainly is in the education and socialization of a child. Education must prepare a child to succeed in life and make a positive contribution to society. *More than that, education is the formation of the human soul.* How can a child be said to be educated who doesn't know the reasons for his birth or the purpose of life or the difference between right and wrong, or even whether God exists? How can we say that we have educated a child if we have not given her a strong moral code or addressed her spiritual nature?

And yet these are all religious issues. *In fact, the questions that religion attempts to answer weave themselves in and out of many academic subjects. They are impossible to avoid.* The problem is that the state must avoid religious discussions, or worse yet, they must by definition give nonreligious answers to religious questions.

They cannot, for instance, discuss the possibility of a Creator but must instead teach all about the origin of the world as if a Creator did not exist. GOD IS DENIED BY OMISSION. In fact, every dimension of life in this world must be taught from the perspective that there is no Creator and therefore no plan, no absolute right and wrong, and no guide for life. Children must be treated as if they had no spiritual dimension but were merely a physical bundle of chemical reactions determined by evolutionary accident. Can we really call this educating a child? *What other society in history would accept this as a definition of education?*

The simple fact is that ANY INSTITUTION THAT CANNOT ADDRESS RELIGIOUS ISSUES HAS JUST DISQUALIFIED ITSELF FROM EDUCATION by definition.

It may be argued that these issues should be addressed at home. This is certainly true. In fact, this is precisely the point. The child's education should reflect the parent's values and beliefs or it will certainly undermine them.

However, this is exactly what the civil government can't do. It must appear to remain absolutely neutral or irreligious. And yet this is impossible. It is impossible to educate anyone and avoid questions and issues that are religious or have religious implications. The state must supply answers that appear to be nonreligious but are really hostile to traditional religion. Because it can't avoid religious issues in education, it ends up teaching the religion of secular humanism or even new age religion and therefore undermines the values and beliefs of the great majority of our families.

The Bible assigns the education of young people to their parents and their faith community.

Hear, O Israel! The Lord is our God, the Lord is one. You shall love the Lord your God with all your heart and with all your soul and with all your might. These words, which I am commanding you today, shall be on your heart. YOU SHALL TEACH THEM DILIGENTLY TO YOUR SONS AND SHALL TALK OF THEM WHEN YOU SIT IN YOUR HOUSE and when you walk by the way and when you lie down and when you rise up.

Deuteronomy 6:4-7

For He established a testimony in Jacob and APPOINTED A LAW IN ISRAEL, WHICH HE COMMANDED OUR FATHERS THAT THEY SHOULD TEACH THEM TO THEIR CHILDREN, THAT THE GENERATION TO COME MIGHT KNOW, even the children yet to be born, THAT THEY MAY ARISE AND TEACH THEM TO THEIR CHILDREN.

Psalm 78:5-6

Note that *the responsibility to educate our children is clearly placed on the shoulders of the parents (and not the government)* and it takes place in the home and all the other venues of daily life. This does not refer to "religious instruction" only, as if it only includes such things as the "Golden Rule" and John 3:16.

The Scripture cited above, Psalm 78, refers to instructing our children in the "Law" which translates the Hebrew word "Torah." The Torah, or Law, is God's authoritative instructions on every area of life. The Bible addresses all areas of life, such as marriage, economics, law, criminal justice and public health. It is a humanistic misunderstanding that restricts the Bible to only "religious truth." The Bible is the foundation for all truth.

Note also that this is a recurring charge that goes from generation to generation as Psalm 78:6 makes clear. This is quite simply God's plan for the raising up of a generation that walks in truth and blessing. *It is how He intends to perpetuate the blessings of salvation from generation to generation and extend His Kingdom on the earth.* To ignore or despise God's plan is to ensure great loss for the generation of our children.

This does not mean, therefore, that all parents must educate their children at home. This would not be possible or prudent. Parents may certainly select others to aid them in educating their children but it must be according to the parent's values and beliefs. The parents and not the state have been charged with the responsibility of educating and training the young. Children have been given to the authority of the parents and not the state or educational bureaucrats. In the final analysis, our kids are just that – OUR kids.

Many Christians seem to have forgotten what King Nebuchadnezzar understood. He defeated Jerusalem and carried off their brightest children. For three years, Nebuchadnezzar took those Jewish youth and put them in Babylonian schools, made them wear Babylonian clothes, listen to Babylonian music, and eat Babylonian food. He figured that they would become Babylonians and that he would own them for life, and he was right (except for four kids who refused it).

IN THE FOOTSTEPS OF DANIEL, JOSEPH, AND NEHEMIAH

If you are a Christian who is involved in public education as a teacher, administrator or support staff, you may be wondering what this means for you. First, let me say that I thank God for you. I thank God that you are serving Him in the public school. Certainly salt and light is needed there and it can be a fruitful ministry. At present, public schools are a reality. If all the public schools closed down tomorrow, we would have chaos. We would have no place to put all the students. We need to continue to have a strategy to minister to our public schools.

However, we must realize that it is only a temporary strategy. In the long run, it will be a losing strategy, if we do not have a plan to restore the responsibility for education back where it belongs – in the hands of parents assisted by the church or whatever entity or organization they choose.

We must strive to glorify Christ in the public schools. But it is not God's plan for us. It is not the promised land. My friend Jim Gilbert loves to point out that both Joseph and Daniel prospered while they were living as captives in foreign lands. Joseph served nobly in Egypt and rose to become Pharaoh's right-hand man. Daniel served the kings of Babylon and Persia and rose to the highest levels. In their respective positions, they did much good for their society, and especially for their people, the Jews. But they never forgot that where they were was not the promised land.

Daniel prayed three times daily facing Jerusalem (Daniel 6:10) and petitioned God mightily for the return of the Jews to the promised land (Daniel 9:1-3, 16-19). Likewise, Nehemiah, although he served the king of Persia as an exile and was very successful, rising to the rank of cup-bearer, nevertheless his heart was with those who had returned to rebuild Jerusalem (Nehemiah 1:1-11). Eventually Nehemiah left his position of power and wealth to return to the promised land and rebuild the Holy City (Nehemiah 2:4-11). In the same spirit, Joseph, although he had attained to the highest rank in Egypt next to Pharaoh, instructed the descendants to look for the coming day that God would give them the promised land, and gave orders that when this day came, his bones should be exhumed and reburied in the promised land (Genesis 50:24, Hebrews 11:22).

Remember, it is good to serve God in the public schools, but it is wrong to settle for that. It is wrong to not support those who are working to establish education according to God's purpose and plan. All of us must support the effort to restore God's boundaries.

The state also threatens to invade the home in areas of family discipline. While the state does have a role in protecting the weak against physical violence in the home, this does not include the right to determine what forms normal discipline, short of that which causes clear injury, should take. These are areas reserved for the family, informed by the church.

While we have largely restricted our argument to that of education and child rearing, much more could be said on this subject and other subjects, such as care for the poor, rehabilitation of substance abusers, juvenile delinquents and the homeless, and many other social programs.

CHAPTER 23

RESTORING GOD'S BOUNDARIES

A football team was being demolished by their opponents. They were nearly ground into the turf each time they tried to carry the ball. So their coach yelled from the sideline, "Give LeRoy the ball!" On the next play, however, someone other than LeRoy carried it, and was quickly crushed by the opposing defense. The coach yelled again, "Give LeRoy the ball!" But once more someone else took it, and was immediately beaten down by the other team. The coach called out a third time for LeRoy to take the ball. This time the quarterback ran over to the sideline and said, "But Coach, LeRoy doesn't want the ball!"

Often we look at problems around us and hope someone else will solve them. Like LeRoy, we don't want the ball. However, as we come to understand ourselves as agents of the rightful King and instruments of His irresistible Kingdom, our belief in what is possible expands and our enthusiasm is stirred.

As citizens in a representative democracy, we are the responsible party for the condition of our society. We are those who are responsible to maintain the proper balance and boundaries of the three spheres of authority in God's earthly government: the family, the church and civil government. The Bible specifically charges us to keep the boundaries which God has set by His own wisdom and authority.

Do not move the ancient boundary which your fathers have set.

Proverbs 22:28

Do not move the ancient boundary or go into the fields of the fatherless.

Proverbs 23:10

The boundary markers being referred to are those that were set up to give each family their inheritance in the Promised Land. God delivered this land into the hands of His people, as He had promised, and then apportioned a share to each family.

So He brought them to His holy land... He also drove out the nations before them AND APPORTIONED THEM AN

INHERITANCE BY MEASUREMENT, and made the tribes of Israel dwell in their tents.

Psalms 78:54-55

God specifically determined each family's inheritance and then had Joshua set up boundary stones during the conquest of the land. These boundary markers ensured that each subsequent generation would receive their inheritance. These boundaries were not to be moved lest the next generation be robbed of their rightful inheritance. God promised a curse on those who moved them.

You shall not move your neighbor's boundary mark, which the ancestors have set, in your inheritance which you shall inherit in the land that the Lord your God gives you to possess.

Deuteronomy 19:14

Cursed is he who moves his neighbor's boundary mark.

Deuteronomy 27:17

Our promised inheritance as Christians is not a literal earthly homeland, but it is all of God's covenant promises to us in the Bible. God has set up spiritual, moral, and jurisdictional boundaries in His Word that ensure His people can live in blessing free from the curse and destruction. These boundary markers allow us to receive our full inheritance which Jesus secured for us by His death and resurrection. Our founding fathers, as well as subsequent generations, labored hard to establish these biblical boundaries in our country to ensure God's inheritance and blessing to their children's children.

Unfortunately, in recent decades, people have gone into the fields and moved our society's God ordained boundary markers. They have changed the moral guidelines, spiritual character, and behavioral standards of our society. They have extended the role of government and attempted to undermine the role of church and family. By so doing, they have robbed not only us, but also our children, of God's blessing and their full inheritance. The result is a society that preys upon the young and naive and an educational system that can only be called "institutionalized child abuse." What else could we label a system in which such a high percentage of our kids are going to be overcome by destructive forces?

It is a system in which not only will a very high number of our children fail academically, but also they will daily be surrounded by temptations that they are unable to manage at their present level of maturity. Worse yet, they are encountering these temptations in an environment where the spiritual, moral and religious beliefs and resources that might help them overcome these temptations are antiseptically removed and even undermined. Many of our youth develop problems during their middle school and high school years that will dominate and plague them for the rest of their lives.

The results of decades of this are predictable. Note the following statistics:

- One million teens attempt suicide every year.
- In 2001, 41.4% of 12th graders reported having used illegal drugs in the past year. Many of these will end up losing their lives to drugs or battle addiction all of their lives.
- Four in ten girls become pregnant during their teen years. Many of these will spend their lives in poverty.
- The three leading causes of death among teens are drunk driving, suicide and murder.
- Teenagers are 3 times as likely to be victims of violent crime as adults.

GAINING GOD'S FULL BLESSING
FOR OUR CHILDREN

Growing up in America is not safe. How could we become so numb to such confusion and suffering and continue to allow it to take place? *God calls us as patriots and parents to restore the ancient boundaries.* We must restore the jurisdictional boundaries (as well as the moral and spiritual ones) in our society. It is vain for us to pray to God for His full blessing upon our children if we do not restore the boundaries in which that inheritance and blessing can come to them. God has committed Himself to fulfill His promises through His proper administrators. We must reclaim the boundaries for our families and churches.

Parents can no longer simply send their children off to church and maybe Bible camps once a year and expect that alone to ensure that their children will love, trust and serve God. We cannot escape the fact that we are our children's primary influence and teachers. Parents must reclaim their boundaries.

Parents must first make sure that they love God with all their hearts and minds and are serving Him in sincerity. They must seek to grow strong in their faith so that they can live lives that are an example and inspiration to their children. They must pray with them and discuss the Scriptures with them. They must show them how a family turns to God and trusts God in all the affairs and troubles of life.

I thank God for the impact that children's workers and youth leaders have had on my three sons, but they can't take my place. Nor can they entirely make up for my failings or shortcomings. God has appointed that my wife and I have the primary shaping influence over our children. We must maintain this boundary and possess it with Jesus' help.

Through our Youth Venture Teen Centers, we have worked with many troubled teens and have witnessed for ourselves the incredible change in those children when their parents come to faith in Christ and begin to operate within God's directions for parents. The results are far beyond what we could ever accomplish with our program alone. Without the parents' involvement, our effectiveness is often limited.

The family must rise up and reclaim their spiritual responsibilities and boundaries.

TRAIN UP A CHILD

In the same way, we can no longer simply blindly send our children off to government schools, trusting them to be responsible to educate our children. It is not enough for us to pray for our schools since God does not want to bless that which is outside of His will. It is not His plan that we relinquish the education of our children to the civil government. He has given children to parents. God will bless His plan, not ours.

This is probably the primary reason why so many Christian parents are not enjoying the promised blessing of Proverbs 22:6:

> *Train up a child in the way that He should go, Even when he is old he will not depart from it.*
>
> Proverbs 22:6

The Hebrew word *"hanak,"* translated *"train up,"* is elsewhere used for dedicating a temple or house (Deuteronomy 25:25; 1 Kings 8:63). In fact, this is its primary usage. It means to "set apart." A child is to be set apart to the Lord by the training and education he receives. A secondary meaning is to "fill the hand." So it also emphasizes that this training must be comprehensive, literally "filling" the child with God's truth and ways. Countering an entire week's worth of humanistic instruction and training with a couple of hours of church or Sunday School does not qualify one to claim this promise with any confidence.

The truth is that many Christians are largely allowing a humanistic state to train up their children. If we want to see our children blessed and receive the full inheritance that only comes to those who continue in the "way they should go," then we must be the ones who train them up.

HOPE FOR NATIONAL REVIVAL

And if we truly want to see the national revival and reformation we pray for, we must do something. We must return to God and to obedience to His way. One of the things this will mean is that the church must make assisting Christian parents in educating and "training up" their children among its highest priorities. This must become more important than building bigger and more luxurious buildings or being the fastest growing church in town. *It will require a huge shift in priorities and resources.*

This will mean that many churches must band together to form schools. I am convinced that lasting revival and national renewal cannot take place as long as children, and Christian children in particular, are educated in secular government schools. It is simply naive to think otherwise. It is vain to pray for national revival if we will not do this thing. *To continue the present course is to reject God's plan for blessing ourselves and our children.*

If we are not satisfied with what is happening with the youth of our nation, and even the children in our own churches, we must be willing to make serious changes. It is not enough to tinker with small changes or to simply throw more money at systems that are fundamentally flawed and wrong-headed. One definition of insanity is to continue to do the same thing and to expect different results. My friend Bill Wilson of Metro Ministries in New York told me of a test to see if mental patients are ready to be released. The examiners stop up a sink and let it overflow. Then they send the candidate in with a mop. If he turns off the faucet first – he's good to go. If he just starts mopping, then it's time to keep him a bit longer.

I know that this is a hard thing for people to hear. This will make people angry. But our problem is that we are a humanistic, lawless generation. *We are always wanting God to accept and bless our choices and plans rather than being willing to learn His ways and conform to them.* Often we feel that there is nothing we can do to fix things. We hope that God will understand and bless us anyway. However, the truth is that whenever we are operating outside of His plans and ways, we bring about much suffering on ourselves. We must be willing to act in order to bring our children into the sphere of protection and blessing.

Today, half an hour north of Bishop, California, there lies a beautiful lake against the majestic Sierra Nevada Mountains, called Convict Lake. Rising up behind Convict Lake is Mount Morrison. Convict Lake and Mount Morrison are so named because in 1871 a group of prisoners escaped from jail in Carson City, Nevada. A posse formed under a leader named Robert Morrison. The posse pursued the convicts and trapped them at the sheer cliffs at the end of Convict Lake. There was a fierce gun battle and Morrison was killed. Several convicts were also killed, and several others escaped and were arrested three weeks later in Bishop.

Robert Morrison risked his life, as did all of the posse members, because they understood something. They had to take responsibility for their world. If they did not want their world to go into chaos with runaway prisoners and criminals, they had to mount up, they had to ride out, they had to put themselves in harm's way. It took courage and sacrifice. As Christians, we must take responsibility. Unlike LeRoy, we must not refuse the ball.

Many people believe that changing things is simply impossible. They do not believe they have resources to do what needs to be done. But this is exactly why we must learn to enter fully into God's Kingdom. In God's Kingdom there are no shortages or lack. In God's Kingdom we become His partner and therefore, *"All things are possible to him who believes* (Mark 9:23)." If we would bring about God's will through His power and riches then we would not need excuses and rationalizations. We would simply inherit the blessings.

CHAPTER 24

THE CONGRESS OF THE KINGDOM

As we have already seen, God's government is distributed through three primary institutions; the family, the church and civil government. As we have seen as well, when the boundaries between these are violated, tragedy results.

This threefold division is evident as far back as the Books of Moses. Israel was organized around three basic offices. Priests were the religious heads, judges (and later kings) represented civil authority, and the elders represented the families and tribes (in later Israel the body of ruling elders became known as the Sanhedrin).

After the Resurrection of Jesus, the church became the pre-eminent focus of the government of the Kingdom of God. While the boundaries are clear between the three spheres of authority, the church is the center of God's redemptive work and now seeks to influence the other two institutions, the family and civil government.

The church attempts to influence family and civil government by changing hearts and minds. It does this by preaching the good news of Jesus Christ and then making men and women disciples by *"teaching them to observe all that I have commanded you"* (Matthew 28:20). Such transformed and trained individuals will in turn renew and bring righteousness to every other institution. In this task, the church works closely with the family, which should train children in the knowledge of God and the laws of His Kingdom. In fact, as we have stated before, ideally, the family is the smallest unit of the church, which is God's own family.

THE AUTHORITY OF THE CHURCH

When Jesus was traveling about Israel and establishing His followers, there were two basic expressions of public religion. There was, of course, the Temple in Jerusalem where the people would go for the annual feasts and which was the only place where the sacrifices were offered. And there was also the synagogue system.

The word, "synagogue" comes from two Greek words, which literally translate "a bringing together" (*sun*, "together," and *ago*, "to bring"). Synagogues were a gathering of Jewish believers. They were very similar to our local churches in that they met weekly for prayer, scripture reading and instruction. A Rabbi or Chief of the synagogue oversaw them. Synagogues were located in nearly every city, town and village in Israel. In fact, there were synagogues in most major cities of the Roman Empire. The only requirement to forming a synagogue was that there were at least 10 Jewish men to attend it.

It may surprise some to realize that the gospels never portray Jesus as referring to His followers as a synagogue. He didn't say that "I will build My synagogue and the gates of Hades will not overpower it." In fact, He did not tell His disciples to go out and plant Christian "synagogues" around the world. No, according to the New Testament, Jesus didn't choose a *religious* word at all to refer the company of His followers. He chose a *secular* word that was commonly used in the world of His day.

EKKLESIA

The word that is used is *"ekklesia,"* which we translate as "church." The word comes from two root words: *"ek,"* meaning "out of" and *"klesis,"* "a calling." It was originally used for the summons to the army to assemble. From the 5th century BC it came to refer to the assembly of full citizens of *"the polis,"* ("city") that met at regular intervals to conduct the city's business. It was a group that was "called out" under authority to act as a legislative-governing body for the city. *Vines Expository Dictionary* defines the word this way; "[It] was used among the Greeks of a body of citizens 'gathered' to discuss the affairs of state." The famous assembly (*ekklesia*) of Athens met 30 to 40 times a year.

The term was in common usage throughout the Mediterranean area in New Testament times. Greek city-states had ruled using this form of government for over 300 years. We see this legislative-governing usage in the Book of Acts. In Acts 19, we find Paul in Ephesus. Paul's ministry is so successful, and so many people are abandoning the idols and false temples, that the silversmiths who made the silver shrines were losing much business. As this was a major trade in Ephesus, it was having a serious economic impact. A riot began, instigated by the silversmiths and led by a man named Demetrius. The crowd spilled into the amphitheater where the town meetings were held. Paul wanted to go in and formally address the charges, but the other believers feared for his life.

And when Paul wanted to go into the Assembly (ekklesia), the disciples would not let him.

Acts 19:30

When Paul could not be found, the crowd mistakenly turned on another Jew who tried to speak to defend himself:

Some of the crowd concluded it was Alexander, since the Jews had put him forward; and having motioned with his hand, Alexander WAS INTENDING TO MAKE A DEFENSE TO THE ASSEMBLY. (ekklesia)

Acts 19:33

As things got increasingly out of hand, the town clerk dismissed the gathering because it was not a legally sanctioned ekklesia, but a mob. Listen to his words:

So then, if Demetrius and the craftsmen who are with him have a complaint against any man, THE COURTS ARE IN SESSION AND PROCONSULS ARE AVAILABLE; let them bring charges against one another. But if you want anything beyond this, IT SHALL BE SETTLED IN THE LAWFUL ASSEMBLY (ekklesia).

Acts 19:38-39

Note that the town official makes several points clear that accord with what we know about the civil affairs of that time. First, the function of the courts was to rule on the law and Demetrius could bring an accusation against Paul there. Second, he mentions that further action could be legislated in the assembly (*ekklesia*) if it were legally noticed and constituted.

This was the common usage of the word at the time. It was a legally called together gathering of people who had authority *to legislate* and "*settle things.*" This is how the first readers of the New Testament understood the word that Jesus chose to describe His followers. According to *The Dictionary of New Testament Theology*, the word was never used by the Greeks to refer to a religious gathering.

It is significant that there were several Greek words to use for "religious gatherings" (chiefly *thiasos, eranos* and *synodos*). The New Testament, however, uses none of these to refer to the company of Christ's followers. Even the word *synagogue* is used only once in relation to Christians in James 2:2. Instead, it uses this secular word, *ekklesia,* which refers to a governing body of assembled citizens. This is the word that we translate as "church."

It is inescapable that Jesus and the Apostles wished to convey the sense that His called-together followers were more than a "feel good" religious club. They constituted a governing body for His Kingdom. The church is the governing and legislating body for the Kingdom of God, which is chief over all the kingdoms of the world. It consists of born-again believers who are enrolled as disciples of Christ and who have been "called out" and elected to govern with King Jesus. As we demonstrated in Chapter 7 in commenting on Ephesians 1:20-23, CHRIST'S PLAN IS TO RULE EARTH FROM HEAVEN THROUGH HIS CHURCH.

Unfortunately, the word "church" has come to mean something very different to us today than what Jesus had intended to convey. Now people use it to mean a religious meeting, or a building that houses "religious activity," rather than what Jesus meant by using the word, which was a *ruling assembly with His authority*. Today, people relate potluck dinners, hymn singing, children's Sunday School programs and poorly-produced Christmas pageants with church, but not ruling or governing the world. Since we think in terms of words, our lack of understanding of the true meaning of the word "church" defines and limits what we expect of it.

Dennis Peacocke has pointed out that of the three main words used in the New Testament to refer to the body of Christ's disciples, *ekklesia* is used most often. The phrase "Body of Christ" or "Body" which emphasizes the "caring community" and "multi-gifted nature" of the church is used 40 times in the New Testament. The term "Bride" or "Bride of Christ" which stresses our worship and love of Jesus as well as our future destiny with Him in heaven is used 20 times. But the word "church," which stresses our governing function under the Kingdom of God, is used 113 times. The church must recover a sense of its call and responsibility to rule and govern with Christ's authority.

God Is in Our Midst

We rejoice that we have been made justified so that God's Spirit can now dwell among us. We rejoice in His presence in our worship. We are built up by the activity of His Spirit's gifts among us. But sometimes we forget that one of His purposes in being restored to our midst is so that He can rule the earth through partnership with us. This is pictured for us in Psalm 82. It opens up with a picture of God in His place of earthly rule and judgment, which is in the center of His covenant community or congregation.

God takes His stand in His own congregation; He judges in the midst of the rulers.

Psalm 82:1

Here we see God in the midst of His ruling assembly, standing up to make a judgment. What follows is a rebuke to that unfaithful generation of delegated rulers, but it also serves as a listing of our commission as God's *ekklesia* for this generation.

How long will you judge unjustly, and show partiality to the wicked? Vindicate the weak and fatherless; do justice to the afflicted and destitute. Rescue the weak and needy; deliver them out of the hand of the wicked.

Psalm 82:2-4

This is our glorious purpose. Through the commission of God, we are to overcome injustice and bring God's merciful rule among our generation. We have received all we need to accomplish it. God has given us His authority, His Word, new regenerated hearts, the indwelling Spirit of God to guide us, and the Baptism of the Holy Spirit to empower us. Through these we have become God's partners, or agents. We exercise His authority and bring about His will, because we empowered by His irresistible Kingdom.

People who understand this cannot be defeated. They are resilient and overcome all obstacles. They change even "impossible" situations because they understand the inevitable victory of God's Kingdom and the surpassing authority and power of Christ Jesus.

For the first seven years of Adoniram Judson's missionary service in Burma, he did not see one single convert to Christ. Still, he worked diligently to bring Jesus' message to the Burmese people. His hope was to eventually translate the Bible into the Burmese language. But because Judson's work was viewed as hostile to the government, he became a political prisoner. His wife, Anne, brought food to him each day and passed it to him through the small barred window just above ground level in his tiny prison cell.

One day Anne told Judson that his Christian supporters had written to discover what his needs were. Without hesitation, after imprisonment and seven years of not reaching a single person for Christ, Judson said, "Tell them to send a communion set. We're going to need it someday." Today, more than 600,000 Christians can trace their roots to this man of faith who saw the need for a communion set. He understood the authority of the church to pull down strongholds and overcome. He knew that the gates of Hell could not overcome the church.

CHAPTER 25

THE FOUNDATION OF THE CHURCH'S AUTHORITY

For us to exercise authority, we must understand the nature of our authority. What is it that gives us authority in our communities? What qualifies us for authority? How do we exercise this authority?

Remember, while God is Creator and owner of the world, He has delegated the rule of it to mankind. This has always been God's purpose for us as He made clear on the day He created mankind.

> *Then God said, "Let Us make man in Our image, according to Our likeness; AND LET THEM RULE over the fish of the sea and over the birds of the sky and over the cattle and OVER ALL THE EARTH, and over every creeping thing that creeps on the earth."*
>
> Genesis 1:26

God gave the rule and authority over earth to us. However, this authority as *delegated* agents of God could only be maintained if we remained in union with Him through obedience. When Adam and Eve fell into sin by believing and obeying Satan rather than God (Genesis 3), we lost a large measure of our authority to Satan. Satan began to exercise a measure of authority over the affairs of mankind and to bring in destruction. (Now, it is important to realize that not only was this true *historically*, so long ago in the garden of Eden, but the principle *continues even today to bring individuals* who believe Satan's lies over God's Word into bondage and destruction).

Ever since then, God has worked to restore mankind's godly authority over the earth by renewing our union with Him through a Covenant and then establishing His covenant people in His covenant Word or Law (*Torah*). It is through living out God's Torah (law/ instruction) that His people would bring God's order back to the world.

In the Old Testament, God began this process by making a covenant with Abraham and his descendants, and then giving them

His law through Moses. God's Kingdom and rule became centered in Israel and especially in Israel's temple.

Unfortunately, Israel was unable to be faithful partners and delegated agents of God's authority. The Old Testament reveals a long history of failure. This is because although they were given God's Torah, they did not have their hearts regenerated yet. This meant that, although they knew God's Law, they were not able to keep it (Romans 7:21-8:4).

THE NEW COVENANT

God promised them a future covenant in which they would not only have the Law (Torah) of God but He would give them new spirits and new hearts with His law written on it.

"Behold, days are coming," declares the Lord, "when I will make a new covenant with the house of Israel and with the house of Judah... But this is the covenant which I will make with the house of Israel after those days," declares the LORD, "I will put My law within them and on their heart I will write it; and I will be their God, and they shall be My people."

Jeremiah 31:31,33

Moreover, I WILL GIVE YOU A NEW HEART AND PUT A NEW SPIRIT WITHIN YOU; and I will remove the heart of stone from your flesh and give you a heart of flesh. AND I WILL PUT MY SPIRIT WITHIN YOU AND CAUSE YOU TO WALK IN MY STATUTES, and you will be careful to observe My ordinances.

Ezekiel 36:26

This promise would be fulfilled in the coming of the Messiah Jesus. Through the perfect obedience of Jesus, even to the point of dying on the cross, mankind's disobedience and rebellion were atoned for. Therefore, mankind's alienation from God was removed, we were made righteous, and union with God was restored. What Adam had lost through rebellion and disobedience, Jesus had restored through submission and obedience.

Therefore, just as through one man (Adam) *sin entered into the world, and death through sin, and so death spread to all men, because all sinned... So then as through one transgression there resulted condemnation to all men, even so through one act of righteousness* (Jesus' obedience on the cross) *there resulted justification of life to all men, for AS THROUGH THE ONE MAN'S DISOBEDIENCE THE MANY WERE MADE SINNERS, EVEN SO THROUGH THE OBEDIENCE OF THE ONE THE MANY WILL BE MADE RIGHTEOUS.*

Romans 5:12,18-19

A very important part of what Jesus accomplished on the cross was to justify those who were joined to Him to stand before God as His delegated authorities once again. But He did something more, He fulfilled the age-old promise of giving us regenerate, spiritually alive hearts so that we could obey and fulfill the Law of God by which we would once again rule.

So also it is written, "The first man, Adam, became a life-giving soul." The last Adam (Jesus) *became a life-giving Spirit.*

1 Corinthians 15:45

For what the Law could not do, weak as it was through the flesh, God did: sending His own Son in the likeness of sinful flesh and as an offering for sin, He condemned sin the flesh, IN ORDER THAT THE REQUIREMENT OF THE LAW MIGHT BE FULFILLED IN US, WHO DO NOT WALK ACCORDING TO THE FLESH, BUT ACCORDING TO THE SPIRIT.

Romans 8:3-4

Now, once again man could rule over the power of Satan. He had been restored to right relationship with God. He had God's law, and finally He had a regenerated heart by which he could embrace that law and therefore once again rule through it.

SONS OF THE MOST HIGH

As we saw in the last chapter, we are restored to our position of rulers over the earth through being part of the ekklesia of God's Kingdom. We become God's co-regents and He rules in our midst. Remember Psalm 82, which we quoted last chapter?

God takes His stand in His own congregation; He judges in the midst of the rulers.

Psalm 82:1

God has restored us to our position of rule under Him. We become identified with Him and His purposes. This explains the incredible words that God addresses to His covenant partners just a few verses later.

> *I said, "You are gods, and all of you are sons of the Most High."*
>
> Psalm 82:6

How, and in what sense can we be called "gods"? How could these Old Testament believers be called "sons of the Most High"? Actually, Jesus Himself gives us the answer in the Gospel of John.

The Jewish leaders had accused Jesus of claiming to be God. Jesus was not yet willing to reveal His true identity as the only begotten Son of God, since they would not have believed nor accepted it. Instead, Jesus uses this biblical text to confound them.

> *Jesus answered them, "Has it not been written in your Law, 'I said that you are gods'?* **If He called them gods, to whom the word of God came** *(and Scripture cannot be broken), how do you say of Him, whom the Father sanctified and sent into the world, 'You are blaspheming,' because I said 'I am the Son of God'?"*
>
> John 10:34-36

Leaving behind Jesus' argument with the Pharisees, look at why Jesus said that those Old Testament believers were called "gods." *It was because the word or law of God had been given to them.* Having received God's law, they had become His viceroys and representatives here on earth. It was because they represented God that they could be called "gods," in that they executed His judgments and represented His authority on the earth. Our authority is based upon our knowing and obeying God's Word.

This is true of all appointed or delegated authority. Judges have great authority, for instance. They grant arrest warrants, determine bail, and assign sentences. In their courtrooms they act like little "gods" (further, it is required that all in the courtroom treat them with the utmost of honor and respect).

Their authority however, does not belong to them. It is only theirs by virtue of the fact that *they have been appointed to enforce the laws of our country.* So it is with the church (the ekklesia of God). We have authority because we have been appointed to represent God and the laws of His Kingdom.

CHAPTER 26

THE BATTLE FOR THE GATES

As we saw in the last chapter, the church does not rule on her own authority, but on the authority of God's law. Judging, governing or managing the world is done according to the Word of God as we are inspired and led by God's Spirit. The church has been given a mandate to bring the world under the authority of Christ's Kingdom. This is the clear meaning of the Great Commission.

Go, therefore, and make disciples of all nations... teaching them to observe all that I have commanded...

Matthew 28:18-19

Our commission is clearly to create disciples who will observe or obey the things that Jesus commanded. In this way, the world will increasingly come under the authority of its **rightful King**. A statement like this will no doubt raise concern among non-Christians. It must be remembered, however, that the church is strictly forbidden from using any coercive power to force God's Kingdom on people. It can only try to win people voluntarily through serving them and influencing them with God's love and truth until they chose to enroll themselves as disciples.

However, this does not mean that the church is not to be aggressive and bold in fulfilling its mandate. Quite the contrary, the church is pictured as storming the very kingdom of Hades.

I also say to you that you are Peter, and upon this rock I will build My church; and the gates of Hades will not overpower it.

Matthew 16:18

Jesus clearly states that gates of Hades will not overcome the church nor be able to stand before its assault. This means that no authority or power will be able to resist or overpower the church, not even death, which is the foundation of Satan's authority (Hebrews 2:14-15), and the final enemy to be completely vanquished (1 Corinthians 15:26). *The church is not to yield before any rebel kingdom or authority to Christ's rule. The church is to march on victorious, assured that Christ's authority and power will be with us.*

THE MEANING OF THE GATES

Christians have often read this passage and wondered how gates could "overpower" anyone. This becomes clear when you realize the ancient concept of the gates of a city. In the ancient world the city gates were very important places.

The city gates were heavily fortified positions that controlled access. Since the cities were protected by high walls, the gates of the city controlled access to the city. When the gates were locked, no one could get in or out. Invading armies could most easily gain access to the city through destroying the city gate, therefore the gates were the most heavily garrisoned by the army and had the greatest battlements on the wall. They became the military headquarters for the city.

The gates were the business and economic centers of the city. Since traveling merchants could only gain access to the city through the gates, they became the central marketplace of the city. Traveling merchants could simply set out their wares outside the city gate, or just within the city gate, where they could be watched (this aided in the city's security). As a result, the economic center of the city was at the gates and it was here that business contracts were made and witnessed (Genesis 34:24; Ruth 4:1,11).

Finally, they were the places where the governing leaders of the city sat and made legal decisions and judgments. It is where kings, such as David, would take their position to hear the requests of the people (2 Samuel 19:8), where fugitives would petition for protection and asylum (Joshua 20:4), where legal actions would be conducted (Deuteronomy 25:7-9), as well as where the elders would give their counsel (Lamentations 5:14).

The gates of a city refer to the legal, social, economic, military and governmental power of the city or kingdom. *To possess the gates of the city is to exercise the controlling influence over a city or society, determining what is allowed in and what is kept out.* To overpower an enemy's gates is to strip them of their power and might and to gain control of their kingdom. This is what Jesus has done to the gates of every other power and enemy, even death. This is a fulfillment of a promise made to Abraham many years ago upon Abraham passing a test from the Lord.

Indeed, I will greatly bless you, and I will greatly multiply your seed as the stars of the heavens and as the sand which

is on the seashore; and YOUR SEED (DESCENDANTS)
SHALL POSSESS THE GATE OF THEIR ENEMIES.
Genesis 22:17

Through Jesus, this promise has been fulfilled for us. Jesus has overcome every other power and authority. He has broken down their heavy doors, removed their strong towers and disarmed their garrisons. **It now remains for us, Abraham's offspring and Christ's followers (His delegated co-rulers), to possess the gates in our cities and begin a reign of righteousness, peace and joy.**

POSSESS THE GATES

Jesus encourages us to do so. Jesus took the occasion of having cast out a demon to declare His victory. In that passage He assures us that He has bound the strong man (Satan), disarmed our enemies, and wants to give us the spoils of war.

> *When a strong man, fully armed, guards his own homestead, his possessions are undisturbed. But when someone stronger than he attacks him and overpowers him he takes away from him all his armor on which he has relied and distributes his plunder.*
Luke 11:21

> *When He* (Jesus) *had disarmed the rulers and authorities, He made a public display of them, having triumphed over them through Him.*
Colossians 2:15

We, as members of Christ's church (*ekklesia*), must see ourselves as those who are meant to occupy the premier place in the gates of our city. In that place of authority, we who have been appointed to Christ's governing assembly and have been given the Law of God, must reign in His power and authority. We must determine what we will allow to enter our city and what will go on in it. We must do this in all the different roles and assignments given us.

In our families, we must model what a Christian marriage is like. We must raise up our children in the discipline and instruction of the Lord (Ephesians 6:4). We must manage the wealth that God entrusts to our family for His glory (1 Timothy 6:17-18). We must welcome the needy into our homes and practice Christian hospitality (Romans 12:13). We must remember that since we are ambassadors for Christ and His Kingdom (2 Corinthians 5:20), our homes are therefore embassies, located in our neighborhood to conduct the business of the Kingdom.

In our role as church members, we must preach the gospel and proclaim our testimony to the faithfulness of Jesus and the power of His saving power in our lives. We must lay hands on the sick and deliver the afflicted of demons. We must gather to pray for a release of God's power and grace for our communities. We must overcome suffering and despair through charitable works of mercy. We must proclaim and teach the Word of God. We must disciple the next generation in our church-run schools and youth groups.

We must likewise serve the King in all our freedoms and responsibilities in the civil realm. As citizens of a democracy, we must register to vote and then actively support candidates, propositions and legislation that lawfully advance righteousness.

Those who hold offices or appointments in the civil realm must act as disciples of Jesus in discharging those duties. Police and firepersons must exercise selfless courage and complete honesty and integrity in their service, trusting in God's strength. Civil servants must discharge their duties in an honorable servant-like way. Elected officials must exercise their authority, not in self-serving ways, but in promoting God's gracious protection and blessing over society.

In the final chapters of this book I would like to tell the story of how these principles we are studying worked themselves out in the history of our church and our city. What I have come to learn of the Kingdom of God came both through the study of Scripture and through experiences as God led us. In other words, God's leading and dealings with us became understandable as we studied Scripture. At the same time, those experiences helped us to understand more fully what the Bible was teaching us. Our church therefore serves as a case study of the principles you have been reading in this book. I believe that what God has done in our church and city can serve as a catalyst for sparking your spiritual imagination for what God might want to do through your church.

CHAPTER 27

OPENING THE GATES

When God called us to El Cajon, California, the city that we are now in, we found that it had great problems. Its population was quite transient and financially pressed. Fifty-nine and a half percent of its inhabitants were renters (in the valley floor it was probably over 80%), and there were relatively few families intact. It had a high crime rate and perhaps worst of all, nationally, it was number one in the production of Crystal Methamphetamine, perhaps the most destructive illegal drug known to man. Nationally syndicated columnist George Will went so far as to label El Cajon the "Medallion of Crystal Meth" in one of his columns (after the Colombian city famous for its cocaine production). This drug, along with rampant alcoholism, produced a high incidence of domestic abuse, crime, gangs, child abuse and neglect. Surprisingly, the city government seemed to have an attitude toward Christian churches that was somewhere between absolute indifference and subtle hostility.

The first order of business was to secure meeting facilities in the city. This proved to be one of the hardest things we would ever do. The city, like so many others, simply did not value churches, since they produce no tax revenue, and was not inclined to give up any commercial, industrial or retail space to one. The city staff was uniformly unhelpful and gave a very unbalanced negative report with a recommendation to deny, even though there was a high vacancy rate in the city.

Worse yet, as unbelievable as it might seem, the El Cajon General Plan, the document that is used to determine proper usages for property in the city, did not even have a single direct reference to churches. In other words, in the view of the city, churches were irrelevant to the future of the city and they had no plans for any more.

Despite their clear discouragement, we made an application for a Conditional Use Permit for a particular industrial building in the city. We were informed by an insider that no church had ever been successful in such an application for industrial space and that they knew of four previous attempts that had either been turned down or had withdrawn amidst city staff opposition. We persevered however, believing that if God wanted us in the city we would prevail despite the obstacles.

The night of the Planning Commission meeting we had little reason to expect a favorable result. Several members had already stated to some people that our proposal was "dead on arrival." Our church gathered at a nearby location to pray during the meeting. The Commissioners were uniformly negative in their comments, each one telling us why they could not support the CUP application. One Commissioner suggested that he might support it if we agreed to move out after 3 years, an impossible requirement, given the amount of money involved to build out the industrial shell into a church. Things looked hopeless, except that our church was praying. I was told later that at a certain time a wonderful sense of God's presence and a sense of victory filled the hall where the prayer was taking place.

When the time came to vote, the vote was 4 to 1 in favor. There was a stunned silence in the council chambers. Dave and I stared at each other in disbelief for a moment and then began to silently praise God. At least one Commissioner seemed flabbergasted. They had all just stated that they could not support us. What happened? To this day I don't know...except that God opened the door for us to go into El Cajon.

For us the following Scripture had become very real.

> *And to the angel of the church in Philadelphia write: He who is holy, who is true, who has the key of David, who opens and no one will shut, and who shuts and no one opens, says this: "I know your deeds. Behold, I have put before you an open door which no one can shut...*
>
> Revelation 3:7-8a

THE LEAVEN OF THE KINGDOM

God's purpose in opening the door for us to locate in El Cajon was that we should be like leaven or like a mustard seed in that city, beginning to transform it and see His Kingdom expand. In those days we were quite a small church but we gave ourselves to God. In the years that followed, we began to reach out to our city. We already had a full regimen of typical church programs such as youth groups, home groups and Sunday services, but we began to add special outreaches to our community.

We began drug and alcohol recovery programs for all ages, and then added a residential drug treatment ranch. We developed our own marriage and parenting courses, seminars and retreats and took many hundreds of couples and parents through them. We opened two community youth centers during the critical hours after school and on weekends, and ministered to thousands of our area youth. We developed a teen mentoring program, a camping program, a bus ministry to area children and youth, apartment visitation, and a large annual youth conference. We hosted many school assembly programs and began ten after-school Christian clubs at area elementary, middle and high school campuses.

We opened two schools, a K-8 and a high school, enrolling several hundred students, a number of them on scholarships. We developed street outreach teams to minister to the homeless of our city, teams to minister in the convalescent homes, teams to minister in the jail. We held a number of large evangelistic crusades with scores of decisions for Christ, conducted community work projects, hosted weekly pastors' prayer groups plus much, much more. Some of the stories of these ministries and their impact are included in the companion book *Breakthrough Kingdom Living*. We were making an impact on the spiritual climate of our city, literally seeing several thousand saved and many marriages and families healed.

We felt especially called to minister to the children and youth of our community. Because of the pervasive presence of drugs, alcohol and other factors, family life was undermined and many children and youth were left exposed to neglect, destructive forces, and temptations. An army of volunteers has been raised up to work with these children and youth. Through our various ministries we currently have over 2,800 ministry contacts a week to the children and youth of our surrounding communities. Some of our after school clubs regularly have over 20% of the entire school's student body in attendance. One student told me, "The club has changed our school."

Just as dramatic is the difference we are making in our neighborhood. For instance, every year our college ministry hosts a Christmas banquet and party for the families of the children who ride our buses to church. (These same children are also visited in their apartment complexes.) At this party, the families are fed a great meal, play games, enjoy entertainment, win prizes in a raffle, and every child receives a gift.

At our most recent banquet, I talked with a woman whose story could echo many others. Her son has ridden the bus for two years and also been sponsored to several of our camps. She told me that it had changed her son's life. Beyond that, she told me they lived in a very large apartment complex. She said, "You can easily see the difference in the children who ride the bus to your church and those who do not; it is the difference between night and day."

In the same way, our Youth Venture teen centers are changing our community. They are open 7 days a week, giving all kids between ages 11 and 18 a safe place to be when they are not in school. In addition, our adult staff takes them through our one-on-one mentoring lessons to give them a solid foundation of God's principles on which to stand. These young people are also taken on three camps a year plus several other camping opportunities and special trips. Since several hundred youth from within walking distance participate in each center, whole neighborhoods are being powerfully impacted. Over the past 9 years, thousands of kids have been impacted by this ministry.

We have witnessed the Holy Spirit and the Word of God transform children and youth from the most destructive backgrounds. We have seen children whose parents are drug addicts and chronically homeless grow up to be productive, godly young people. In some cases, we have seen parents delivered of drug addiction and seen whole families healed and restored. In other cases, our members have opened up their homes and loved and parented these children as their own. Some of these kids we have even put through our schools on scholarships. Some have gone on to become interns in our programs. Their lives have been forever changed.

One of the most rewarding experiences I can remember took place recently. One of our staff pastors, Jim Deyling, made a video for his daughter's birthday. (She is one of our volunteers working with youth.) The video was put together from footage shot at some of our recent weekly programs, youth camp, after school clubs, and annual youth conference. It showed hundreds of different children and youth, from all different backgrounds and circumstances. They were all worshiping God. The footage was from different settings, but it all showed kids and young people worshiping God with abandon, literally caught up in the glory and presence of God. Some were kneeling, some were weeping, most had arms raised. Many of these young people are from very dis-advantaged backgrounds, but they have been radically connected to their Heavenly Father and they will never be the same. As I watched the video, I was overcome with emotion and overwhelmed with the power of the Holy Spirit to produce change even in the worst situations.

The wonderful truth is that we can see a difference in the spiritual climate of our city.

THE MUSTARD SEED FACTOR

But the Kingdom of God also has a claim in the civil realm. The influence of King Jesus must also be appropriately felt in the realm of civil society. The leaven of the Kingdom must work in the civil realm as well as in the realm of the family and the church. As we mentioned before, the attitude of the governing authorities was not sympathetic to the church.

An extreme example of their position was reflected in a newspaper quote by one of the City Council members when she voted against allowing a church to hold a concert in the park. She stated that, "it was inappropriate to allow proselytizing on public property." In other words, the right to free speech should stop when that speech includes the word "God."

Having experienced the anti-Christian bias of city government, and being aware that in our form of democracy we were responsible for who our leaders were, we approached a local businessman who was known for being a strong Christian and prevailed upon him to run for the office of City Councilman. It took much persuasion since he was a very busy, successful man and had never been particularly interested in politics. He was, however, very interested in serving Jesus. We pointed out how much he could serve Jesus in such a position.

My brother and I got involved in his election, along with many other Christians, and he won the election. The incumbent that he defeated was the very one whom I quoted above who didn't think Christians should be allowed to talk about Jesus on public property. Once elected, he proved to be a perfect example of what a Christian elected official should be.

One day as he was walking past the post office, he noticed the pornographic newspapers that were being sold through coinoperated machines out front. It stunned him that they were being sold there where any child with 75 cents could buy one. He bought one and was shocked at what was inside. He took it to the next City Council meeting with the intention of doing something about it. He distributed a copy to each of the other City Council members. They were informed by the City Attorney that it was beyond their jurisdiction and would have to be addressed at the state level

But Councilman Bob McClellan wasn't done. He convinced the El Cajon City Council to mail typical copies of the porn tabloids, along with a letter signed by the Mayor to more than 200 mayors, legislators, and boards of supervisors where newsracks were being considered – hoping to shock them into reality with the content of the papers. He personally underwrote all the costs associated with this and continued to direct the process of cooperating with other jurisdictions and generating momentum in the state legislature.

Finally, AB 17 was introduced to the State Legislature, which would prohibit the sale of pornography through coin-operated newsracks. Later, when State Assemblyman Steve Peace sought to amend the bill to "make it useless," McClellan solicited support from other legislators and Attorney General Dan Lundgren. The entire process took 17 months, but Governor Pete Wilson signed AB 17 into law, and the bill went into effect without Peace's amendment as of January 1, 1995.

As a result of this action, James Dobson and his organization, Focus on the Family, awarded Bob McClellan with its annual "Hometown Hero of the Year" award for 1994.

In the next election, a second Christian man, Mark Lewis, was elected. Two years later, when the Mayor's seat became vacant, Mark ran for it as well. To everyone's great surprise, he pulled off a great upset and won the seat. As Mayor he attempted to honor God in all his duties. He instituted prayer before the City Council meetings and even convened pastors' prayer meetings to pray for God's protection and blessing for the city and to pray that the City of El Cajon might come to truly honor God. The city was changing.

Just as importantly, a great injustice was finally able to be rectified. As I stated earlier, the General Plan of the city made no mention of churches, meaning that churches were almost certain to be opposed by the City Planning Department. This unforgivable situation was allowed to continue and was not rectified by the Planning Commission or City Council, even though I brought it to their attention on at least three occasions. It was obviously the way they wanted it.

Working with the new Mayor, we were able to correct this situation. He brought forth before the Council a motion to include in the General Plan language which would give churches favorable standing when they made application before the city staff. This put the other City Council members in a hard place. It would be hard to justify voting against the obvious fairness of including churches in the General Plan. The motion passed and helpful language was included. The impact of this was immediate.

In the next two years, six new churches were able to locate in El Cajon. Three of these located in industrial space, of which we had been the first and only church to do so in the history of El Cajon. One of the pastors notified me that city staff had told him specifically that if the General Plan had not been changed, they would have rejected that church's application. One open door leads to another. The city was changing.

CHAPTER 28

POSSESSING THE GATES
OF THE CITY

The promise that God gave to Abraham that his seed would "possess the gates of their enemies" (Genesis 22:17) is one that passes down to us as well, since we are his seed. All of those who belong to Christ are Abraham's descendants.

> *And if you belong to Christ, then you are Abraham's descendants, heirs according to promise.*
>
> Galatians 3:29

The promises spoken to Abraham were ultimately spoken to Jesus and to those who would be joined to Jesus by faith.

> *Now the promises were spoken to Abraham and to his seed. He does not say, "And to seeds," as referring to many, but rather to one, "And to your seed," that is, Christ.*
>
> Galatians 3:16

> *Therefore, be sure that it is those who are of faith who are sons of Abraham.*
>
> Galatians 3:7

It is not correct to restrict these promises of dominion and overcoming to the nation of Israel alone. They were certainly fulfilled during the reigns of King David and King Solomon. But God's promises of help and victory belong to all of Abraham's descendants. They were fulfilled just as surely in the lives of the Apostles Paul and Peter, and in the lives of Martin Luther, John Wesley, Charles Finney and countless thousands of others. **God blesses and elevates His people to demonstrate HIS POWER AND GLORY**.

> *The Lord has declared you to be His people, a treasured possession, as He promised you, and that you should keep all His commandments; AND HE SHALL SET YOU HIGH ABOVE ALL NATIONS which He has made, FOR PRAISE, FAME AND HONOR, and that you shall be a consecrated people to the Lord your God, as He has spoken.*
>
> Deuteronomy 26:18-19

As God is the Sovereign ruler of the universe, He elevates His followers to influence and power to demonstrate His praise and glory. His fame and honor are demonstrated as He elevates those who worship and follow Him. In so doing, He also shows forth His love for His people, and brings about His purposes on the earth. As made clear above, in order for this to happen, we must reflect His nature and character by keeping the commandments of the covenant. God has always sought for an obedient and faithful covenant people that He could bless and elevate to dominion.

> *Now it shall be, IF YOU DILIGENTLY OBEY THE LORD YOUR GOD, being careful to do all His commandments which I command you today, the Lord your God WILL SET YOU HIGH ABOVE ALL THE NATIONS OF THE EARTH. All these blessings will come upon you and overtake you if you obey the Lord your God: Blessed shall you be in the city, and blessed shall you be in the country. Blessed shall be the offspring of your body and the produce of your ground and the offspring of your beasts, the increase of your herd and the young of your flock. The Lord shall cause your enemies who rise up against you to be defeated before you; they will come out against you one way and will flee seven ways.*
>
> Deuteronomy 28:1-4, 7

> *THE LORD WILL MAKE YOU THE HEAD AND NOT THE TAIL, AND YOU ONLY WILL BE ABOVE, AND YOU WILL NOT BE UNDERNEATH, if you listen to the commandments of the Lord your God, which I charge you today, to observe them carefully.*
>
> Deuteronomy 28:13

God elevates us to power and influence by granting us to "possess the gates." Rather than retreating from positions of power and influence in society, thinking them somehow "worldly and unspiritual," Jesus would have His disciples bring His word to bear on society from these positions of influence. The "elders" belong sitting at the city gate (Lamentations 5:14). This does not happen by magic as we sit in our prayer closets, but rather as we begin to engage our social and political processes, depending upon God and His word. This is how such Bible heroes as David, Joseph, Daniel, and Nehemiah rose to places of power and influence where God could use them.

SITTING AT THE GATES

As we stated earlier, one of the prerogatives of "possessing" the gates of a city is that *whoever possesses the gates determines what comes into the city and inversely what is kept out. When you sit at the city gates you can do much to open up the city to the grace and mercy of God.*

One of my most rewarding memories is of gathering with a group of pastors in the City Chambers, at our Mayor's request, and joining him in asking for God's mercy and help for our city. We further dedicated our city to be pleasing to God. This was, I believe, an important alliance of spiritual and civil gatekeepers joining in agreement to invoke God's blessing in our city. Together we opened up the gates and invited in God's presence.

> *LIFT UP YOUR HEADS, O GATES, AND BE LIFTED UP, O ANCIENT DOORS, THAT THE KING OF GLORY MAY COME IN. Who is the King of Glory? The Lord strong and mighty, the Lord mighty in battle. Lift up your heads, O gates, and lift them up, O ancient doors, that the King of Glory might come in.*
>
> Psalm 24:7-9

Only those who had charge of the physical gates of Jerusalem could open them to let people in. Likewise, only those who had possession of the civil, spiritual and social gates of Jerusalem could open the city to the Lord. In the same way, only when we assume the positions of leadership and influence and power that the Lord would elevate us to can we invite Him in.

On that day, when we stood in the City Chambers and as gatekeepers invoked God's name and blessing over our city, it was only possible because there were those of us who had planted, established, and/or maintained churches, and others that had run for and attained public office. Only those who control the gates can open up the city. I have seen first hand the difference. I have seen the day when churches were restricted and evangelistic crusades were turned away. And now I see a new day.

Will the churches of your city be vibrant, full of life, and centered on God's word, or dead, compromised, and without direction? It depends upon who controls the gates of the church. What activities will be encouraged in your city and which ones discouraged? It depends upon who sits at the gates of government. What will the children be taught about right and wrong, the existence of God, and their purpose and place in the universe? It depends upon who sits in the gates of education.

It is simplistic to think that cities will change *simply because* people without power or influence gather on mountaintops and shout at demonic principalities and powers or make "prophetic declarations" against them. This is not how life works. The New Testament does not teach these as being particularly significant in the way in which demonic strongholds are pulled down. This is not how the early church changed their world. (For a more biblical understanding of spiritual warfare, study carefully such passages as Ephesians 6:10-20; 2 Corinthians 10:3-6; 2 Corinthians 6:7; Acts 26:16-18; and Revelation 12:10-11.)

Prophetic declarations and acts no doubt have their place, as they did that day with our Mayor in the City Council Chambers, but they alone are certainly not decisive.

In our city we decided to exercise our authority, as gatekeepers, not only to determine what would come in, but what would be kept out as well. As far as possible, we want to bring our city into agreement with heaven. In the Lord's Prayer, we pray:

> *Our Father, who is in heaven, hallowed be Thy Name. Your Kingdom come, your will be done, ON EARTH AS IT IS IN HEAVEN.*
>
> Matthew 6:9-10

This prayer is more than a request. It is a declaration of our desire and purpose. We purpose to be God's instrument in bringing to pass this state of affairs for which we pray.

We commit, as Jesus' followers, to make it our highest purpose to make earth agree with heaven. We want the peace, justice and righteousness of heaven to become realized on earth. We want the blessings of heaven on earth. Likewise, we do not want to encourage on earth what is not permitted in heaven.

In heaven, worship and praise ascends before the throne of God night and day, therefore we want to encourage worship of God and His only Son Jesus in our communities. On the other hand, in heaven there is no exploitation nor corruption of what God has created. So we want to try and eliminate those things which victimize our citizens and families, and which corrupt our youth with temptations for which they are unprepared.

What this means is that we want to encourage churches, families and parental authority, for instance, and want to discourage gambling, alcohol, lewd behavior and lawlessness. While this may seem obvious to many reading this book, it is amazing how often our cities reverse this in their ordinances and practices.

In the next chapter I will share with you a true story of how upside down things have sometimes gotten and what can happen when God's people begin to operate in the gates of their city.

CHAPTER 29

OPENING AND CLOSING THE GATES

As we have seen, God has promised that we His followers would possess the gates of the city. God's plan is to bring His peace and righteousness to a city by assisting and elevating those to power and influence who will lead by the principles of His Word.

When God's people understand this, and are willing to step out in faith, then God will establish them and promote them to leadership. When you are placed at the gates of the city you can open up the city to blessing and righteousness, and you can close the city gates to unrighteousness and destruction. Let me give you an additional example of how Christians in our city shut the gates to perversion and exploitation.

Let me begin the story by quoting from an editorial that I wrote in the *San Diego Union-Tribune*.

> A church attempts to relocate a few miles away from its present location and build a new, larger facility. It takes 10 years and 5 million dollars to receive their Major Use Permit. A strip club applies for a Minor Use Permit to open and receives it in 10 working days, at a cost of $1,130. What do these two projects have in common?

> What they have in common is that both of them took place here in our own East County area under the jurisdiction of the County Board of Supervisors. The church is Skyline Church in Rancho San Diego, which continues its battle to get its sanctuary built. The strip club was Dream Girls, which was set to open in the former Dunn Edwards paint store near the corner of Magnolia and West Bradley in El Cajon.

> If this seems unfair to you, then read on.

> This incredible set of events actually took place. A very fine church was delayed for ten years and was forced to pay out $5 million in fees, studies, and other considerations to

receive their Major Use Permit. As I write this, they are still attempting to win final approval to build their sanctuary. The strip club did not require a Major Use Permit. Nor were they required, as was the church, to notify all neighbors and participate in open hearings.

In the rest of the editorial, I explained how this state of affairs could take place. The fact is, except for hazardous waste sites, possibly no other use merits such scrutiny and opposition from local governments as churches. Perhaps the major reason for this would be the fact that they do not produce the all-important property and sales tax revenue for the municipality. The second reason would seem to be a "professional blind spot." Somehow, in their education and training, public bureaucrats receive an incredibly stubborn inability to recognize the benefits that churches bring to a community.

It is in this way that a strip club could be welcomed while a church could find it nearly impossible to locate in the same jurisdiction. This is obviously unfair and unwise. A strip club brings with it many documented problems for the community. These include an increase in prostitution, drugs, and sexual assaults. On the other hand, churches bring tremendous blessings to the communities wise enough to welcome them.

If you love the people of your community and believe that God has called you to sit in the gates of the city, then you must do more than just complain. You must act in faith and become responsible.

Going Into Action

The strip club in question was to be opened just 630 feet from our church in a commercial zone. The man who intended to open it already operated several other clubs in the county. He only needed to receive his liquor license to open. It was this notification for application of a liquor license (which is required by state law to be posted in the window of the building to be occupied) that was the first anyone knew of the proposed strip club.

Immediately, some people in our church got busy. As always, our first step was to organize prayer. At our two weekly prayer meetings, and through our prayer society (a group of over 600 prayer warriors in our church who have committed to interceding at least 2½ hours a week for specific prayer assignments), prayer was raised toward heaven.

Next, local residents and businessmen were contacted and a coalition was formed. An organization was created called Concerned Citizens of East County and a web site set up. A meeting was arranged with our County Supervisor Dianne Jacob.

At that meeting, we were informed by Supervisor Jacob that there was nothing they could do to stop the club from opening in the building, since the permit had already been granted. However, she was determined to make sure that something like that could never happen again. She and her staff proved to be tireless workers with us in what was to come.

We made the situation known through press conferences, radio interviews, and the web site. An old truck was turned into a billboard alerting the community as to the planned strip club, and was parked in front of the proposed site. God helped us by assembling just the right people with the right skills for the project. One businessman in particular, John Gibson, who was also a member of our church, proved especially instrumental because of his background as a commercial broker. The first order of business was to try and stop the liquor license application.

In order to try and fly under the radar screen, the applicant had made the unusual step of bypassing the local office and applying for the license directly from the state office. Our first goal was to get the application sent back down to the local level. Signatures were collected on a petition and included with a letter from Supervisor Diane Jacob requesting to have the application reviewed locally. These were presented to the State Office of Alcohol Beverage Control by our State Assemblyman, Jay LaSuer (a Christian in whose election campaign many of us had worked). We were successful, and the application was sent down for local review.

With the help of the Sheriff's office, we were able to demonstrate that the area had a high crime rate and had already received an overabundance of liquor licenses. In addition, the nearby Lakeside Planning Group had voted 14 to nothing against it. Based on these facts, the license was denied by the Alcohol Beverage Control Board.

The owner of the Dream Girls club was furious. He promised to open the club anyway as *a totally nude club* (at that time clubs that did not serve alcohol could be totally nude). In retaliation for our sign truck being parked in front of his empty building, he began to park his lewd Dream Girls vans in front of our church.

Through our networking with a national anti-pornography group, Citizens for Community Values, we were able to locate an attorney who specialized in ordinances designed to curb X-rated businesses. A businessman from our church paid him to come out and consult with Diane Jacob's office. They were so impressed that they retained him as a consultant to try to write the toughest possible laws that could stand up in court.

The so-called adult entertainment industry had been big political contributors to some of the other supervisors, so we knew that we could not take their votes for granted. We mounted a public relations blitz, bringing in a former dancer from Spokane, Washington and recruiting a young 18-year-old girl that I had previously known from our Youth Venture Program. She had been recruited as a dancer and had just recently quit. She told me, "It ruined my life." We also found and recruited a former male employee to report what he had seen firsthand.

Six television and radio stations conducted interviews with them (the eighteen year-old was incognito). They told of the drugs, prostitution, and various other unsavory and illegal activities that are associated with the clubs. They told their own heartbreaking stories of what happens to the girls who are recruited as dancers. In addition to the portions that were broadcast, a fuller version of the interviews, which contained materials not suitable for television, was prepared for the Board of Supervisors meetings.

While all this was going on, our nation's eyes were riveted on an investigation, taking place here in San Diego, into the disappearance of a young girl from her own bed during the night while her parents were home. After weeks of searching for Danielle Van Dam, her decomposed body was found in our East County area. This horrified our community and turned public opinion strongly against the idea of locating a strip club in close proximity to a church, dance studio and arcade, all of which were frequented by children.

The day of the Board of Supervisors meeting found us all downtown together for the hearing. Many spoke out on our behalf and several very strong presentations were made. Portions of the videotaped interviews were shown. The ordinances passed that day by the Board of Supervisors exceeded any that we would have hoped for when the process began many weeks before.

They started by passing strict zoning ordinances. So-called "adult entertainment" establishments could no longer be located in commercial zones, only industrial zones. The requirements concerning their distances from schools and churches were increased. Under these new restrictions, only a very few parcels in the county would now qualify. The building planned for the new Dream Girls strip club would be illegal under both provisions. Further, any adult entertainment establishments presently in violation of these new requirements would have to shut down within three years. This meant that 3 businesses presently operating would have to relocate or shut down in three years.

But the Supervisors, guided by the specialist that we brought in, went far beyond this. They made totally nude entertainment illegal *anywhere* under their jurisdiction. Further, they made private dancing, that is dancing off the main stage in a dark corner or back room in front of a patron (known as "lap dancing"), illegal. They made any touching between the patron and the dancer illegal, and they made direct tipping of the dancer by the patron illegal. This deals a potentially lethal financial blow to the so-called strip clubs, or "gentleman's clubs," as they are presently operated.

We had helped "close the gates of the city" to perversion, exploitation and sexual addiction by helping to shut the gates against strip clubs. This was especially gratifying to me since I had first-hand experience with seeing the above-mentioned young, naive girl's life scarred by being recruited and exploited by the industry.

Righteous Gatekeepers

Who will sit in the gates of the city? Whoever does will decide whether destruction or blessing comes into the city. It is an important question. A city needs righteous gatekeepers. It needs faithful and trustworthy people in the gates.

> *...for the four chief gatekeepers WHO WERE LEVITES, WERE IN AN OFFICE OF TRUST.*
>
> 1 Chronicles 9:26

The Gatekeepers were those who carried much responsibility and held a sacred public trust. The city's safety depended upon their character and honor as much as upon the strength of the walls. The city was only as secure as the faithfulness of the Gatekeepers.

History records this truth. Many cities fell because Gatekeepers were bribed. Ancient China is an example of this.

The Chinese people wanted security against the barbaric peoples to the north, so they built the Great Wall of China. It was so high they believed no one could climb over it, and so thick nothing could break it down. They settled in to enjoy their security. During the first hundred years of the wall's existence, China was invaded three times. Not once did the barbaric hordes break down the wall or climb over it. Each time they bribed a gatekeeper and then marched right through the gates. The Chinese were so busy relying on walls of stone, they forgot to teach character and honesty to their people.

A family, a church, or a city without faithful gatekeepers is a dangerous and scary place. Strangers with evil intent come upon the unprepared and unwary. The young and naïve become as sheep led to the slaughter. As the citizens slowly become enticed and held in bondage, addiction, and confusion, the homes of the community cease to be places of safety and nurture. They become like polluted springs. Where they should be places of rest and refreshment and life, they become polluted and toxic. Schools become places of spiritual child abuse. Even churches can be overcome and offer no life.

At such time people must arise to become faithful Gatekeepers.

Oh that there were one among you who would shut the gates.
                                                              Malachi 1:10

When you allow the Lord to seat you at the gates of the city, you can decide what will come in and what will be kept out. In our city, the believers decided to begin to occupy the gates. We decided that we would open up the gates and allow churches in, so we changed the General Plan of the City. A number of churches came in.

We decided that we would let Jesus back into the lives of students at our public schools, so we began on-campus Christian clubs. Our church operates on-site Bible Clubs at 10 schools, but in this we are merely joining in with many other churches, because there are presently a total of 61 Christian clubs operating in our East County public schools through the efforts of many churches and four para-church agencies. These clubs operate in elementary, middle, and high schools. Some are on campus and some meet in homes in the evening. All of them are attempting to bring Jesus into the lives of students who might otherwise never learn of Him.

Christians also opened up the gates and brought Jesus into the prisons, hospitals, retirement homes, apartment complexes, and neighborhoods. But we also shut the gates against so-called adult entertain-

ment. By interceding for our city, preaching the gospel, and ministering the love of Jesus, we daily shut out loneliness, despair, suicide and
hopelessness.

The victories that I have been writing about throughout this book
were only possible because 10-15 years earlier, some area Christians
heard God's call and began to aspire to seize the gates of the city for
Jesus' sake. It was those earlier decisions to plant churches, start ministries, organize for prayer, run for elected office, register to vote, and
work in political campaigns that led to these victories.

THE POWER OF PERSEVERANCE

Lest anyone misunderstand and think that such victories come easily – let me assure you that you will get nowhere unless you persevere.
For instance, I was on the losing side in the first four political campaigns I was involved in. Sometimes we lost for heartbreaking reasons
when we expected to win. Another time it was because we split the vote
between two conservative Christian candidates, neither of whom
would drop out. Once it was because a highly unethical hit piece, fund-
ed by outside special interest money, went out the day before the election. (Several of these stories are told in *Breakthrough Kingdom Living*.)

One particularly disheartening defeat involved our High School district. Liberal, humanistic elements had gained control of the school
board and were attempting to put forward a radical homosexual agenda into our schools. Parents and churches were incensed. Hundreds of
parents and concerned citizens packed out the board meeting. Dozens
spoke out against the proposed change. That night, one of the more
moderate board members changed their vote.

The next year a more radical board member replaced the moderate.
One of the first actions of the new board was to reintroduce their radical homosexual agenda.

Once again, hundreds of parents and district citizens jammed the
gymnasium, with many others being turned away. This time, however,
homosexual activists from around the state had come to support the
liberal majority on the school board. Although these activists were significantly outnumbered, they were very loud. A number of parents, as
well as local pastors, most notably Jim Garlow, Pastor of Skyline Wesleyan Church, spoke against the plan.

This time the liberal majority ignored the clear wishes of the parents in the district and voted 3 to 2 to implement their agenda. Pastor Gary Cass, one of the two dissenting board members, spoke eloquently in objection.

Immediately a recall effort was launched against the board chairman who was the main force behind putting forth the homosexual agenda. It was necessary to collect 22,506 signatures to place the recall election on the ballot. Our consultants told us that since many signatures on petitions were always rejected due to illegibility, incomplete address, people who were not currently registered, or who actually lived outside the district boundaries; we should aim at turning in 28,000 signatures to ensure that we would have enough valid ones. This would prove to be a huge undertaking. On the day of the deadline, we turned in 28,500 signatures. We were elated. Several days later, however, we received the very discouraging news that our petitions had a higher than expected rejection of signature rate, and that we fell just short of what we needed. To make matters worse, the day after the deadline, one of our volunteers found over 1,400 more signatures sitting on top of a file cabinet in the recall office that had not been turned in. This was very discouraging news.

The liberal activist board members were ecstatic and begin to try, along with the school superintendent, to punish and marginalize the two Christian board members. They further put together a slate of liberal candidates to defeat the Christian board member who was up for reelection (along with two other members) in the next election. These liberal candidates received large donations, not only from the local teachers' union, but the state teachers' fund, as well as homosexual activists across the entire county and state. In addition, *The San Diego Union-Tribune* weighed in heavily against the Christian candidates.

Once again it seemed like David versus Goliath. However, after much prayer and hard work, when the election was over, the Christian conservative candidates swept all three open seats and now have a four-seat majority on the school board. And the liberal chairman that we tried unsuccessfully to recall, well, he is gone, having come in sixth place. The truth is, perseverance is necessary to win Kingdom victories. Christians who expect to lose and expect everything to get worse quit. However, Christians who understand the Kingdom persevere.

The truth is that progress does not usually come easily. Every step forward has required faith, perseverance and patience. Every advance has to overcome demonic opposition. Every ministry has required perseverance over delays, opposition from neighbors, city officials and other setbacks. Paul said it well when he said:

Through many tribulations we must enter the Kingdom of God.

Acts 14:22

Jesus likewise told us that the world would oppose us and cause us tribulation but likewise we are assured that because He has overcome the world, if we persevere, we too shall overcome.

In the world you will have tribulation, but take courage, I have overcome the world.

John 16:33

But you have need of endurance, so that when you have done the will of God, you may receive what was promised.

Hebrews 10:36

Let us not lose heart in doing good, for in due time we will reap if we do not grow weary.

Galatians 6:9

Only through great perseverance, faith, and patience can the greater victories of God's Kingdom be gained. However, when we press forward together in unity and persevere, we can see Heaven touch Earth and change our cities.

SELF-SERVING SHEPHERDS AND SHORT-SIGHTED CHURCHES

Churches and church leaders that refuse to interrelate and join in cooperative efforts or who shrink back from doing anything controversial and who run from criticism just don't get it. *Jesus is interested in much more than their Sunday morning attendance figures. Jesus wants to develop disciples, pull down strongholds, seat His followers at the gates to the city and establish His Kingdom "on earth as it is in heaven."*

It is God's desire that His people, guided by His Word and inspired by His Spirit, should judge and govern the world. It is our destiny.

Or do you not know that THE SAINTS WILL JUDGE THE WORLD? If the world is judged by you, are you not competent to constitute the smallest law courts? DO YOU NOT

KNOW THAT YOU WILL JUDGE ANGELS? HOW MUCH MORE MATTERS OF THIS LIFE?

1 Corinthians 6:2-3

God promised us that we would "possess the gates of our enemies" (Genesis 22:17). He promised that the "Gates of Hades would not prevail against us" (Matthew 16:18). It is time for Christians to set aside their personal, selfish and worldly agendas and together possess the gates. The very best of us must give ourselves to this grand commission rather than be caught up in the race to acquire more and more personal possessions. There is no higher or better course to pursue than to serve Jesus in pulling down the strongholds of wickedness and bringing in the reign of Christ's peace and righteousness. Let us put aside doctrines of men and demons (I Timothy 4:1) that bring about defeatism among God's people and instead obey Jesus' directive. God will work with us to give us success.

The evil will bow down before the good, and the wicked at the gates of the righteous.

Proverbs 14:19

CHAPTER 30

THE LORD BUILDS WHILE
THE WORKERS LABOR

About two years ago, an opportunity came up for us to relocate our church to a retail center, known as Town Center, in the downtown area of our city. The retail center included a closed multiplex movie theatre and a number of large and small retail spaces. The entire center had failed once, been redeveloped as the first project of the Redevelopment Agency about twenty years earlier, and had failed a second time. It presently stood about 80% vacant and the owners were facing bankruptcy because, despite over two years of an aggressive marketing campaign, they had not been able to locate any developer willing to develop the property according to the parameters imposed on them by the city. There were simply no developers who believed the city's desires for the property were realistic.

It seemed like we would be the ideal fit. We would turn this empty, chronically under-performing property into a vibrant center of life and activity seven days and evenings a week. Thousands of people a week would come down into the area because of the church to help revitalize the retail district. More importantly, we would be able to greatly increase our services to the community, which an independent study estimated already would cost the city over $700,000 yearly to duplicate. Nevertheless, as expected, we ran into solid opposition.

Even before they had an opportunity to consider the merits of our proposal, several Council members and city staff jumped into action. On a 3 to 2 vote, they dismissed the chairman of the Planning Commission because they suspected he would favor the plan. Since the new provisions in the General Plan pertaining to churches had been added, he had voted in their favor and been friendly to them. He was the most qualified Commissioner and was so well respected by his colleagues that they had voted him chairman. Nevertheless, he was removed from office by the three City Council members, although they could not agree as to why. This signaled the no-holds-barred war against the church and its proposal.

As part of our application process, the city required that an independent firm conduct an economic study of the impact of the project on the city and its revenues. Wanting to make the strongest case, we asked several Planning Commissioners which firm enjoyed the city's highest confidence. We were directed to a firm that had been employed by the city itself on several occasions.

We contracted with that firm. They issued the findings of their study and it was very favorable for our project. The city then did an unusual thing. They took tax money and hired another firm to conduct a second study. This new study was apparently based upon wrong information and contained several glaring material errors of fact, which, upon being pointed out, were admitted to by the firm the study. However, the opponents continued to use these now-admitted highly inflated numbers. Enough has already been stated to show that the deck was stacked. However, Christians do not look at the "things which are seen, but the things which are unseen" (2 Corinthians 4:18). Consequently, after seeking the Lord's will through further prayer, we felt led to proceed forward.

The response to our application was not surprising. The staff report recommended against it. The Planning Commission voted against it and we lost on appeal to the City Council on a 3 to 2 vote. But if we thought it was over, we were wrong. Two events took place in the next several weeks. First, a religious rights attorney friend of ours, Brad Dacus, told us of recent legislation that he thought was important to our situation.

Congress had recently passed the Religious Land Use and Institutional Persons Act, otherwise known as RLUIPA. This legislation was an attempt to halt the widespread discrimination of city governments against churches. Municipal opposition to church land use issues most often was based upon the fact that churches pay no taxes to local government. So widespread and serious is this discrimination that the legislation passed both the Senate and House of Representatives *without a single dissenting vote*. One of the last acts of President Clinton was to sign the bill into law. Brad, the director of Pacific Justice Institute, which is a religious rights legal organization, felt that our case was perhaps just the right case to establish this new law and offered to take the case *pro bono*, that is, for no money.

The second event that changed the apparent closed door to relocation was the sudden and unexpected immediate resignation of one of the City Councilmen who had voted against the project in the 3 to 2 defeat. As a result of the fallout of dismissing the Planning Commissioner, some unsavory things had publicly surfaced concerning this Councilman (including his anti-Christian bigotry), and it was assumed that this was the reason for his shocking resignation.

WHAT ABOUT COURTS AND POLITICS?

Perhaps here it is necessary to look at an issue over which some Christians are in disagreement with one other. That question is to what extent such Christians should become involved in politics or the legal process. Some Christians feel that political involvement and legal actions are *carnal or fleshly efforts*. They feel that Christians ought to limit themselves to *spiritual acts* like prayer and evangelism to affect their world.

It won't surprise anyone who has read this far to learn that I do not believe that is the proper Kingdom view. Remember, we saw that the Kingdom of God rules over all three basic realms: the church, the family and civil society. Each of these has its own proper domain and its own proper tools to bring righteousness to bear. As we saw, for instance, the church has the keys and civil government has the sword.

A Christian must seek to be salt and light in all three arenas. It is spiritual to serve Jesus in all three arenas. As we pointed out previously, although our spirit and attitude must be the same as we serve Jesus in each realm, our responsibilities are different.

Earlier, we contrasted a particular Christian's different duties as a policeman on Saturday and, say, a Sunday School teacher on Sunday. In each realm, he has a somewhat different calling and certainly different tools to accomplish those tasks. As a policeman, his primary duty is to protect people and property and one of his tools is a gun, which is certainly an inappropriate tool in Sunday School. In church on Sundays, he must pray for the safety of his city, *but on Monday he must put on his gun and trust Jesus to use him to help answer that prayer.*

This balance is illustrated in the following verse from Psalm 127.

> *Unless the Lord builds the house, they labor in vain who build it. Unless the Lord guards the city, the watchman keeps awake in vain.*

Psalm 127:1

Here we see that both the Lord must build and the laborers must labor. Likewise, the Lord must guard the city but, just as importantly, the watchman must stay awake. It is not carnal to fulfill our responsibility in each realm using the proper tools. Some Christians discount any effort beyond prayer and preaching the gospel to effect societal change. However, it is wrong to just pray and neglect your other duties as a Christian.

The book of Nehemiah is a fascinating study of the interplay between the human actors and Divine oversight. Nehemiah is an inspiring model to us of how to courageously cooperate with God in rebuilding a city against overwhelming odds. Nehemiah's understanding of practical spirituality is reflected throughout the book in such verses as Nehemiah 4:8-9.

> *All of them conspired together to come and fight against Jerusalem and to cause a disturbance in it. But WE PRAYED TO OUR GOD, and because of them WE SET UP A GUARD against them day and night.*
>
> Nehemiah 4:8-9

Nehemiah both held a prayer meeting to pray for God's protection, and set human guards in place. Throughout the book, Nehemiah understands how God works through the processes of everyday life to accomplish His purposes. Nehemiah prays concerning the abysmal conditions in Jerusalem, and then offers himself to God as the instrument of deliverance (Nehemiah 1:1-11). He used his position and influence as the king's cupbearer to get the king to finance the construction in Jerusalem, commenting that the king gave him his request, "because the good hand of my God was upon me" (Nehemiah 2:8).

We must not be childish in our understanding of the ways of God and always insist that God work in spectacular ways. We must realize that God gives rights, opportunities, and proper tools to enable us to see our prayers answered.

Laws are not passed in heaven, but on earth through the prayers and appropriate faithful efforts of God's people. Laws are passed by lawmakers involved in the political process in which we as Americans are called to be involved. Those laws are only good if they are enforced, which sometimes involves the use of courts.

If God graciously gives us legal rights like those provided by RLUIPA, it is ingratitude to not exercise them. It is not carnal to use the appropriate God-given tool, for instance the courts, to appeal the actions of those who may be breaking the law. It is no more wrong to call upon the courts to enforce the laws than it is wrong to call a policeman to enforce the laws (although the Bible counsels us that it is usually better to suffer loss than to sue a Christian brother or sister in secular court – 1 Corinthians 6).

This is especially true when going to court may benefit your brothers and sisters around the country and allow the cause of Christ to go forward. Remember that the apostle Paul was not shy about using his full rights as a Roman citizen to protect himself and further the preaching of the gospel. Paul understood that his legal rights were gifts from God to further God's righteous purposes.

Paul pressed his legal rights as a Roman citizen to escape a scourging (Acts 22:25-29). In Jerusalem, he asserted his rights as a Roman citizen to a Roman commander, in order to defend himself before a mob (Acts 21:39-40), and in Acts 16:35-39, he demanded an apology from the magistrates of Philippi for mistreatment, based upon his citizenship rights (Acts 16:35-39).

What was most telling to us in making our decision was the example of Paul before Festus, the Roman governor of the province of Judea. Paul, fearing that due to the influence of the Jewish leaders upon Festus, he would not be able to get a fair or favorable hearing, appealed to Caesar. In other words, he used his right to sue to a higher authority to review the actions and anticipated decisions of a lower authority (Acts 25:1-11).

With this understanding, we filed for an injunction against the city to bar their decision as being in violation of the Religious Land Use and Institutional Persons Act. We also prepared to become involved in another campaign for the open City Council seat.

Gaining the Majority

The very Planning Commissioner who had been removed from the Planning Commission because he refused to follow the antichurch philosophy of city hall was willing to run for the open seat. We saw an historic opportunity for El Cajon to undergo a profound change in the spirit and attitude of its city government.

We knew that the Commissioner would be viciously opposed by the entrenched powers at City Hall, as well as our largest and most influential newspaper. We knew this from the experience of previous elections. Dave (my brother and co-pastor) and I called several other Christian leaders and went to work. All of our activities would be done in our roles as independent, community-minded citizens. Absolutely no church money, materials or staff time was ever used in any of our activities. Many Christians, however, were tired of the anti-church attitudes of the status quo and were anxious to become involved. Some of the city bureaucrats and councilmen had made statements that they would like to turn back some of the advances made by churches; this added to the urgency of our efforts.

Unfortunately, as always, we were greatly hindered by the same limitations we always encountered in trying to marshal a united Christian effort. Many pastors and church leaders are unmotivated to act beyond their narrow self-interest. If it will not directly add to the attendance figures on Sunday morning or the size of the offering, they are not interested in investing any time or effort in the project, no matter how greatly it might benefit the Kingdom of God or the wider Christian mission. Secondly, many pastors and church leaders are unwilling to become involved in anything that might be controversial or for which they might receive criticism. Their motto might be summed up as, "Above all, never rock the boat and never risk offending potential church members."

As always, it seems, the responsibility would land on just a small handful of people. Several people would make huge sacrifices to win a victory that would be enjoyed by many churches and Christians. The battle was even worse than we could have imagined. The most scurrilous charges were made by the opposition. Facts and statistics that they knew to be lies and in error were continually and repeatedly stated even when categorically being demonstrated to be false. Slander and religious bigotry were employed. As the campaign progressed, they seemed to get more and more desperate and their true spirit began to show.

Someone from their side called in the liberal group Americans United for the Separation of Church and State, headed up by Barry Lynn, the radical former national director of the ACLU. The main agenda for this group seems to be to try and intimidate Christians from their rights as citizens. Someone else called the IRS and tried to instigate audits against us and several other churches. Our crime? We were in a large industrial park with 16 other tenants. The landlord of the park had put up several campaign signs on the extreme west and east ends of the park. Because we rented space in that park, they tried to make the argument that we were in some sort of violation. Of course, the IRS refused to even investigate.

These actions pulled off the mask of those opposing us and revealed their spirit. One of the Councilmen who was very active in the election called several pastors and threatened them with reprisals for their support of his rival's candidate. Toward the end of the campaign, our candidate (who was always cordial and gracious) was even physically assaulted by his opponent after a radio debate, which resulted in a restraining order being issued by the courts against the other candidate.

All of these attacks would seem as nothing when Election Day rolled around and our candidate won by a comfortable margin of 8 %. A new day had dawned with a new spirit on the City Council. Instead of the threats that had recently been made, churches could now look forward to fair treatment.

Meanwhile, our suit based on the new law RLUIPA moved excruciatingly slowly through the legal process. Having lost the election, the City Attorney recommended that they settle the lawsuit. As a result, the city agreed to rewrite their zoning laws that were discriminatory against churches, to allow churches to locate in the commercial zone without having to obtain a Conditional Use Permit (which is how cities traditionally discriminate against churches that pay no taxes), and to pay all attorney and legal fees (including being able to pay Pacific Justice that had offered their services for free). This was a huge victory for all churches. Pacific Justice Institute issued a press release calling this an important victory. The story ran in newspapers across America. I received a phone call from someone who read the story in the *New York Times*.

The settlement had an immediate effect in El Cajon. Because our battle with the city took nearly 2 years we had lost the option to buy the Town Center Property where we had hoped to locate our church. Facing financial ruin, the property owners had split the parcel and had entered into a "lease with an option to buy" agreement with a local business for half of the property. The remaining half was not large enough for us.

However, we were able to find four smaller churches for whom the remaining space was more than enough for their present needs.

Now, under the new laws, they would not have get permission from the city to locate there. The remaining property was purchased. Each of the churches was able to move into a theatre in the multiplex with a bare minimum of cost. The remaining storefronts were built out to house a daycare and two Christian schools. In addition, several theatres were left open for various uses by the community, including a Christian theater group.

Despite losing the property, our prayers were answered for a strong evangelical presence to be located in downtown El Cajon. To put the icing on the cake, one of the schools that relocated into the property was our own high school. This solved for us our most pressing need and allowed both of our schools to expand.

God's plan all along had been different and even bigger than we had planned when we followed His leading in applying for the property against all odds. God had changed the laws of the city affecting all its churches, had changed the balance of power on the City Council, and had established four churches in the city's downtown.

This was a better outcome than our having gotten the property, since we would have faced huge engineering and construction problems in converting the property to our needs. The adaptation of the property to its current use made it much easier and less expensive to get building permits.

What is next for us and our city? I don't know, except that Jesus is continuing His plan to bless our community and grant to us our prayer that His "Kingdom would come and His will be done on Earth as it is in Heaven."

SECTION FOUR

For Pastors and Church Leaders

Shepherd the flock of God among you, not under compulsion, but voluntarily, according to the will of God; and not for sordid gain.

1 Peter 5:2

CHAPTER 31

THE STRUGGLE FOR THE SOUL OF THE CHURCH

Today there exists a great struggle for the soul of the church. The great question facing the church is whether she will be "Kingdom centered" or "church growth centered."

History reveals that every generation struggles with some issue over the identity, mission and future of the Church. Names like the Apostle Paul, Athanasius, Martin Luther, and John Wesley are famous largely because of their efforts in winning these struggles and defining the identity and mission of the Church.

The twentieth century was no exception...During the first fifty years of this century, the so-called "higher critical" methodologies of Biblical criticism were sweeping through the seminaries and churches of America. The great question before the church was, "Would the church be conservative and Bible believing (holding that the Scriptures were infallibly inspired), or liberal, viewing the Bible as a human (and therefore fallible) document?" This question has largely been settled in favor of those who believe that the Bible is literally true, and that its original manuscripts were without error. The mainline liberal denominations have waned in numbers and influence while the conservative evangelical churches, seminaries, and movements have boomed.

From the 1960's through the 1980's, a new issue faced the church focusing on the charismatic renewal. Would the church at large accept or reject this renewal with its praise and worship choruses, praying for the sick, ministry of deliverance, and the practice of spiritual gifts? The question seems to be largely settled. Persecution and exclusion of charismatics is largely a thing of the past. Most believers have moved in a more charismatic direction and much of the style and practices of the renewal have become standard even in churches and denominations that were at one time quite hostile.

Today there is a new question facing the church, one born out of yet another great struggle for her very soul. The question facing us today is *whether we will be Kingdom-centered or church-growth centered.*

The Church Growth Movement began with the work of Donald MacGavran, C. Peter Wagner, and the Charles E. Fuller Institute of Evangelism and Church Growth School at Fuller Seminary in Pasadena California. It began as an attempt to identify sociological factors that growing churches shared as well as identify factors that marked non-growing or declining churches. Its aim was to supply information that would help local churches to reach out to their communities and grow. Certainly, the movement has been successful in this aim.

Its very success has, however, contributed to a new problem. This is because the principles and methods identified by the movement *do* work. However, because they are *sociological rather than spiritual*, they will work for any organization, religious or secular. These are the same methods and principles used to market any product or business. They will cause the growth of a church in terms of attendance and budgets, if for no other reason than, they make the church that employs them *more appealing to religious consumers* than other churches, not so adept at marketing skills.

Such techniques and methods invite great abuse as the focus of church leaders can shift to "working" the principles rather than depending on the Holy Spirit. Large "churches" can be built on the cleverness of a man and his market-tested programs rather than on the revelation and anointing of the Holy Spirit. In the hands of ambitious or insecure self-promoters with wrong motives, these principles can actually set back the advance of the Kingdom.

Further, when marketing practices turn community churches into competitors, one church can grow by merely emptying others. The growth of any one congregation or even several congregations does not mean that the Kingdom of God is advancing, or even that the church in the area is stronger. Often the result is merely a rearranging of Christians from one church to another, much like reshuffling the same 52 cards.

For instance, I know of one notable church in the South that started as a small church plant and exploded in growth until it had more than 10,000 people in attendance. I later read that in one 3year period (which coincided with the church's fastest growth), over 100 small churches in their area shut down and closed their doors. It would be impossible to measure the true impact of this megachurch, or to quantify "church growth" without taking both of these factors into account.

It is undeniable that the era of the "church growth movement" has not produced Kingdom growth. According to Focus on the Family's H.B. London, $500 billion dollars has been spent on ministry in the U.S. in the last 15 years *with no appreciable growth* (Pastors Briefing, Feb. 22 1999). In fact, according to pollster George Gallup, North America is the **only continent** where Christianity is not growing (George Gallup, Church in the World Today)!

Clearly, our focus on building our own local church has not advanced the Kingdom! **We will not advance until we replace our "church growth" mentality with a "Kingdom growth" mentality**.

Let me explain briefly how I am using the term "church growth" so as not to give unnecessary offense. Certainly, many people have gone to church growth conferences with right hearts and motives and have gleaned helpful principles. They have incorporated these principles into their ministries, yet they are not "Kingdom growth" people. Undoubtedly, many people who conduct church growth seminars are "Kingdom growth" people. This is by no means a wholesale condemnation of church growth principles or leading individuals in the movement.

I am not trying to establish a false "us versus them" divide. I do, however, see a serious problem in the thinking of many church leaders and pastors, and am using the term "church growth" in a particular way in order to contrast it with a proper Kingdom mentality. In one sense, this approach is unfair because it emphasizes the worst shortcomings of the age of "church growth" without fairly speaking of the benefits and successes of the movement. However, perhaps the reader will overlook such generalizations in order to consider the finer points being made.

By a "Kingdom growth mentality" I mean a person who has a perspective that is "big picture." One whose primary commitment is to the well-being and advance of the whole church in their area and the overall cause of Christ in their city and world. Such a person realizes that true Kingdom advance entails social justice, political righteousness, cultural influence, building strong families, and other God-ordained institutions. This is someone who is committed to these and not just their individual church or ministry. It is a person who is committed to using the "tools and keys" of the Kingdom rather than relying on the secular tools of man's wisdom.

For many today, the growth of their individual church or ministry has come to take precedence over the priorities of Jesus. *Jesus told us to preach the gospel, heal the sick, care for the poor and transform society. He did not tell us to work to build a successful church or ministry (by the world's standards) for ourselves.*

The spirit and values of our age have infiltrated the church. For many, it's all about their individual statistics and numbers (which actually may tell you very little about real Kingdom advance). While it is normal and right for all of us to want to see our individual churches and influence grow, for many the desire for numerical growth has dwarfed all other goals. We compete for such titles as "biggest" and "fastest-growing." All of us feel the pressure. Our worth as ministers seems to be judged on the basis of our attendance and numerical growth. This definition of "success" is taking a toll on our spiritual life.

An uncritical pragmatism is replacing prayerful soul-searching. Attending Church Growth seminars is replacing seeking God's face for direction. The seemingly all-important goal of growth in Sunday morning attendance often leads to an uncritical "whatever works" mindset.

Unfortunately, the result is often organizational growth without spiritual reality. Enamored with the trappings of "success," many have fallen into what Professor Donald Bloesch has labeled "a secularized evangelicalism that prizes success and worldly acclaim over theology and biblical fidelity." Churches seemingly throw biblical discernment to the wind and increasingly adopt the methods of modern advertising and marketing to enhance growth. The bottom line is increasingly, "Does it produce growth?" rather than "Is it biblical?"

In our efforts to be "seeker-sensitive" we can deform and dilute both the message and the nature of the church. When increasing our "appeal" to the *unchurched* becomes our primary focus, then compromise becomes a huge danger. Ingenuity, "relevance," and change become valued over fidelity and steadfastness (instead of them all being held in an equal balance and tension). *Churches begin to become more of a reflection of society than a molder of society.* In his book, *Dining with the Devil*, Os Guiness warns of the effect that our market and poll-driven strategies are having on the church when he writes:

> The problem is not that Christians have disappeared, but that the Christian faith has become so deformed. Under the influence of modernity, we modern Christians are literally

capable of *winning the world while losing our own souls*, (p.43).

In our efforts to be appealing and "seeker sensitive" we adopt strategies that change the nature of the church. Our preference for *counting* attendance rather than *forming* disciples can alter our mission and goals. We have replaced divine guidance with "market research," prayer and fasting with church growth manuals, and Elijah the Seer with George Barna the polltaker. At conferences, too often, instead of hearing "Thus sayeth the Lord," we hear "the latest research suggests..."

Where once we strove to be holy in order to please God, now we strive to be casual and entertaining to please men. In our efforts to be trendy and appealing to people we have merely exchanged the vice of being "holier than thou" with the vice of being "trendier than thou."

Some of this is due to changes in our society. Sunday, which was once known as the Lord's Day, a day set aside to worship God, has now become "my day," as in "it's *my* only day to sleep in" and "its *my* only day to relax." We have largely capitulated to this current cultural attitude of self-absorption rather than challenge and overcome it.

In our drive to fill our parking lots and padded chairs we have produced "consumer oriented" churches that offer products and services to meet the desires and perceived needs of our potential consumers.

Whereas Jesus challenged his hearers to become disciples, we entice our target audience to be merely attenders. Jesus, in the Sermon on the Mount, continually raised the bar, whereas we are in danger of removing it all together, as in the case of one mailer sent to my house by one of our local "growing" seeker-sensitive churches. It read: "Come visit our church. We won't ask you to do anything, be anything, give anything or say anything."

In our efforts to be "seeker friendly," we are in danger of becoming "church lite" (Lite Church: everything you wanted in a church, but less). We have narrowed the topics of our shortened sermons to "felt needs," and eliminated or de-emphasized prayer, personal soul searching, confession of sin, and true worship. We have used the extra time for entertaining dramas and "special music" to make people feel good. We have developed consumer-oriented churches where "the customer is always right." We have aimed low and avoided anything that might give offense. What is next? How about ten-minute sermons and a 6% tithe? What about valet parking?

In many cases, churches are surrendering to the current self-indulgence of our culture. The old Christian virtue of sacrifice is out. One pastor of a "seeker driven" church told me that he no longer gave to missions because "we are the mission." In many churches, money that was once spent on foreign missions is now spent on advertising and improving and remodeling facilities so that people will feel good about themselves while they are at church.

What we are in many cases settling for is a "feel good" religion where God is unnecessary because our techniques and programs have created a "positive" and "pleasing" experience that keeps the church full. We have often settled for being entertaining rather than striving for a true supernatural encounter with God. We may have "satisfied customers," but do we have true converts, self-denying disciples who have entered the Kingdom and are able to defeat Satan?

The real need of people is not that they "feel good about themselves." *What they truly need is an encounter with God and His Word that leaves them completely undone, ready to be converted to Christ and His righteousness and the power of His resurrection.* We need to bring people to the state that Isaiah was in when he said:

> *Woe to me, for I am ruined! I am a man of unclean lips, and*
> *I live among a people of unclean lips.*
>
> Isaiah 6:5

Only after this insight can a person be truly converted so that they can say with Paul:

> *I have been crucified with Christ; and it is no longer I who*
> *live, but Christ lives in me and the life that I now live in the*
> *flesh I live by faith in the Son of God, who loved me and gave*
> *Himself up for me.*
>
> Galatians 2:20

This must not be merely a one-time event but a continual awareness and way of life that disciples of Jesus walk in. Our efforts to make people feel good about themselves may do little more than to produce religious Pharisees rather than true converts and disciples.

Our worship services must be just that, worship. Only in this way will people meet God and be converted. Too often our efforts are aimed at entertaining the flesh instead of crucifying it. A church service that centers around entertainment will not dethrone the flesh. The true power to draw and hold people must come from the Presence of God and not from entertainment. Only when God is enthroned can the flesh be dethroned. *A church can make no greater mistake than to surrender the supernatural in order to be merely entertaining.*

Each of us must aspire to attend and serve a church that only God could build. People's real need is to meet God. The Book of Acts records explosive Kingdom (and church) growth as a result of the power of God and the ministry of the Holy Spirit expressed in signs, wonders, miracles, deliverances and spiritual gifts. The Book of Acts is a picture of how Jesus intends to build His church. He has not changed His methods.

Yet we too often build religious organizations in exactly the same way that secular organizations and corporations are built. Recently a pastor friend attended a Church Growth conference that promised to "empower Christian churches to reach their communities for Jesus Christ." My friend gave me the conference syllabus and his notes to look over. Rather than drawing from biblical insights, the conference was based solely on sociological and marketing principles.

The seminar taught you to build your church through first developing a clear identity that people would recognize and would distinguish you from other churches. Next, you were to communicate the "product benefits" that you offered through various recommended marketing and advertising strategies. Then you were to develop programs and policies that would turn attenders into members, and finally you were to train people to invite others to your services.

Perhaps you noticed that these principles would work for starting any business. You could just as easily build a health club, car dealership or Buddhist Temple as a Christian church.

Further, we are taught to practice "niche marketing" by carefully tailoring our approach and message to reach a very narrow socioeconomic and racial target group. Niche marketing may help you "slice off" a piece of the pie by emphasizing and exploiting what separates and divides people. It may help to build your "ministry," but it will blow up in our collective faces. It will divide us even further by race, age and social class. It will leave us poorer, with the young without the wisdom of the elder, the "rich" isolated from the poor, and everyone cut off from what they can gain from those different from themselves. This approach is clearly against the purposes of God, as a study of Scripture will make plain. This approach has fragmented and weakened our society and will do so for the church as well.

In the seminar, we are taught to appeal to people's self interest by clearly listing the "product benefits" that will be theirs by coming to our services. We are also given 52 outreach ideas "Guaranteed to Attract Visitors." These included advertising in the phone book, building a website, hosting a celebrity, serving outstanding food, hosting a voting booth, giving visitors' gifts, and promoting hobby clubs. Out of the list of 52, not one was utilized in the Book of Acts, nor were any of the methods of evangelism that took place in the book of Acts listed in the syllabus.

Certainly there is nothing wrong with any of these activities and, in fact, they could be useful (but remember, they will work for any organization – good or bad). But the point is obvious. We no longer need God to build our "growing" churches. Instead of belonging to a church that only God could build, we can have a church built without need of God. *In fact, we must be careful lest our efforts result in a kind of church that He would never want built.* We may be growing, but what is the use of making good time if we are running the wrong race?

My friends, such an approach may fill seats but it will not gain the Kingdom. We have certainly increased the choices and options for church consumers, but as we have seen, we have not significantly increased the overall amount of church-goers or produced effective disciples. *The tragic result is that we have made church-goers more discriminating and demanding, but not more Christ like.* Now, church hoppers and shoppers bounce from one spiritual "boutique" to another until they land (for awhile) in a satisfying spot. Many attend three or more churches but belong nowhere.

Indeed, in our efforts to "win the world" we are in danger of "losing our soul." We have increasingly surrendered the "power of His Holiness" for the flashy appeal of relevance and trendiness.

Pastors flock, by the thousands, to church-growth seminars hosted by mega churches to learn the "secrets" to their success. We hope to learn marketing and accounting methods that we could employ at our church to get the same results as the big boys. I attended one such conference at which I was taught such things as: what are the best advertising strategies, how to organize parking lot teams, how to follow up with visitors and even what color to paint the ceiling.

At that same conference, our sincere and likeable host said, "If you see anything you like take it home and use it, you don't have to give us credit. Use our methods, systems, and even printed materials. You are welcome to go home and preach any of my sermons since they are not copyrighted." Pastors return from such conferences and try to turn their church into an exact clone of the church that hosted the conference.

While the generosity of the host pastor is to be applauded, we would have been better served by counsel more like the following: "Now that you have gained a vision of what God can do with a church, go home and get on your face and dedicate yourself to God, then seek His face for your own direction and anointing. Learn how to hear the leading of God for yourself and how to depend upon the empowering of the Holy Spirit. Only in this way will *He* build *His* church."

Our carnal nature merely wants to "organize," but in order to enter the Kingdom we must "agonize." We must agonize in prayer, in crucifying the flesh, and in living out "the fellowship of His sufferings and the power of His resurrection" (Philippians 3:10).

It is human nature to want to go to a book or conference to receive a "sure-fire" technique or program that will ensure success and effectiveness. Everyone wants a map to show us how to become "successful." But God doesn't give us a map. He gives us a guide. That guide is the Holy Spirit. Only He knows the way. And that way can only be learned through humility and brokenness.

CHAPTER 32

THE KINGDOM-DRIVEN CHURCH

Do you truly want to affect your world for Christ? Do you want to be an instrument of the Kingdom of God? How can your church serve the Kingdom?

We can be grateful for what we can learn from churches that host conferences aimed at helping us to see our churches grow. Certainly at our church we have been sensitized to the need to make our church more accessible to visitors. We have employed some "borrowed" ideas that we believe have improved our ability to minister to our community. However, we who are evangelical Christians must turn to the Bible as our ultimate guide and model. Let me suggest a model church from the New Testament for aspiring church planters and pastors to study. The Church is the New Testament Church at Antioch.

> *Now there were at Antioch, in the church that was there, prophets and teachers: Barnabas, and Simeon who was called Niger, and Lucius of Cyrene, and Manaen who had been brought up with Herod the tetrarch, and Saul. While they were ministering to the Lord and fasting, the Holy Spirit said, "Set apart for Me Barnabas and Saul for the work to which I have called them."*

Acts 13:1-2

Let us look very briefly at this model.

1. **IT HAS THE NEW TESTAMENT FORM OF FIVE-FOLD, CITYWIDE CHURCH LEADERSHIP.**

Notice that the leadership represented the entire body of believers in the city ("Now there were at Antioch, in the church that was there..." verse 1). Rather than each individual fellowship of believers being independent of each other, there was a common leadership team that brought unity and a common vision to the citywide church. No leader was alone and isolated. Each was accountable and supported.

In the same way, notice that leaders were ordained and set in place by the leaders of the citywide church. It was not a case of some independent "spiritual entrepreneur" deciding to begin "their" church or ministry, rather they were ordained by the united leadership ("Then when they had fasted and prayed and laid their hands on them...." verse 3).

It is essential today that pastors and church leaders reaffirm their submission to the larger Body of Christ in their area. If we would be Kingdom-growth people we must lay down our self-serving personal agendas and serve Christ's larger purpose. *Self-exalting competition must give place to Christ-exalting cooperation.*

Notice also that the church at Antioch functioned with the five-fold model ministry that Jesus ordained (Ephesians 4:11-13). We read specifically that the church contained "prophets and teachers" (verse 1). Barnabas and Paul are about to be set aside and ordained as apostles (verse 3). We can safely assume that the church had pastors and probably evangelists as well. Each of the five ministry offices contributes a different aspect of Jesus' gifting and anointing to the Body of Christ. Only Jesus functioned in all five offices during His earthly ministry.

Only when all five are fully functioning can the church be fully functional. (Otherwise it must be dysfunctional.) This is how Jesus guides and equips His church, as a study of Ephesians 4 and related passages make clear. It is not necessary that each individual congregation have all five ministry offices (in fact, this will probably rarely, if ever, take place). What is necessary is that each congregation is submitted to and drawing from the citywide church which does have all five offices functioning. It is further necessary that pastors are guided and supported by apostles and prophets.

This Apostolic form of New Testament government is in contrast to the modern corporate model of many churches today with Department heads, an Executive Pastor, a Business Pastor and a Senior Pastor who functions as a CEO.

2. THE PRIORITY OF THE LEADERSHIP TEAM IS PRAYER AND MINISTRY TO THE LORD.

In Antioch the leaders were involved in praying and ministering to the Lord ("While they were ministering to the Lord and fasting...." verse 2). This was the apostolic priority for leadership. In Acts Chapter

6, the Apostles surrendered the daily oversight of money and the daily management of ministry. These responsibilities were given over by the apostles to "deacons" with these words:

But we will devote ourselves to prayer and to the ministry of the word.

Acts 6:4

The Apostolic priority in leadership is that the upper leadership must make ministry to the Lord and hearing from the Lord on behalf of the congregation their first priority. The spiritual dimension of church life takes clear precedence over the business side of the church. They lead by virtue of having heard from the Lord and then being anointed to accomplish what Jesus has just directed them to do. Their first priority, therefore, is to stay in union with Jesus and abide in the fullness of His Spirit.

In the modern corporate model, church leaders are managers. They lead by virtue of overseeing the management process. The tendency is to become buried in management and administration. The reality is that many pastors do not have an active private life with the Lord Jesus. The average workweek of the average pastor is 50-60 hours or even more. The great bulk of this is in administration and attending meetings. Most pastors are forced to function more like "deacons" if we look at their actual job description.

This state of affairs had led to a spiritually dry climate in the church. Pastors are seen more as managers rather than as spiritual directors. Os Guiness in his book *Dining with the Devil* quotes a Japanese businessman who said, "Whenever I meet a Buddhist leader I meet a holy man. Whenever I meet a Christian leader I meet a manager."

If we would see the Kingdom come to our churches, church leaders must reaffirm the priority of waiting on the Lord and seeking His face.

3. DIRECTION IS DETERMINED BY THE REVELATION AND LEADING OF THE HOLY SPIRIT.

The leaders of the Church in Antioch sought the Holy Spirit for direction. ("While they were ministering to the Lord and fasting, *the Holy Spirit* said..." verse 2). They didn't just try to copy what seemed to be working at some other church. They looked to the Lord Jesus for guidance through the Holy Spirit. They followed the Holy Spirit, not the latest fad.

What is needed today is not a market-driven church but a *prophetic* church. The great need of the church is to get reconnected to the leadership of its Head, Jesus Christ, through the prophetic and revelatory ministry of the Holy Spirit. Jesus promised to continue to guide us through the Holy Spirit.

> *But when He, the Spirit of Truth, comes, He will guide you into all the truth: for He will not speak on His own initiative, but whatever He hears, He will speak: and He will disclose to you what is to come. He will glorify Me, for He will take of Mine and will disclose it to you.*
>
> John 16:13-14

> *For all who are being led by the Spirit of God, these are the Sons of God.*
>
> Romans 8:14

> *He who has an ear to hear, let him hear what the Spirit says to the churches.*
>
> Revelation 2:7

Our way into the riches and power of the Kingdom will not come through some pre-cooked methodology that we get at some conference. Rather it will be a way we must discover ourselves as we listen to the Holy Spirit and are led by Him. This is because the "way in" isn't a way at all, but a Person. It is through union with and submission to the Lord Jesus, as mediated to us through the ministry of the Holy Spirit, that the Kingdom will open up.

Our "answer" will not be in some handbook we can buy. It will not be some formula to follow. It will not be that easy or simple. Our answer will most certainly be "outside the box," that is, it will be outside of our comfort zone. It will be beyond our wisdom. It will be uniquely *His way for us.* It will take us beyond ourselves. It will require the overthrowing of our ways and wisdom. It will even require at times a fresh crucifixion of ourselves. It will take us out of ourselves into a greater self. It will stretch us and enlarge us. It will not leave us unchanged. And in the end we will become what He is calling us to be and our churches will be something that only He could have built.

Conferences and books are good because the Holy Spirit can instruct us and speak to us through these. However, we must, with great determination, seek for the revelation and leading of the Holy Spirit for ourselves and our church, and not just copy methods.

4. IT IS A YIELDED AND OBEDIENT CHURCH.

The Church at Antioch followed the direction and appointment of their Head, Jesus Christ ("...Set apart for Me Barnabas and Saul for the work to which I have called them" verse 2).

Perhaps some of the other leaders had wanted to be set apart and sent out as apostles to experience the danger and glory of missionary work. Perhaps Barnabas and Paul received the commission that others secretly desired.

Perhaps Paul and Barnabas did not want to leave. Perhaps they wanted the prestige and honor of leading the huge, important church at Antioch.

Nevertheless, all accepted the Lord's right to call and ordain whom He chose. Submission to the Lord's will trumped everything else. The commitment to obey Jesus and see His Kingdom come was more important to them than personal ambition or personal desires. Everyone trusted in the wisdom and care of God. They understood that ultimately nobody else can receive what God has set apart for you. In this way, they were set free from strife and envy.

If we are to receive the Kingdom we must individually, as leaders, lay down our "rights" and personal agendas and acknowledge joyfully Christ's right to appoint whom He chooses. We must lay aside jealousy and strife and each seek to fulfill God's assignment to us.

5. IT IS AN OUTREACH-ORIENTED CHURCH.

They understood that taking the gospel of the Kingdom to others was central to their reason for existing ("Then, when they had fasted and prayed and laid their hands on them, they sent them away" verse 3). The rest of the chapter details some of the places that they were sent.

This is a message that the church needs to grasp today. In a recent survey, when church members were asked what the purpose of the church is, 85% said the purpose of the church is to meet their family's needs, and only 15% said the purpose of the church is to reach the lost (Thomas Clegg, ASCG *Journal of Church Growth*).

The church in Antioch was committed to reaching "distant" people. Paul and Barnabas were sent to people of cultures different from the people of their church. They were sent to idol worshiping people who had never heard of Jesus. This would involve great hardship and even danger. It required great consecration and courage.

They did not merely send out invitations to come to their services. They went outside their four walls, outside their comfort zone and penetrated someone else's world.

The world will never be won with bulk mail. Very few people will consider going to church simply because they receive an advertisement in the mail. Such mailers will attract the "nearly churched" but not the truly "unchurched." It may reach those who were formerly churched in their previous community, those who were raised in church but have become inactive, and those people who, because of some crisis in their life, are looking for a church.

THE NEARLY CHURCHED

In other words, the "nearly churched" are those who are probably going to wind up in someone's church sooner or later. By frequent use of bulk mail and other advertising that builds a high name recognition in their community, a church can increase their "market share" of this group and see their attendance swell. I have even seen churches grow quite large by spending large sums exclusively advertising in purely Christian publications. But this cannot substitute for evangelism. This does not satisfy Jesus' command to *"Go out..."*

Imagine a series of concentric circles. Inside the center circle are those who are at least moderately involved in a church. We will call these "the churched." In the next circle out are the "nearly churched." Let's say that this group comprises 20% of those who are not churched. This would include those new in town who attended church in their previous hometown, and those who dropped out because of some unwelcome change in their previous church. It would also include those who were raised in church but dropped out as they reached young adulthood. They are not far from the church. The church does not seem foreign or strange to them. They are not hostile to the church, in fact, they are favorably predisposed or "church friendly." They are interested in church and may be just waiting for someone to ask. Advertising's main effect will be to get them to choose your church over someone else's church.

Outside of these circles, however, are several more circles that comprise the remaining 80% or so of the unchurched (at least here in Southern California). These people are not "church friendly." Many don't understand the church, are indifferent to it, distrust it or are even downright hostile to it. Some families have been unchurched for generations. Some of these people are born into different religions or don't speak our language. Many people in these groups have never set foot in an evangelical church and certainly will not do so just because they receive "junk mail" from one.

Very, very few of these people will be reached if all we do is sit behind our four walls and address bulk mailings or raise money for billboards. It will take *more* than that. To reach these people takes sacrifice, hard work and patience. Once evangelized, they will take longer to disciple. It is a much slower way to grow a church than to simply compete for the "nearly churched."

More and more of the church's resources are being used to reach the already churched and the "nearly churched." Churches noticed the rapid growth of other churches who aggressively advertised. Wanting similar growth, they began to enroll with the same advertising firms and send out similar mail pieces. Ten years ago it was very rare to receive a mailing from a church at my home. Now I receive them frequently.

The obvious result is "diminishing returns." More and more churches are aggressively competing for the same small group of people. Fewer and fewer resources, in both people and money, are available to reach those people who are not in the "nearly churched" category.

Great effort is invested in reaching these "nearly churched" who are *already willing* to come to our churches. Multiple teams of people direct their cars in the parking lot, greet them 3 or 4 times before they sit down (starting in the parking lot), escort their children to Sunday School, serve them in the visitor lounge, sing special songs, act in entertaining dramas and spruce up the bathrooms and hallways during service. Following the service we address cards (and maybe cookies) to be sent to their homes. *The result is that almost all the human resources of the church are invested in putting on the big show on Sunday morning. Very little is left for outreach beyond the four walls.*

These "nearly churched" do need someone to help them to find a church and make a place for them. But this is not the same as truly evangelizing our culture. The present "focus" of so many churches appears to be a contest over who gets to these "nearly churched" first and who can win their hearts. They are the closest to us and therefore the most easily reached.

The church in Antioch, however, attempted to reach everyone that Christ had died for. Their focus was on reaching beyond their own demographic comfort zone. They sought not just those who were "close" but they extended themselves to those who were "far away" both socially and geographically.

Transforming Our Culture

In comparing these two church models, I do not mean to say that it is either/or. That it is either Antioch or "church growth seminar" model. It is not either/or, but it is 90/10. That is, we must get 90% of our guidance and inspiration from the model of the Church of Antioch and 10% from the helpful "management techniques" of the "church growth" specialists. *After all, in the final analysis, we are not called to plant or "grow" a church, we are called to proclaim, demonstrate and live out the Kingdom of God.*

The "church growth mindset" (as I am defining it) is a sure recipe for continued failure. Despite our substantial efforts and expenditures to make our individual churches grow, society seems to be moving away from Biblical values as quickly as ever. *Our call is to affect culture, not just build a "successful church."* The truth is that none of us can claim to be successful just because our church is growing if we are losing the community and the Kingdom is not advancing in our city. *How can any of us rejoice and be gleeful over "my success" and growing attendance if we are losing our city and our generation?*

It is human nature to strive for personal affluence and the aura of "success" while missing the greater call. This was the trap that many leaders of Elijah's day fell into. God's rebuke of them is a lesson to us.

> *Thus says the Lord God, "Woe to the foolish prophets who are following their own spirit and have seen nothing. O Israel, your prophets have been like foxes among ruins. You have not gone up into the breaches, nor did you build the wall around the house of Israel to stand in the battle on the day of the Lord."*
>
> Ezekiel 13:3-5

Foxes living near a defeated and sacked city care nothing for the city nor its inhabitants. They have no burden to rebuild the city walls or fortifications in order that the city might become safe and prosperous again. They care not that the survivors are in danger from raiders and thieves. They see only in the ruins an opportunity to build for themselves a nice cozy den.

In Ezekiel's time, Israel was in peril. Her moral and spiritual walls were in collapse. Her people practiced idolatry, immorality and injustice. Her protection from God was being removed. The prophets, however, were blind. They were only interested in building their own ministries and reputations and feathering their own nests. None was broken for the people. None sought hard after the face of God in order to get God's word to restore the city.

Like foxes among the ruins of a city wall, they had merely looked for places to build dens among the ruins. They had not cared about the welfare or spiritual survival of the city. They neglected their true task, which was to band together and, relying on God, restore the spiritual protection and blessing to the people. Instead, each looked only to his own "ministry," working to have success in his career.

In order to be faithful men and women of God, we must lay down our personal agendas and work to see the Kingdom of God come to our city. If we work for our individual success, and don't seek first the progress of the Kingdom of God, the advancement of the entire church and the welfare of the city, then our heart is not right. If we only have vision and energy for "our church" or "our ministry" then we need to check to see what spirit we are of. It certainly is not the Holy Spirit that is directing us.

We must set our goal higher than the Sunday morning attendance figures. After all, the Church is not something that only exists one hour a week. It cannot be measured and evaluated by one single meeting on Sunday. The Church of Jesus Christ is a 24/7 phenomena.

We must get past the idea that church is a meeting. Rather the Church is a regional-wide Body which is animated by a Spirit (God's very Spirit) and directed by a Head (Jesus Christ Himself).

This one Body must follow the leading of the one Head and be inspired and empowered by one Spirit. When it does so, this Body will do the same things He did in His fleshly body 2000 years ago. We must be as He was and do what He did.

The Body of Christ must get past its overemphasis on putting on a "Big Show" once a week and begin to transfer some energy and money into other "Kingdom building" efforts like education, family building, civic and political leadership, and penetration into the many new religious and ethnic groups that are coming into our nation. The gifts and anointing given to the Body of Christ are not just for gathering a meeting on Sunday morning. Rather, they are for transforming every facet and institution of modern life with the presence of the Kingdom of God. The efforts of Christ's Body must go into every facet of society.

Further, we must make a commitment to do so with the very tools with which God has supplied us. We must aim to do the same things that Jesus did when He walked among us nearly 2000 years ago. This is what Jesus promised us:

> *Truly, truly, I say to you, he who believes in Me, the works that I do, he will do also; and greater works than these he will do; because I go to the Father.*
>
> John 14:12

We must do those same things that caused Jesus to stand out among all the competing movements and groups of His day. We must not settle for the same marketing and advertising tools that are employed by secular businesses. Rather, we must press into God until His mighty works of the Kingdom are evident among us. We must fast and pray and intercede and learn to wait on God's leading until we see the full release of the gifts of the Spirit and the signs and wonders of His Kingdom. Only in this way can that which is of God be distinguished from that which is of man or that which is a spiritual counterfeit. Only in this way can the fullness of His Kingdom come.

It is time for us to lay down the "Corporate America" model of the Church and let it get back to what it was in the New Testament. In the New Testament the church was a family. The leaders were elders and fathers, not entrepreneurs, managers or CEO's.

The goal of the elders was to bring to birth and then to raise up and train sons and daughters in the faith who could defeat Satan and extend Christ's Kingdom. Our goal today must be the same.

We are not called to manage a "fast growing organization" but to father and mother God's precious children. This is true apostolic New Testament ministry. The amount of believers that a minister has fathered and brought through to fruit-bearing maturity is a truer measure of his "success" than Sunday morning attendance figures. Our true success is measured in the quantity and quality of our successors. Jesus certainly understood this. He spent His greatest efforts developing twelve (and in a larger sphere 70) men to succeed him. This is how He measured His success.

A KINGDOM GROWTH CHURCH

So what does a Kingdom growth congregation look like? Let me describe one such church that I know.

This particular church is founded on worship and intercession. Every part of the church from children's church on up makes worship a high priority. This is true for home fellowships as well as youth group meetings. God's presence is courted and enjoyed. A sense of awe pervades meetings of the Body. Out of that rich sense of His presence God speaks to individuals and to the whole church. Many have given testimony of having been converted to Christ by just walking in and sensing the Lord's presence during the opening worship time.

The last 25 to 30 minutes of the Sunday service (and many other meetings for that matter) is unscripted. The church simply ministers to the Lord and waits on the Holy Spirit. At first it was a scary thing to do. But the Holy Spirit does show up and take charge and direct. The most powerful encounters with God and the most wonderful works of the Holy Spirit take place during this time. Part of the reason for this is that over 500 people are part of the Prayer Society, which have committed to intercede for the church 3 hours per week.

Except for special evangelistic meetings and campaigns, the bulk of preaching on Sunday morning is geared toward challenging believers to place their whole lives under Jesus as Lord and Savior so that their lives will be powerfully transformed and they receive His Kingdom blessings into every dimension of their lives. In this way they become living testimonies to the reality of God wherever they go. Evangelism is focused outside of the church walls and put in the hands of these transformed disciples wherever they go.

The leadership team makes prayer and waiting on God a priority. Direction for the church comes out of prayer. Rather than trying out whatever is "hot" in the Body of Christ, the Holy Spirit is sought for revelation about how to minister in their unique setting. Besides regular times of prayer, twice each year the entire pastoral staff takes four days and goes on a retreat together to worship, pray and wait on God for direction for the church.

The church makes discipleship and leadership development a priority. Just like a family, sons and daughters are birthed and then brought up to maturity and productivity. This is accomplished through an emphasis on one-on-one mentoring, a vital church-wide small group ministry (that begins with Junior High), internship programs, and leadership mentoring by the Senior Pastors.

As a result, the church, which has undergone significant growth and has a large staff, has never gone outside of the church to hire for *any* pastoral or support staff position. In fact, the large majority of staff (both pastoral and support) found Christ at the church or in the previous ministry of the pastors. When a staff member's production is less than what is desired, the pastors work with the individual to encourage, challenge and equip him or her rather than fire them. After all, isn't that what a family does? As a result there has been very, very little turnover of staff.

The church focuses its dollars and efforts at reaching the lost. It expends its greatest efforts outside the church walls. It has developed outreach clubs at 10 schools, operates several youth community centers, an outreach bus ministry, as well as outreach programs operating in apartment complexes, neighborhoods, convalescent homes, jails and city streets.

The church supports the efforts of the entire church in the area. The pastors have participated in weekly pastor prayer groups for 15 years. The church has participated in nearly every multi-church effort during that same period. They have worked for and helped spearhead many victories that have benefited all churches. Each weekend service they pray for a different church and pastor in the area.

Besides what they have given to foreign missions, the church has given many thousands of dollars to other area ministries and churches. They have helped other churches with their building programs. When they had Sunday night meetings they would give the evening's offering to a different area church or ministry each week.

This particular church realizes that the Kingdom of God involves more than just church meetings. They have worked hard to strengthen families, developing several different parenting classes and groups, marriage groups, marriage retreats, financial planning and family counseling. They assist Christian parents to raise their children by operating schools from Kindergarten through twelfth grade and by assisting home school parents. They have encouraged and recruited Christians to run for public office. They have worked to affect public policy and have laws changed.

The key to an exciting, vibrant church is to allow your church to be driven by its original purpose. That purpose is nothing more and nothing less than to be a living, visible expression of the Kingdom of God, which encompasses the dynamic power, righteous government and loving family of God. Do you hear His call? His Kingdom awaits you.

ABOUT THE AUTHOR

Mark Hoffman (B.A., Point Loma College, M. Div., Bethel Seminary West) lives in La Mesa, California, with his wife, Linda, and three sons, Neil, Brice, and Will.

Along with his brother, David Hoffman, he co-pastors Foothills Christian Fellowship in El Cajon, California, which they founded in 1985. He is also the executive Director of Youth Venture and author of Breakthrough Kingdom Living

ORDERING INFORMATION

Additional copies of *On Earth as it is in Heaven*, as well as *Breakthrough Kingdom Living*, may be obtained at:

www.CSNbooks.com

Or by contacting:

Mark Hoffman c/o
Foothills Christian Fellowship
350-B Cypress Lane
El Cajon, Ca 92020
(619) 442-7728